NEW ORTHOGRAPHY

HUGO'S
RUSSIAN
GRAMMAR
SIMPLIFIED

THE <u>ONLY</u> REAL SELF-INSTRUCTOR

EXERCISES, KEY AND VOCABULARIES

WITH THE
PRONUNCIATION OF EVERY WORD
EXACTLY IMITATED

"STANDARD" EDITION

Revised and re-written.   All rights reserved.

WILDSIDE PRESS

INTRODUCTORY REMARKS.

It is agreed by all who have succeeded in acquiring a foreign language correctly, that it is impossible to do so without a certain amount of grammatical explanation. It is of the utmost importance, however, that a grammar should not contain more than is absolutely necessary to explain the various changes which words undergo, and the principal points of difference between English and the foreign idiom.

It is comparatively easy to speak and write a foreign language for the purposes of ordinary conversation and correspondence, if students are content to use simple language.

"Simple language" does not mean childish language; it is the knack of using short clear sentences which cannot be misunderstood.

Hugo's claim that this book fulfils all the required conditions, and that it is the only grammatical guide by which it is possible to acquire the leading principles of the Russian Language in 100 hours.

The principal features of Hugo's Russian Grammar are :

1. The Russian is guaranteed correct, and is such as is used by the educated classes. Every word has been written by a Russian University man, and carefully revised by other educated Russians.

2. The rules are simply and clearly explained on the Hugo principles, and with the abundant examples, leave no room for doubt.

3. Clear Rules of Pronunciation are given, as well as the Imitated Pronunciation of every word, arranged in the Vocabularies for easy reference.

HUGO'S RUSSIAN GRAMMAR SIMPLIFIED.

4. Exceptionally distinct and accented type is used, specially cast for this work.

5. Specimen pages of Handwriting, in clear modern style, are given.

6. Enormous saving of Student's time is effected by having the Russian and the English on the same page, thus admitting of instantaneous comparison. This is indispensable in such a highly inflected language as Russian.

HOW TO USE THIS GRAMMAR,
so as to obtain satisfactory results in 100 hours.

The great thing is to obtain quickly a GENERAL IDEA of the leading principles of Russian grammar; this is far more important than mastering each individual rule and verb thoroughly in the beginning.

It does not matter much if occasional mistakes are made, so long as students can see WHY the Russian in the exercises is used as it is.

There are 80 pages of exercises, half of each page being in Russian, and half in English. The key to each language therefore appears on the same page as the exercise.

After having gone through the alphabet and the words on page 10 carefully, the student should put the Russian on page 11 into English, and afterwards the English into Russian, checking each translation by comparing it immediately with the book.

Each page of exercises should be done two or three times. An hour and a quarter is ample allowance for this, inclusive of reading the rules and examples.

With the Verbs, students will find putting English into Russian the easier process. Each word and phrase should be carefully compared with its translation, and the grammar page opposite referred to for explanation. The Russian of the exercises should be written at least once, as this assists the memory.

By proceeding in this way—simply by frequent repetition and comparison—students cannot fail to learn the words, rules, and verb terminations.

HINTS ON THE IMITATED PRONUNCIATION.

If the Imitated Pronunciation is read as if it were English, but slowly and distinctly, **sounding the stressed syllable more fully than the remainder of the word,** every Russian speaking person will understand.

By attending to the following points, the pronunciation will be greatly improved :

h and kh represent the guttural sound of the Scotch CH in LOCH, but the K must not be heard as in KING ; for this reason the guttural sound at the beginning of a word is indicated by h only, to be strongly aspirated.

E, EE, and I stand for I in PIT, and represent the difficult sound bI, which, when accented, resembles a very short OO^E.

ăh, ĕh, to be sounded shorter than 'ah, eh.'

aw to be pronounced very short, somewhat like O in NOT.

j like S in PLEASURE, or J in the French J'AI ; but not like J in JAM.

Y is always like Y in YES, never like Y in MY.

W is used to indicate the hard L, except where 'w' at the end of a syllable would produce the wrong sound. In such cases L is used.

In spite of the division of the words into Russian syllables, the various parts must be read like one word.

The part of the word printed in **thick type** must be more strongly sounded than the rest.

The sign ^ between two vowels shows that they are to be pronounced with one emission of the voice, like O^Y in BOY.

The sign , between a consonant and a vowel indicates that they ought to be connected by a very slight and short I or Y sound (as in IT or YES). But unless this sound can be made very short, it is better omitted. Such an omission is less offensive to Russian ears. This slight Y sound is only distinctly heard in the middle of a word if the accent rests on it.

The sound (,) is in many words scarcely heard, **but it must be sounded distinctly at the end of every Verb in the Infinitive.** It then sounds like a very slight guttural, almost as if drawing up one's breath, or sighing slightly.

THE RUSSIAN ALPHABET.

The following is the order of the 32 Russian letters, with their names and English equivalents :
(Capitals and Small Letters practically only differ in size).

1. A a	2. Б б	3. В в	4. Г г	5. Д д	6. Е е
ah (a)	beh (b)	veh (v)	gay (g)	deh (d)	yeh (e)
7. Ж	8. З	9. И	10. Й	11. К	12. Л
jeh*	zeh (z)	ee (i)	ee (i short)	kah (k)	ell (L)
13. М	14. Н	15. О	16. П	17. Р р	18. С
em (m)	en (n)	aw (o)	peh (p)	err (r)	ess (s)
19. Т	20. У	21. Ф	22. Х	23. Ц	24. Ч
teh (t)	oo (u)	eff (f)	khah*	tseh (ts)	tcheh (ch)
25. Ш	26. Щ	27. (Ъ) ‡	28. Ы	29. Ь	
shah (sh)	sh-tchah (sh-tch)	(hard sign)	yeh-rи	soft sign	
30. Э	31. Ю	32. Я			
ay (a)	yoo (u)	yäh			

*7. j like s in 'measure.' 28 or er˘e.
22 kh guttural = ch in 'loch.'

There are nine Vowels in Russian :

а	е	и	о	у	ы	э	ю	я
1 ah	6 yeh	9 ee	15 aw	20 oo	28 er˘e	30 ay	31 yoo	32 yäh

There are three semi-vowels in Russian :

Й 10 is used only after vowels with which it forms a diphthong.
Ь 29 no sound ; indicates that preceding consonant must be pronounced soft.

‡ The letter **Ъ** 27 is no longer used at the end of words to show that the preceding consonant is to be sounded hard. In the middle of a word it may be retained or replaced by an apostrophe.

All the remaining letters are CONSONANTS.

NOTE.—The letters given in brackets below have been abolished from the Russian language and only occur in books published in Russia before 1918.

(I) И 9 is used instead | (Ѣ) Е 6 is used instead
(Ѳ) Ф 21 is used instead

SPECIMEN OF MODERN RUSSIAN HANDWRITING.

See also pages 228 and 229.

Students should use Russian handwriting from the first, but need not use CAPITALS.

1. А 2. Б 3. В 4. Г 5. Д or Д 6. Е
7. Ж 8. З 9. И 10. Й 11. К 12. Л 13. М 14. Н 15. О
16. П 17. Р 18. С 19. Т 20. У 21. Ф 22. Х 23. Ц 24. Ч 25. Ш
26. Щ [27. Ъ] 28. Ы 29. Ь 30. Э 31. Ю 32. Я

HUGO'S RUSSIAN GRAMMAR SIMPLIFIED.

The pronunciation of every word being clearly imitated in the Lessons, students should not lose time by studying the Rules of Pronunciation, which are for reference only.

Proceed at once to Lesson I., page 10.

FOR REFERENCE ONLY.

SIMPLE RULES OF PRONUNCIATION.

The VOWELS, when stressed, are pronounced in the same way as their names, given in the Alphabet on page 4. (Letter 28 excepted, as explained on page 7).

The Vowels a, я, e, o, WHEN NOT EMPHASIZED, change their pronunciation thus:

o when coming before the stressed syllable generally sounds like 'ăh,' short. Examples:

одúн	погóда	хорошó	господúн
ăh-deen	păh-gaw-dăh	hăh-răh-shaw	găh-spăh-deen
one	weather	well	gentleman

Stressed o, and o NOT coming BEFORE the stressed syllable.

но	дом	винó	дóктор
naw	dom	ve-naw	dok-torr
but	house	wine	doctor

Final o when not stressed is sometimes (principally in adverbs) pronounced like A in 'soda'.

пúво	мнóго		рáно
pee-vaw	mnaw-gaw *or* mnaw-gă		rah-nă
beer (Noun)	much (Adverb)		early (Adverb)

a when not stressed sounds like a short 'ăh.'

бумáга	кóмната	багáж	карандáш
boo-mah-găh	kom-năh-tăh	băh-gahj	kăh-răhn-dahsh
paper	room	luggage	pencil

Stressed a: да   как?   дáма   стакáн
             dah   kahk?   dah-mäh   stäh-kahn
             yes   how?   lady   glass

The unstressed **a** is sometimes pronounced (principally after the hissing letters, ш, ч, ж, щ) like A in 'soda.' This will be shown in the Imitated Pronunciation.

я, not stressed, sounds either like 'yĕh' or 'yăh.'

     дéвять   глядúте!   дя́дя   úмя   врéмя
   d'yeh-v'yĕht,   gl'yĕh-dee-t,ĕh!   d'yah-d'yăh   eem-yăh   vr,em-yăh
       nine   look!   uncle   Christian name   time

Stressed я: я   пять   меня́   шля́па   для
            yah   p'yaht,   m,ĕh-n'yah   shl'yah-păh   dl'yah
            I   five   of-me   hat   for

е, when stressed, is often pronounced 'yaw.'

This is shown by ё (two dots over e), but only in educational books.

     её   не   всё   день   Пётр
   yĕh-yaw   n,ĕh   fs,aw   d,en,   p'yawtrr
     her   not   everything   day   Peter

Unstressed е:

     ему́   перó   áдрес   семья́   дáйте!
   yĕh-moo   p,ĕh-raw   ah-dr,ess   c,em-yăh   die-t,ĕh!
   to-him   pen   address   family   give!

е, ё only sound 'eh' and 'aw' if coming after one of the hissing sounds:

        (ж j,   ч tch,   ш sh,   щ sh-tch)

   женá   чей   ещё   шесть   счёт
  jăh-nah   tchĕh˜e   yesh-tchaw   shest,   sh˜tchawt
   wife   whose   yet   six   bill

Ы (yeh-rɛ) is sounded almost like Y in 'pity.'

Most books give the sound as 'we' or 'oo˜e' (short), but this is hardly correct.

(For full explanation, see Difficult Sounds on page 9).

THE SEMI VOWELS.

Ъ (hard sign), or apostrophe, as explained on page 4, is placed between a consonant and a vowel when they must be pronounced separately.

Ь (soft sign)—see 'Difficult Sounds' on next page.

Й this letter can only be used after vowels with which it forms one syllable. It is pronounced without pausing between the letters.

ОЙ=OI in OIL	**АЙ**=IE in TIE
ЕЙ=YA in YALE	**УЙ**=the French OUI

ИЙ=ee͡e like ILLE in the French word FILLE.

The following CONSONANTS are pronounced thus:

Ж (7)=s in 'measure'	**Ч** (24)=ch in 'church'
Х (22)=h aspirated guttural like ch in 'loch'	**Ш** (25)=sh in 'shut'
Ц (23)=ts in 'nuts'	**Щ** (26)=sh-tch; sounds like sh and ch in 'fresh cheese'

Р (17) is to be rolled on the tongue, like a Scotch r.

В (3) sounds like V, but like F before or after sharp consonants: К, С, П, Т, Ф; hissing: Ш, Щ, Ч, and Ц, Х.

Г (4) like g in 'go,' but ГО, the Genitive termination of Adjectives and Pronouns, is pronounced vaw (short). At the end of a word and when followed by К it is often guttural.

The soft **Л** in Russian is almost like the L in 'million'; it is liquid, like the Spanish LL, and does not present any difficulty.

L is always soft before one of the soft vowels: (Я, Е, И, Ю, Ь).

DIFFICULT SOUNDS IN RUSSIAN.

The difficult sounds in Russian are:

     hard **Л**;   soft sign **Ь**;   **Ы** (yeh-rE *or* er͡e)

The hard **Л** has no equivalent in English. Its sound is produced by pressing the tongue against the roof of the mouth. Try to pronounce L with closed teeth, and in the throat.

    In North Britain the L is pronounced in a similar manner.

In Central Russia (Moscow, etc.) its pronunciation resembles that of the English W, and thus it is given in the Imitated Pronunciation, this being the nearest for English speaking people.

The hard L at the end of a word or syllable is imitated by L, where W would produce the wrong sound in English.

Ы (yeh-re) is another difficult sound, which occurs very frequently. It is the sound of I in FISH, PIT, pronounced deep down in the throat, and with closed teeth.

If ILL or BILL is pronounced with closed teeth, and in the throat, the exact sound of the Russian ы in был (was), and also of the Russian hard л is produced.

This sound is given in the Imitated Pronunciation by E.

The most difficult sound of all is that of the soft sound ь. This was in ancient Russian pronounced like и ; but nowadays it only sounds like a very short i (e) or yer, hardly heard. In our Imitated Pronunciation this is shown by the sign , after the consonant.

вы	мы	сын	часы́	был	была́
ve	me	cen	tchăh-ce	bel	be-wăh
you	we	son	watch, clock	was	she was
сло́во	стол	бы́ли	соль	для	ле́то
swaw-vaw	stol	be-lee	sol,	dl,ăh	l,eh-taw
word	table	were	salt	for	summer
мать	знать	день	то́лько		
maht,	znaht,	d,en,	tol,-kaw		
mother	to know	day	only		

The great thing to get a good **RUSSIAN PRONUNCIATION** is to put plenty of stress on the emphasized syllable, and to pronounce clearly and distinctly.

The remaining parts of the word are to be pronounced easily and without stress. If this is done, it does not matter if the exact shade of pronunciation is not obtained.

FIRST LESSON.
READING AND PRONUNCIATION.
(For "Hints on the Imitated Pronunciation," see page 3).

1. address   а́дрес
   ah-dr‚ess
2. house   дом
   dom
3. luggage   бага́ж
   băh-gahj
4. restaurant   рестора́н
   r‚ĕh-stăh-rahn
5. table   стол
   stoL (hard L)
6. ticket   биле́т
   bee-l‚et

All Nouns ending in consonants are MASCULINE.

7. booking-office   ка́сса
   kah-săh
8. hotel   гости́ница
   găh-stee-ne-tsăh
9. newspaper   газе́та
   găh-z‚eh-tăh
10. room   ко́мната
    kom-năh-tăh
11. street   у́лица
    oo-le-tsăh
12. telegram   телегра́мма
    t‚ĕh-l‚ĕh-grah-măh

All Nouns ending in a are FEMININE.

13. business   де́ло
    d-yay-lo or d‚eh-waw
14. letter   письмо́
    peess‚-maw
15. pen   перо́   *p‚ĕh-raw*

All Nouns ending in o are NEUTER.

WHERE?   где?   THIS   э́то   THERE   там
gd‚ĕh? or gd-yay?   *ay-to or a-taw (aw short)*   *tahm*

HERE IS *or* THERE IS   вот
                  vot (= the French 'voilà')

	MASCULINE.	FEMININE.	NEUTER.
OUR	наш	на́ша	на́ше
	nahsh	*nah-shăh*	*nah-shĕh*
YOUR	ваш	ва́ша	ва́ше
	vahsh	*vah-shăh*	*vah-shĕh*

These words take the same Gender and Number as the Noun.

1. A and THE are not translated in Russian, unless emphasized, and therefore дом may mean HOUSE, A HOUSE or THE HOUSE.

1. Translate into English.

The small figures indicate the number of the word in the Vocabulary.

1. дом,² комната,¹⁰ перо¹⁵; 2. наш билет,⁶ наша газета,⁹ наше письмо¹⁴; 3. ваш багаж,³ ваша гостиница,⁸ ваше дело¹³; 4. улица,¹¹ наш адрес,¹ ваш стол⁵; 5. наше дело,¹³ ваша телеграмма,¹² наш ресторан.⁴

1. Re-translate into Russian (Key to above).

1. a house, the room, a or the pen ; 2. our ticket, our newspaper, our letter ; 3. your luggage, your hotel, your business ; 4. a or the street, our address, your table ; 5. our business, your telegram, our restaurant.

2. Translate into English.

1. Где гостиница ? 2. Это ресторан. 3. Вот касса. 4. Ваш багаж там. 5. Это наш стол. 6. Где ваша комната ? 7. Вот наша улица. 8. Ваше перо там. 9. Это наш дом. 10. Вот ваше письмо. 11. Где ваш билет ? 12. Вот наш адрес.

IS, as a rule, is not rendered in Russian.

2. Re-translate into Russian (Key to above).

1. Where is the hotel ? 2. This is a restaurant. 3. Here is the booking-office. 4. Your luggage is there. 5. This is our table. 6. Where is your room ? 7. There is our street. 8. Your pen is there. 9. This is our house. 10. Here is your letter. 11. Where is your ticket ? 12. Here is our address.

2. The GENITIVE is formed in the following manner:
(OF in the GENITIVE is not translated by a separate word).

the house	дом	of-the-house	дóма
the pen	перó	of-a-pen	перá
the lady	дáма	of-the-lady	дáмы

IMITATED PRONUNCIATION.—daw-măh, p̆eh-rah, dăh-mE.
E stands for Ы, pronounced like I in PIT, with closed teeth.

These examples show that **A** is added where the Masculine ends in a consonant; that the Neuter Termination **O** becomes **A**; and that the Feminine ending **A** becomes **Ы**, as illustrated in the following table:

	MASCULINE.	NEUTER.	FEMININE.
NOMINATIVE:	consonant	o	a
	adds	becomes	becomes
GENITIVE:	a	a	ы

POSSESSIVES like 'the father's hat' must be translated by 'the hat of the father'; his friend's room=the room of his friend.

3.
HIS	егó	HER	её	THEIR	их
	yĕh-vaw		yĕh-yaw		eekh

Notice the exceptional pronunciation of the first two words.
The above three words are invariable in Number, Gender and Case.

16. brother   брат
       braht
17. doctor   дóктор
       dok-torr
18. flat   квартúра
       kfăhr-tee-răh
19. friend   друг
       drook *or* drookh

20. glass   стакáн
       stăh-kăhn
21. lady   дáма
       dah-măh
22. number   нóмер
       naw-m͵err
23. wine   винó
       ve-naw

4. Singular: WAS был
               bEL (boo͡iL)

FEMININE.   NEUTER.
былá   былo
bE-wah (boo͡e-wah)   bE-waw

Plural: WERE бы́ли
              bE-lee (boo͡e-lee)

Plural the same for Masculine, Feminine and Neuter.

(For Exercises, see page 15).

3. Translate into English.

The small figures indicate the number of the word in the Vocabulary.

1. его гостиница,[8] её адрес,[1] их дело[13]; 2. ресторана,[4] телеграммы,[12] пера[15]; 3. его письма,[14] их улицы[11]; 4. кассы,[7] её багажа[3]; 5. номер[22] дома[2]; 6. багаж дамы[21]; 7. друг[19] её брата[16]; 8. брат его друга; 9. квартира[18] их доктора[17]; 10. номер[22] её комнаты[10]; 11. квартира дамы[21]; 12. стакан[20] вина.[23]

3. Re-translate into Russian.

1. his hotel, her address, their business; 2. of the restaurant, of the telegram, of the pen; 3. of his letter, of their street; 4. of the booking-office, of her luggage; 5. the number of the house; 6. the lady's luggage=the luggage of the lady; 7. her brother's friend=e friend of her brother; 8. his friend's brother=the brother of his friend; 9. their doctor's flat; 10. the number of her room; 11. the lady's flat; 12. a glass of wine.

4. Translate into English.

1. Это дом их брата. 2. Где касса? 3. Вот ваша телеграмма. 4. Багаж дамы там. 5. Где гостиница его друга? 6. Это номер их дома. 7. Вот адрес его доктора. 8. Наша улица там. 9. Вот стакан вина.

4. Re-translate into Russian.

1. This is their brother's house. 2. Where is the booking-office? 3. Here is your telegram. 4. The lady's luggage is there. 5. Where is his friend's hotel? 6. This is the number of their house. 7. Here is his doctor's address. 8. Our street is there. 9. There is a glass of wine.

SECOND LESSON.

5. PERSONAL PRONOUNS (NOMINATIVE or SUBJECT)

SINGULAR.				PLURAL.	
1. I	Я yăh	1st person	1. WE	МЫ mE (moo͡e)
2. thou	ТЫ tE (too͡e)	2nd ,,	2. YOU	ВЫ vE (voo͡e)
3. HE	ОН on	3rd ,, (m.)	3. ⎫		
4. SHE	ОНÁ äh-nah	,, ,, (f.)	4. ⎬ THEY	ОНИ́ äh-nee
5. IT	ОНÓ äh-naw	,, ,, (n.)	5. ⎭		

Students who cannot understand the pronunciation of vE, mE, tE, may follow the less correct way : voo͡e, moo͡e, too͡e, as given in most books ; but be careful to pronounce with closed teeth.

AM, IS, and ARE not being rendered in Russian, Я may mean I and I AM, ВЫ YOU and YOU ARE, ОН HE and HE IS, etc.

6. ADJECTIVES AS PREDICATE (SHORT FORM)

I am ready   Я готóв   yăh găh-tof
she is not ready   онá не готóва   äh-nah n,eh găh-taw-văh
we are not ready   мы не готóвы   mE n,ĕh găh-taw-vE
they are ready   они́ готóвы   äh-n,eh găh-taw-vE
it is ready   готóво   gah-taw-vaw

(The Neuter is generally used without the Pronoun).

These terminations are the same as those of the Nouns : consonants, А, О ; Plural for all : Ы.

24. at (the place of) у (requires Genitive) oo	27. glad рад rahd
25. at home дóма daw-măh	28. here здесь zd,ess,
26. busy зáнят zah-n,ăht	29. right прав prăhf

5. Translate into English.

The small figures indicate the number of the word in the Vocabulary.

1. я рад,²⁷ вы пра́вы,²⁹ он не гото́в; 2. она́ за́нята,²⁶ они́ не пра́вы,²⁹ они́ ра́ды²⁷; 3. я был, она́ была́, мы бы́ли; 4. он не* был, вы не бы́ли, они́ не бы́ли; 5. был ли† он? не была́ ли она́? 6. мы не бы́ли, не бы́ли ли вы? не был ли он?

* HE (n-yay or n‚eh), NOT, is put before the Verb.
† In questions, ЛИ (lee) is put after the Verb. ЛИ has no meaning.

5. Re-translate into Russian.

1. I am glad, you are right, he is not ready; 2. she is busy, they are not right, they are glad; 3. I was, she was, we were; 4. he was not, you were not, they were not; 5. was he? was she not? 6. we were not, were you not? was he not?

6. Translate into English.

1. Он не был здесь.²⁸ 2. Не была́ ли она́ там? 3. Мы бы́ли до́ма.²⁵ 4. Бы́ли ли вы у²⁴ до́ктора¹⁷? 5. Я не был у²⁴ его́ дру́га.¹⁹ 6. Он не рад.²⁷ 7. Бы́ли ли вы пра́вы²⁹? 8. Они́ не за́няты.²⁶ 9. Не бы́ли ли они́ гото́вы? 10. Мы бы́ли у²⁴ её бра́та.¹⁶ 11. Они́ у²⁴ до́ктора. 12. Не бы́ли ли вы там?

6. Re-translate into Russian.

1. He was not here. 2. Was she not there? 3. We were at home. 4. Were you at the doctor's? 5. I was not at his friend's. 6. He is not glad. 7. Were you right? 8. They are not busy. 9. Were they not ready? 10. We were at her brother's. 11. They are at the doctor's. 12. Were you not there?

7. The Past Tense changes in the Plural, Feminine, and Neuter, like был (was), see par. 4.

I knew я знал   she knew она́ зна́ла
they knew они́ зна́ли

(For the Infinitive of the following Verbs, see page 18).

30. bought	купи́л koo-peeL	34. saw	ви́дел vee-d,eL
31. did, made	де́лал d,eh-wăhL	35. sold	про́дал praw-dăhL
32. knew	знал znăhL	36. smoked	кури́л koo-reeL
33. read (Past)	чита́л tche-tahL	37. wrote	писа́л pe-sahL
38. cigar	сига́ра ce-gah-răh	40. sister	сестра́ c,ĕh-strah
39. officer	офице́р ăh-fee-ts,err	41. ready	гото́в găh-tof

8. The Accusative of Nouns has the same form as the Nominative, see page 10.

Masculine: дом, house   Neuter: де́ло, business

Exceptions:

(*a*) The Accusative of Masculine Nouns, referring to Persons and Animals, is the same as the Genitive, see page 12, rule 2.

brother: Nom. брат   Gen. & Acc. бра́та

(*b*) Feminine Nouns change their ending **a** into **y** in the Accusative.
This refers to ALL Feminine Nouns in a, including Persons and Animals.

lady: Nom. дама́   Acc. да́му
newspaper: „ газе́та   „ газе́ту

The English must be changed when translating, thus:
did he see? *or* has he seen? into: SAW HE?
I did not write *or* I have not written, into: I NOT WROTE.
have you not bought? *or* } NOT BOUGHT (ли) YOU?
did you not buy?

7. Translate into English.

1. я курил,[36] он не курил, курили ли вы?
2. она писала,[37] мы не писали, писали ли они?
3. мы продали,[35] я не продал, продали ли вы?
4. он купил,[30] купила ли она? не купили ли они? 5. мы знали,[32] знали ли вы? они не знали;
6. я читала,[33] не читал ли он? мы не читали.

7. Re-translate into Russian.

1. I smoked, he did not smoke, did you smoke? 2. she wrote, we did not write, did they write? 3. we sold, I have not sold, have you sold? 4. he bought, did she buy? have they not bought? 5. we knew, did you know? they did not know; 6. I (f.) read, has he not read? we did not read.

8. Translate into English.

1. Курили[36] ли вы сигару[38]? 2. Он писал[37] письмо. 3. Продал[35] ли он ваш дом? 4. Я не купила[30] газеты.* 5. Знали[32] ли вы её брата? 6. Мы не читали их письма.[14] 7. Я видел[34] его друга.[19] 8. Не купили ли они пера? 9. Офицер[39] курил сигару.[38] 10. Она писала телеграмму.[12] 11. Читала ли она письмо её сестры[40]? 12. Видели[34] ли вы комнату их брата?

8. Re-translate into Russian.

1. Did you smoke a cigar? 2. He wrote a letter. 3. Has he sold your house? 4. I (f.) did not buy a paper. 5. Did you know her brother? 6. We did not read their letter. 7. I saw his friend. 8. Did they not buy a pen? 9. The officer was smoking a cigar. 10. She wrote a telegram. 11. Did she read her sister's letter? 12. Have you seen their brother's room?

* see Rule 9.

THIRD LESSON.

9. After a NEGATION, the Genitive is always used instead of the Accusative.

I saw the house	я ви́дел дом
I did not see the house	я не ви́дел до́ма
he read the paper	он чита́л газе́ту
he did not read the paper	он не чита́л газе́ты
we saw the lady	мы ви́дели да́му
we did not see the lady	мы не ви́дели да́мы

10. The PAST TENSE in Russian is very easy. It is formed by changing the ending ть of the Infinitive into л (Fem. ла, Neut. ло, Plur. ли), see page 16.

As there is only one Past Tense in Russian, 'I smoked, I have smoked, I was smoking, I have been smoking,' etc., are all translated by the same word (кури́л) in Russian.

30.	to buy	купи́ть	34.	to see	ви́деть
		koo-peet,			vee-d͵et,
31.	„ do, make	де́лать	35.	„ sell	прода́ть
		d͵eh-wäht,			präh-daht,
32.	„ know	знать	36.	„ smoke	кури́ть
		znaht,			koo-reet,
33.	„ read	чита́ть	37.	„ write	писа́ть
		tche-taht,			pe-saht,

The numbers correspond with those of the Past Tense on page 16.

11. The GENITIVE must be used after the NUMBERS two, three, and four.

42.	два часа́ two hours	Nominative:	час
	dvăh tchăh-sah		tchahss
43.	три мину́ты three minutes	„	мину́та
	tree me-noo-tɛ		me-noo-tăh
44.	четы́ре сло́ва four words	„	сло́во
	tchĕh-tɛ-r͵ĕh swaw-văh		swaw-vaw

Notice that in Russian the Noun is in the Singular.

9. Translate into English.

1. два стола,⁵ три дамы, четы́ре пера¹⁵; 2. две* ко́мнаты,¹⁰ три слова́,⁴⁴ четы́ре часа́⁴²; 3. вот на́ша гости́ница,⁸ э́то её де́ло¹³; 4. вот ваш биле́т,⁶ э́то на́ша кварти́ра¹⁸; 5. где их бага́ж³? 6. но́мер их до́ма, а́дрес да́мы; 7. я был здесь, она́ не была́ там, бы́ли ли они́ до́ма? 8. я рад²⁷; 9. он не был гото́в.⁴¹

*две is used instead of два before Feminine Nouns.

9. Re-translate into Russian.

1. two tables, three ladies, four pens; 2. two rooms, three words, four hours; 3. here is our hotel, this is her business; 4. there is your ticket, that is our flat; 5. where is their luggage? 6. the number of their house, the lady's address; 7. I was here, she was not there, were they at home? 8. I am glad; 10. he was not ready.

10. Translate into English.

1. Я ви́дел³⁴ её бра́та. 2. Они́ не купи́ли³⁰ гости́ницы. 3. Мы не прода́ли³⁵ их до́ма. 4. Ви́дели ли вы его́ сестру́⁴⁰? 5. Я не писа́ла³⁷ телегра́ммы.¹² 6. Чита́ли³³ ли вы газе́ту? 7. Зна́ла ли она́ ваш а́дрес? 8. Не кури́л³⁶ ли он сига́ры³⁸? 9. Бы́ли ли вы у его́ сестры́? 10. Они́ ви́дели его́ дру́га. 11. Мы не́ были у до́ктора.

10. Re-translate into Russian.

1. I saw her brother. 2. They did not buy the hotel. 3. We have not sold their house. 4. Did you see his sister? 5. I (f.) did not write the telegram. 6. Did you read the paper? 7. Did she know your address? 8. Did he not smoke a cigar? 9. Were you at his sister's? 10. They have seen his friend. 11. We were not at the doctor's.

12. PERSONAL PRONOUNS (continued from page 14).

GENITIVE AND ACCUSATIVE (have both the same form).

ME, of me   меня   **HIM**, of him   его
     men-yăh, better: m‚ĕh-n‚ah   yĕh-vaw

OF HER, Genitive: её   **HER**, Accusative: её
     pronunciation of Genitive and Accusative: yĕh-yaw

US, of us   нас   **YOU**, of you   вас
     nahss   vahss

THEM, of them   их   **THEE**, of thee   тебя
     for Masc., Fem., and Neuter: eekh   teb-yăh or t‚ĕh-b‚ah

13. Example of the Regular Verbs: TO KNOW, знать.

The Terminations of the PRESENT of most Verbs are added by changing the ть of the INFINITIVE, thus:

I know	я знаю	we know	мы знаем
thou knowest	ты знаешь	you know	вы знаете
he knows	он знает	they know	они знают

     IMITATED PRONUNCIATION: yăh znah-yoo, tE znah-yesh, on znah-yet; mE znah-yem, vE znah-yĕh-t‚ĕh, ăh-nee znah-yoot.

I do, etc., я делаю, ты делаешь, он делает мы делаем, вы делаете, они делают.

     IMITATED PRONUNCIATION: d‚eh-wăh-yoo, d‚eh-wăh-yesh, d‚eh-wăh-yet; d‚eh-wăh-yem, d‚eh-wăh-yĕt-t‚eh, d‚eh-wăh-yoot.

I do not read, я не читаю; does he read? читает ли он? she reads, она читает; we do not read, мы не читаем; do you not read? не читаете ли вы? they do not read, они не читают.

     IMITATED PRONUNCIATION: yăh n‚ĕh tche-tăh-yoo; tche-tăh-yet le on? ăh-nah tche-tah-yet; mE n‚eh tche-tah-yem; n‚ĕh tche-tah-yĕh-t‚ĕh le vE? ăh-nee n‚ĕh tche-tah-yoot.

45. ask	спрашивать	47. meet	встречать
	sprah-she-văht,		fstr‚ĕh-tohăht,
46. invite	приглашать	48. understand	понимать
	pre-gwăh-shaht,		păh-ne-maht,

11. Translate into English.

1. я не понима́ю, понима́ет ли она́? он не понима́ет; 2. мы спра́шиваем, не спра́шиваете ли вы? они́ спра́шивают; 3. я зна́ю вас, он не зна́ет меня́, зна́ете ли вы их? 4. мы не приглаша́ем его́, приглаша́ют ли они́ её? они́ не приглаша́ют её; 5. я не встреча́ю, встреча́ют ли они́? 6. мы ви́дели её.

11. Re-translate into Russian.

1. I do not understand, does she understand? he does not understand; 2. we are asking, do you not ask? they are asking; 3. I know you, he does not know me, do you know them? 4. we do not invite him, do they invite her? they do not invite her; 5. I do not meet, do they meet? 6. we saw her.

12. Translate into English.

1. Он чита́ет газе́ту. 2. Я не зна́ю его́ дру́га. 3. Встреча́ете ли вы до́ктора? 4. Она́ писа́ла телегра́мму. 5. Мы не понима́ем её письма́. 6. Я приглаша́ю их. 7. Не зна́ете ли вы́ их а́дреса? 8. Мы зна́ем у́лицу, но не зна́ем но́мера до́ма. 9. Они́ понима́ли меня́, но я не понима́л их. 10. Не зна́ете ли вы, где она́?

12. Re-translate into Russian.

1. He is reading the paper. 2. I do not know his friend. 3. Are you meeting the doctor? 4. She was writing a telegram. 5. We do not understand her letter. 6. I invite them. 7. Don't you know their address? 8. We know the street, but (но) don't know the number of the house. 9. They understood me, but I did not understand them. 10. Don't you know where she is?

FOURTH LESSON.

14. The GENITIVE must be used after all Prepositions, unless the contrary is pointed out.

for me, для меня   from him, от него*

dl‚äh m‚ĕh-n‚ah   äht n‚eh-vaw

without the officer, без офицéра, b‚ez äh-fe-ts‚eh-räh

*The following examples show that Personal Pronouns beginning with **е** or **и** must prefix an **н**(n) after any Preposition.

him, of him	егó	at his place	у негó
her, of her	её	at her place	у неё
them, of them	их	at their ,,	у них

егó his, **её** her, **их** their, take no **н** when followed by a Noun.

15. TO HAVE meaning TO POSSESS has to be changed when translating into Russian, thus:

I have a book
= by me (is) a book   } у меня кнúга
                                   oo-m‚ĕh-n‚äh k-nee-gäh

has he the ticket?
= is by him ticket?   } есть ли у негó билéт?
                                yesst‚ le oo n‚ĕh-vaw be-l‚et?

In questions, **есть** (is) must be expressed in most cases.

we have no luggage
= by us no luggage   } у нас нет багажá
                              oo-nahss n‚et bäh-gäh-jah

have they no house?
= is not by them house? } нет ли у них дóма?
                                  n‚et le oo-neekh daw-mäh?

	NOMINATIVE.			GENITIVE.	
	MASC.	NEUT.	FEM.	MASC. & NEUT.	FEM.
16. THIS	э́тот	э́то	э́та	э́того	э́той
THAT	ay-tot	ay-taw	ay-täh	ay-täh-vaw	ay-toy
MY	мой	моё	моя́	моегó	моéй
	moy	mäh-yaw	mäh-yah	mäh-yĕh-vaw	mäh-yĕh͡e

MASC. & NEUT.	FEM.		MASC. & NEUT.	FEM.
OF OUR нáшего	нáшей	OF YOUR	вáшего	вáшей
nah-shĕh-vaw	nah-shĕh͡e		vah-shĕh-vaw	vah-shĕh͡e

13. Translate into English.

1. мой карандашъ,⁵⁷ моя шляпа,⁵⁴ моё мѣсто⁵⁸; 2. этотъ господинъ,⁵³ эта книга,⁴⁹ это слово⁴⁴; 3. нашего дома, нашей улицы¹¹; 4. вашего дѣла,¹³ вашей шляпы⁵⁴; 5. моего карандаша,⁵⁷ моей сестры; 6. этого офицера,³⁹ этой книги*; 7. безъ моего друга, отъ этой дамы; 8. для этого господина, у вашей сестры; 9. у меня билетъ; 10. у него нѣтъ вашего конверта⁵²; 11. есть ли у васъ моя телеграмма? 12. нѣтъ ли у нихъ нашего багажа? For Vocabulary, see page 24.

13. Re-translate into Russian.

1. my pencil, my hat, my place; 2. this gentleman, that book, this word; 3. of our house, of our street; 4. of your business, of your hat; 5. of my pencil, of my sister; 6. of this officer, of this book; 7. without my friend, from this lady; 8. for that gentleman, at your sister's; 9. I have got the ticket; 10. he has not got your envelope; 11. have you my telegram? 12. have they not got our luggage?

14. Translate into English.

1. Есть ли у васъ мой карандашъ? 2. Нѣтъ, у меня нѣтъ вашего карандаша. 3. Есть ли у него мѣсто⁵⁸? 4. Нѣтъ ли у нихъ нашей книги?* 5. Не понимаетъ⁴⁸ ли онъ моей телеграммы? 6. Мы встрѣчаемъ⁴⁷ нашего друга.

14. Re-translate into Russian.

1. Have you got my pencil? 2. No, I have not got your pencil. 3. Has he got a place? 4. Haven't they got our book? 5. Does he not understand my telegram? 6. We are meeting our friend.

* After gutturals (г) и must be used instead of ы in the Genitive.

49. book	книга k-nee-găh	56. no (*or* there is not)	нет n‚et *or* n-yet
50. dog	собака săh-bah-kăh	57. pencil	карандаш kăh-răhn-dahsh
51. English =in English	по-английски păh-ăhn-glee^e-ske	58. place (room)	место m‚eh-staw
52. envelope	конверт kăhn-v‚errt	59. Russian =in Russian	по-русски păh-roo-ske
53. gentleman	господин găh-spăh-deen	60. who ? ktaw ? *or* khtaw ?	кто ?
54. hat	шляпа shl‚ăh-păh	61. what ? shtaw ? *or* tchtaw ?	что ?
55. a-little =not much	немного n‚ĕh-mпaw-gaw	62. yes dăh	да

17. Besides the Verbs which add ю, ешь, ет, ем, ете, ют, instead of the Infinitive ть, there are Verbs which add: ю, ишь, ит, им, ите, ят.
        yoo,   eesh,   eet,   eem, eet-yĕh, yăhtt.

TO SPEAK, TO say, TO TELL, говорить (găh-văh-reet,)

I speak я говорю	we speak мы говорим
thou speakest ты говоришь	you speak вы говорите
he speaks он говорит	they speak они говорят

yah găh-văhr-yoo, tE=twe găh-văh-reesh, on găh-văh-reet, mE=mwe găh-văh-reem. vE=we găh-văh-ree-t‚ĕh, ăh-nee găh-văhr-yăht.

63. to praise	хвалить khfăh-leet,	65. to tease	дразнить drăh-zneet,
64. to smoke	курить koo-reet,	66. to thank	благодарить bwăh-găh-dăh-reet,

When translating into Russian, the English must be changed thus: I do not thank=I not thank ; is she thanking ?=thanks she ? they are not smoking *or* they do not smoke=they not smoke ; are you not speaking ? *or* do you not speak ?=not speak you ?

15. Translate into English.

1. я курю́, ты ку́ришь, он не ку́рит; 2. мы ку́рим, ку́рите ли вы? они́ не ку́рят; 3. я благодарю́, не благодари́ть ли она́? мы не благодари́м; 4. хвали́те ли вы? они́ хваля́т, не хвали́т ли она́? 5. он дразни́т меня́, я не дразню́ её, не дразня́т ли они́ вас? 6. благодарю́ вас, он не благодари́т нас.

15. Re-translate into Russian.

1. I smoke, thou smokest, he does not smoke; 2. we are smoking, do you smoke? they do not smoke; 3. I thank, does she not thank? we do not thank; 4. do you praise? they are praising, is she not praising? 5. he teases me, I do not tease her, don't they tease you? 6. (I) thank you, he does not thank us.

16. Translate into English.

1. Говори́те ли вы по-ру́сски? 2. Да, я говорю́ немно́го. 3. Говори́т ли ваш друг по-англи́йски? 4. Нет, но он понима́ет. 5. Она́ не благодари́ла меня́. 6. Не благодари́те ли вы их? 7. Ку́рит ли он сига́ру? 8. Кто говори́т? 9. Она́ писа́ла по-ру́сски. 10. Они́ спра́шивают по-англи́йски. 11. Кто ку́рит здесь? 12. Что вы говори́те?

16. Re-translate into Russian.

1. Do you speak Russian? 2. Yes, I speak a little. 3. Does your friend speak English? 4. No, but he understands. 5. She did not thank me. 6. Don't you thank them? 7. Is he smoking a cigar? 8. Who is speaking? 9. She wrote in Russian. 10. They are asking in English. 11. Who is smoking here? 12. What do you say?

67. in-the-evening	вечером	71. to-day	сегодня
	v‚eh-tchĕh-rom		c‚ĕh-vaw-dn‚ăh
68. in-the-morning	утром	72. very	очень
	oo-trom		aw-tchen‚
69. only	только	73. when ?	когда ?
	tol‚-kaw		kăh-gdăh
70. thanks	спасибо	74. yesterday	вчера
=I thank you	spăh-cee-baw		ftchĕh-rah

REMARKS on DECLENSION OF NOUNS.

All Russian Nouns end in one of the following NINE terminations:

MASCULINE.		FEMININE.		NEUTER.	
HARD.	SOFT.	HARD.	SOFT.	HARD.	SOFT.
consonants	й, ь*	а	я, ь*	о	е, мя*

The above endings are part of the word, as it appears in dictionaries and lists of words. This form is often called the NOMINATIVE.

So far, only Nouns with the HARD ENDINGS have been used; that is to say, MASCULINES ending in CONSONANTS, FEMININES ending in **a**, and NEUTERS ending in **o**.

The above Table shows that BESIDES THE ONE HARD ENDING each Gender or Declension has also TWO SOFT ENDINGS.

Although there are SIX SOFT ENDINGS, these words are, from a practical point of view, far less important than the THREE HARD ENDINGS.

* There are about ten Nouns ending in **мя**, only three or four of which are of importance. Nouns ending in the soft sign are not numerous, but they are important. Some of them are Masculine, some Feminine. The best plan is to consider them all as Feminine, and to learn the Masculines as they occur.

Names of PERSONS retain their natural GENDER, no matter how they end.

RECAPITULATORY PRACTICE.

1. Где ваш брат? 2. Я не видел моего брата. 3. Он знает нашего друга. 4. Продали ли вы ваш дом? 5. Эта дама моя сестра. 6. Не видели ли вы моей квартиры? 7. Кто читает нашу газету?

    1. Where is your brother? 2. I did not see my brother. 3. He knows our friend. 4. Did you sell your house? 5. This lady is my sister. 6. Did not you see my flat? 7. Who reads our newspaper?

8. Я был очень занят вчера вечером. 9. Она не была готова. 10. Я делаю это только для вас.—Спасибо. 11. Мы встретили этого офицера у нашей сестры. 12. У них были две дамы и два господина.

    8. I was very busy yesterday in-the-evening. 9. She was not ready. 10. I am doing this only for you.—Thanks. 11. We met this officer at our sister's. 12. At their-place were two ladies and two gentlemen.

13. У неё четыре комнаты. 14. Нет ли у вас карандаша?—Есть. 15. У моего брата нет билета. 16. Есть ли у вас багаж? 17. Мы купили это для нашей сестры. 18. Когда вы писали эту* телеграмму? 19. Вы курите? 20. Они курят только сигары.

    13. She has got four rooms. 14. Haven't you got a pencil (=is not by you pencil)?—I have (is). 15. My brother has no ticket. 16. Have you got any luggage? 17. We have bought this for our sister. 18. When did you write this telegram? 19. Do you smoke? 20. They only smoke cigars.   *see page 28.

FIFTH LESSON.

18. Learn the following forms of the ACCUSATIVE which must always be used with any Feminine Noun in the Accusative:

OUR	на́шу	nah-shoo	YOUR	ва́шу	vah-shoo
MY	мою́	măh-yoo	THIS, THAT	э́ту	ay-too

This ending is the same as that of the Feminine Nouns in a.

The Accusative of these Pronouns for Masculine and Neuter is like the Nominative; but when followed by a Masculine Noun, referring to a living being, the endings are like the Genitive.

75.	always	всегда́	80.	pound	фунт
	fc,eg-dah			weight, money	foont
76.	answer	отвеча́ть	81.	present	пода́рок
	ăht-f,ĕh-tchaht,			(Noun)	păh-dah-rok
77.	believe	ве́рить	82.	send	посыла́ть
	v,eh-reet,			păh-ce-wăht,	
78.	give	дать	83.	truth	пра́вда
	daht,			prahv-dăh	
79.	pay	заплати́ть	84.	yet	еще́
	zăh-pwăh-teet,			yĕh-sh^tchaw	

19. PERSONAL PRONOUNS (continued from page 20).

DATIVE or INDIRECT OBJECT.

SINGULAR.			PLURAL.		
ME, to me	мне		US, to us	нам	
	mn,yeh or mn,ĕh			năhmm	
thee, to thee	тебе́		YOU, to you	вам	
	teb-yeh			văhmm	
HIM, to him	ему́		THEM, to them	им	
	yĕh-moo			imm or eem	
HER, to her	ей		For MASC., FEM., and NEUTER.		
	yĕh,e or yĕh^e				

The DATIVE must be used in sentences like: he sent me (=to me) the parcel; we gave the boy (=to the boy) a book.

17. Translate into English.

1. он не отвеча́ет[76] мне, отвеча́ют ли они́ вам? 2. я не ве́рю[77] ему́, не ве́рите ли вы им? 3. мы даём[78] вам э́то, не даю́т ли они́ ей? 4. кто говори́т? говори́т ли она́ вам? 5. я заплати́л[79] им, не заплати́ли ли вы ему́? 6. кто чита́ет мою́ газе́ту? ви́дели ли вы на́шу кварти́ру? 7. она́ встреча́ет[47] э́ту да́му, она́ зна́ет на́шу сестру́.

1. he does not answer (to-) me, do they answer (to-) you? 2. I do not believe (to-) him, don't you believe (to-) them? 3. we give (to-) you that, don't they give (to-) her? 4. who is speaking? does she tell (to-) you? 5. I paid (to-) them, did you not pay (to-) him? 6. who is reading my newspaper? did you see our flat? 7. she is meeting this lady, she knows our sister.

18. Translate into English.

1. Я отвеча́ю[76] ему́ по-ру́сски.[59] 2. Писа́ла[37] ли она́ вам? 3. Они́ не ве́рят[77] нам. 4. Купи́ли[30] ли вы мне газе́ту? 5. Она́ заплати́ла[79] им два фу́нта.[80] 6. Они́ даю́т[78] ей пода́рок.[81] 7. Что вы посыла́ете[82] ему́? 8. Я писа́ла ему́ письмо́ вчера́.[74] 9. Он всегда́[75] говори́т мне пра́вду.[83] 10. Про́дали[35] ли вы им э́тот дом? 11. Мы купи́ли[30] ему́ шля́пу.[54]

1. I answer (to-) him in-Russian. 2. Did she write to you? 3. They do not believe (to-)us. 4. Did you buy (to-) me a newspaper? 5. She paid (to-) them two pounds. 6. They give (to-) her a present. 7. What do you send to him? 8. I (f.) was writing to him a letter yesterday. 9. He always tells (to-) me the truth. 10. Did you sell (to-) them that house? 11. We bought (to-) him a hat.

85. taxi driver шофéр
    sho-fair
86. how much ? скóлько?
   or how many ? skol‚kaw
87. to-morrow зáвтра
    zahf-träh
88. why ?   почемý ?
   păh-tchĕh-moo ?

20. The terminations of the DATIVE of Nouns are :
MASCULINE and NEUTER change the last letter of the NOUN into y.

брат to the brother брáту | перó to the pen перý
braht   brah-too p‚ĕh-raw   p‚ĕh-roo

FEMININE NOUNS change the a into e.

дáма dah-măh   to the lady дáме dah-m‚ĕh

21. The DATIVE forms of Pronouns, used so far, are :

         MASC. & NEUT. FEM.   MASC. & NEUT. FEM.
TO-MY моемý моéй   TO-OUR нáшему нáшей
        măh-yĕh-moo măh-yeh^e   nah-shĕh-moo nah-shĕh^e
TO-YOUR вáшему вáшей   TO-THIS э́тому э́той
        vah-shĕh-moo vah-shĕh^e   TO-THAT ay-taw-moo ay-toy

22.   FUTURE of TO BE, БЫТЬ boo^it,

I shall be   я бýду | we shall be мы бýдем
thou wilt be ты бýдешь | you will be вы бýдете
he will be   он бýдет | they will be они́ бýдут

IMITATED PRONUNCIATION.—yăh-boo-doo, tE boo-d‚esh, on boo-d‚et ; mE boo-d‚em, vE boo-d‚ĕh-t‚ĕh, ăh-nee boo-doot.

I give, etc., is regular, except for the accented ё.

   я даю́, даёшь, даёт, даём, даёте, даю́т.
   dăh-yoo, dăh-yosh, dăh-yot, dăh-yom, dăh-yot-yĕh, dăh-yoot.

Notice the position of the Subject in questions beginning with a word of interrogation.

The Russian for : how much did HE pay ?=how much HE paid ? what do YOU say ?=what YOU say ? why were THEY not here ?= why THEY not were here ? ли is not used in such cases.

19. Translate into English.

1. моему́ бра́ту, мое́й сестре́ ; 2. э́тому сло́ву, э́той ко́мнате ; 3. на́шему ме́сту, ва́шей у́лице ; 4. я не бу́ду, бу́дет ли он ? она́ не бу́дет ; 5. мы бу́дем, не бу́дете ли вы ? они́ бу́дут ; 6. не бу́дут ли они́ ? бу́дете ли вы до́ма ? я бу́ду там за́втра[87] ; 7. мы ему́ ещё[84] не заплати́ли,[79] он нам ещё не писа́л.

1. to my brother, to my sister ; 2. to this word, to that room ; 3. to our place, to your street ; 4. I shall not be, will he be ? she will not be ; 5. we shall be, will you not be ? they will be ; 6. won't they be ? will you be at home ? I shall be there to-morrow ; 7. we have not paid (to-) him yet, he has not yet written to us.

20. Translate into English.

1. Ско́лько[86] вы заплати́ли[79] э́тому господи́ну ? 2. Мы отвеча́ем[76] ва́шему дру́гу.[19] 3. Бу́дет ли он там сего́дня[71] ? 4. Мы не бу́дем до́ма сего́дня ве́чером.[67] 5. Говори́ли ли вы э́то ва́шей сестре́ ? 6. Она́ даёт кни́гу э́той да́ме. 7. Почему́[88] вы не посыла́ете[82] письма́ моему́ бра́ту ? 8. Не бу́дут ли они́ у вас за́втра[87] у́тром[68] ? 9. Заплати́ли[79] ли вы ва́шему шофёру[85] ?

1. How much did you pay (to-) this gentleman ? 2. We are answering (to-) your friend. 3. Will he be there to-day ? 4. We shall not be at home to-day in-the-evening (= this evening). 5. Did you tell that to your sister ? 6. She is giving a book to that lady. 7. Why do you not send a letter to my brother ? 8. Will they not be at your place to-morrow in-the-morning ? 9. Did you pay (to-) your taxi driver ?

To be referred to constantly,

UNTIL THOROUGHLY MASTERED.

RUSSIAN DECLENSIONS SIMPLIFIED.
(See also page 26. For Exercises, see page 35.)

1. When studying the Russian Declensions, it is important to know that only the HARD DECLENSIONS have to be learnt.
2. The SOFT DECLENSIONS need no learning, because the terminations of the SOFT NOUNS can be formed from the HARD ENDINGS by the following simple rule:

| а becomes soft я | у becomes soft ю |
| о ,, е | ы ,, и |

NOTE.—Terminations not containing one of these vowels have the same ending for Hard and Soft Nouns.

EXAMPLES.—The GENITIVE of HARD MASCULINES ends in а, therefore the GENITIVE of the SOFT MASCULINES must end in я.

HARD: дом   Genitive: дома
therefore the Soft Endings must be:

музе́й Genitive музе́я | рубль Genitive рубля́
moo-z͡eh͡e museum moo-z͡eh-yăh   roobl,   rouble   roob-l̯ah

The GENITIVE of HARD FEMININES ends in ы, therefore the GENITIVE of SOFT FEMININES must end in и.

HARD: шля́па   Genitive: шля́пы
therefore the Soft Endings must be:

а́рмия Genitive а́рмии | ночь Genitive но́чи
arr-mee͡yăh army arr-mee͡ye   notch   night   naw-tche

The GENITIVE of HARD NEUTERS ends in а, therefore the GENITIVE of SOFT NEUTERS must end in я.

HARD: перо́   Genitive пера́
therefore the Soft Endings must be :

мо́ре Genitive мо́ря | и́мя Genitive и́мени*
maw-r‚eh   sea   maw-r‚äh   ee-m‚äh   name   ee-m‚ĕh-ne

The ACCUSATIVE of HARD FEMININES ends in y, therefore the ACCUSATIVE of the CORRESPONDING SOFT FEMININES (я) must end in ю.

HARD: у́лица   Accusative у́лицу
therefore the Soft Endings must be :

а́рмия Accusative а́рмию | соль Accusative соль †
arr-mee͡yäh   army   arr-mee͡yoo   sol‚   salt   sol‚
† Accusative Feminine soft sign same as Nominative.

The DATIVE of HARD MASCULINES ends in y, therefore the DATIVE of SOFT MASCULINES must end in ю.

HARD: стол   Dative столу́
therefore the Soft Endings must be :

чай   Dative ча́ю | Царь   Dative Царю́
tchie   tea   tchah-yoo   tsarr‚   Tsar   tsäh-r‚yoo

The DATIVE of HARD FEMININES ends in e and according to the note following Rule 2, page 32, the DATIVE of SOFT FEMININES must be the same.

HARD: да́ма   Dative да́ме
therefore the Soft Endings must be :

пу́ля   Dative пу́ле | дверь   Dative две́ри ‡
poo-l‚äh   bullet   poo-l‚ĕh   dv‚err‚   door   dv‚eh-re
‡ Feminine soft sign take И.

The DATIVE of HARD NEUTERS ends in y, therefore the DATIVE of SOFT NEUTERS must end in ю.

HARD: письмо́   Dative письму́
therefore the Soft Endings must be :

мне́ние Dative мне́нию | вре́мя Dative вре́мени*
mn‚eh-nee͡yäh opinion mn‚eh-nee͡yoo   vr‚eh-m‚äh time vr‚eh-m‚ĕh-ne
* one of the ten exceptions in МЯ.

CONVERSATIONAL SENTENCES.

1. Гдé онá?—Онá дóма. 2. Вот он! Я здесь. 3. Они́ там. 4. Кто[1] э́то?—Э́то мы. 5. Что э́то?—Э́то наш карандáш. 6. Когдá вы бы́ли у них? 7. Сегóдня[2] ýтром.[3]

1. Where is she?—She is at home. 2. There he is! I am here. 3. They are there. 4. Who is this?—This are we (=it is we *or* us). 5. What is this?—This is our pencil. 6. When were you at their place? 7. To-day in-the-morning (=this morning).

8. Где вы бы́ли вчерá[4]? 9. Я был у моегó дрýга. 10. Был ли он дóма?—Был. 11. Понимáете ли вы по-рýсски[5]? 12. Нет, не понимáю. 13. Ви́дели ли вы моегó брáта сегóдня[2]? 14. Да, ви́дел; он был здесь ýтром.[3] 15. Не спрáшивал ли он, где я? 16. Нет, не спрáшивал.

8. Where were you yesterday? 9. I was at my friend's. 10. Was he at home? — (He) was. 11. Do you understand Russian? 12. No, not understand (=I don't). 13. Have you seen my brother to-day? 14. Yes, saw (=I have); he was here in the morning. 15. Didn't he ask, where I (am)? 16. No, not asked (=he didn't).

17. Знáет ли он э́того господи́на? 18. Да, э́тот господи́н егó друг. 19. Кто[1] э́та дáма? 20. Не знáю, кто онá. 21. Что[6] вы дéлали вчерá[4] вéчером[7]? 22. Я писáл письмó и читáл кни́гу.

17. Does he know that gentleman? 18. Yes, this gentleman is his friend. 19. Who is this lady? 20. (I) do not know who she is. 21. What did you do yesterday (in the) evening? 22. I wrote a letter and read a book.

IMITATED PRONUNCIATION: 1. ktaw. 2. c,ĕh-vaw-d,năh. 3. oo-trom. 4. ftchĕh-rah. 5. păh-roo-ske. 6. tchtaw. 7. v,eh-tchĕh-rom.

PRACTICE on SOFT DECLENSION NOUNS.
(For explanation, see pages 32 and 33).

These words, some of which are not in the Vocabulary, are given in Nominative, Genitive, Dative, and also in the Accusative when different from Nominative or Genitive.

1. музе́й, музе́я, музе́ю; 2. слова́рь, словаря́, словарю́; 3. торго́вля, торго́вли, торго́вле, торго́влю; 4. дверь, две́ри, две́ри; 5. здоро́вье, здоро́вья, здоро́вью; 6. Кита́й, Кита́я, Кита́ю.

IMITATED PRONUNCIATION.—1. moo-z‚eh^e, moo-z‚eh-yăh, moo-z‚eh-yoo; 2. swăh-varr‚‚, swăh-văh-r‚ah, swăh-văh-r‚oo; 3. tarr-gov-l‚ăh, tarr-gov-le, tarr-gov-l‚ĕh, tarr-gov-l‚oo; 4. dv‚err‚‚, dv‚eh-re, dv‚eh-re; 5. zdăh-rov-yĕh, zdăh-rov-yăh, zdăh-rov-yoo; 6. ke-tie, ke-tah-yăh, ke-tah-yoo.

1. museum, of the museum, to the museum; 2. a dictionary, of a dictionary, to a dictionary; 3. trade, of trade, to trade, trade (Accus.); 4. the door, of the door, to the door; 5. health, of health, to health; 6. China, of China, to China.

7. мой дя́дя, моего́ дя́ди, моему́ дя́де, моего́ дя́дю; 8. наш учи́тель, на́шего учи́теля, на́шему учи́телю; 9. э́та ночь, э́той но́чи, э́той но́чи, э́ту ночь; 10. ва́ше мне́ние, ва́шего мне́ния, ва́шему мне́нию.

IMITATED PRONUNCIATION.—7. moy d‚ah-d‚ăh, măh-yĕh-vaw d‚ah-de, măh-yĕh-moo d‚ah-d‚ĕh, măh-yĕh-vaw d‚ah-d‚oo; 8. nahsh oo-tchee-t‚el‚‚, nah-sheh-vaw oo-tchee-t‚ĕh-l‚ăh, nah-sheh-moo oo-tchee-t‚ĕh-l‚oo; 9. ay-tăh notch, ay-toy naw-tche, ay-toy naw-tche, ay-too notch; 10. vah-shĕh mn‚eh-ne^yĕh, vah-shĕh-vaw mn‚eh-ne^yăh, vah-shĕh-moo mn‚eh-ne^yoo.

7. my uncle, of my uncle, to my uncle, my uncle (Acc.); 8. our teacher, of our teacher, to our teacher; 9. this night, of this night, to this night, this night (Accus.); 10. your opinion, of your opinion, to your opinion.

SIXTH LESSON.

23. The Terminations of the INSTRUMENTAL are:
MASCULINE and NEUTER: **OM** FEMININE: **ой (or ою)**

ой is the more usual of the two, being the shorter form.

The "Instrumental Case," as its name implies, denotes the INSTRUMENT, PERSON, MANNER, MEANS, by which something is done or caused.

with-a-knife	ножóм	by-a-word	слóвом
	năh-jom		swaw-vom
with-a-newspaper	газéтой or газéтою		
	găh-z,eh-toy, găh-z,eh-taw-yoo		

The examples show that these PREPOSITIONS are simply rendered by the INSTRUMENTAL, and are not translated separately.

But if WITH means TOGETHER WITH, it must be rendered by **с** or **со**, followed by the INSTRUMENTAL.

we were with your brother	мы бы́ли с ва́шим бра́том
	me be-le s'vah-sheem brah-tom

24. The INSTRUMENTAL of PRONOUNS, used so far, is:

	MASC. & NEUTER.	FEMININE.		
BY MY	мои́м	моéй	or	моéю
BY YOUR	ва́шим	ва́шей	,,	ва́шею
WITH OUR	на́шим	на́шей	,,	на́шею
WITH THIS	э́тим	э́той	,,	э́тою

Masc. & Neut.: măh-eem, vah-sheem, nah-sheem, ay-teem. Fem.: măh-yĕh^e or măh-yĕh-yoo, vah-shĕh^e, nah-shĕh^e, ay-toy or ay-taw-yoo.

25. The FUTURE is formed by placing the INFINITIVE after the Future of TO BE (rule 22).

I shall know	я бу́ду знать
he will not speak	он не бу́дет говори́ть
will he understand ?	бу́дет ли он понима́ть ?

This FUTURE form can only be used with IMPERFECTIVE Verbs (see p. 48).

21. Translate into English.
(For Vocabulary, see page 41).

1. карандашо́мъ, бума́гой,[107] перо́мъ; 2. мое́й кни́гой,[49] ва́шимъ биле́томъ,[6] на́шей телегра́ммой; 3. э́тимъ а́второмъ,[89] э́той да́мой, по́ездомъ[116]; 4. съ мои́мъ ученико́мъ,[109] съ на́шей сестро́й; 5. чай[114] съ са́харомъ,[113] съ лимо́номъ,[100] съ молоко́мъ[101]; 6. я не бу́ду кури́ть,[64] не бу́детъ ли онъ рабо́тать[121]? 7. мы бу́демъ говори́ть, не бу́дете ли вы писа́ть? 8. они́ не бу́дутъ знать, бу́дутъ ли они́ понима́ть?

1. with a pencil, with paper, with a pen; 2. with my book, with your ticket, with our telegram; 3. by this author, by that lady, by train; 4. together-with my pupil, together-with our sister; 5. tea with sugar, with lemon, with milk; 6. I shall not smoke, will he not work? 7. we shall speak, will you not write? 8. they will not know, will they understand?

22. Translate into English.

1. Не бу́дете ли вы говори́ть сего́дня[71] съ ва́шимъ хозя́иномъ[99]? 2. Я бу́ду писа́ть карандашо́мъ и́ли перо́мъ. 3. Онъ не бу́детъ кури́ть э́той сига́ры.[38] 4. Они́ бу́дутъ обѣ́дать[92] за́втра[87] съ ва́шимъ бра́томъ. 5. Я бу́ду у васъ съ мое́й жено́й[120] ве́черомъ.[67] 6. Э́та кни́га напи́сана[122] мои́мъ дру́гомъ.

1. Will you not speak to-day with your landlord? 2. I shall write with a pencil or with a pen. 3. He will not smoke this cigar. 4. They will dine to-morrow with your brother. 5. I shall be at your place with my wife in the evening. 6. This book is written by my friend.

26. PERSONAL PRONOUNS (continued from page 28.)

The Instrumental Case.

WITH or BY ME	мной* mnoy	WITH or BY US	нáми nah-me
,, ,, thee	тобóй* tăh-boy	,, ,, YOU	вáми vah-me
,, ,, HIM	им im *or* yim	,, ,, THEM	и́ми ee-mee *or* yee-me
,, ,, HER	ей* yeh^e	*or мнóю, тобóю, éю mnaw-yoo, tăh-baw-yoo, yĕh-yoo	

As explained on page 22, after a Preposition an н is prefixed to Pronouns beginning with е or и, thus :

together with her ;—with them   с нéю ;—с ни'ми

co is used before two consonants : with me   со мной

27. The INSTRUMENTAL is used after the following PREPOSITIONS :

BEFORE	пéред p,eh-r,ed	BEHIND	за zăh
OVER	над năhd	UNDER	под pod

These Prepositions (except над) only govern the Instrumental Case when a state of rest is implied, i.e., when answering the question 'where ?'

before the house   пéред дóмом

28. The CONDITIONAL is formed by adding бы AFTER, and sometimes BEFORE, the PAST TENSE.

I should know   я знал бы
they would not know   они́ не знáли бы

If бы comes before the PAST, the Pronouns я, etc., cannot be omitted.

éсли (IF) in the CONDITIONAL is joined with бы :

if he would know it   éслибы он знал э́то

Soft Masculine and Neuter Nouns must end in ем as the hard ones end in ом. Soft Feminine Nouns end in ей as the hard ones end in ой.—Feminine ending in soft sign takes ью.

with a teacher   с учи́телем   by night   нóчью

23. Translate into English.
(For Vocabulary of New Words, see page 41).

1. со мной, с ними, с ней; 2. перед нами, за вами, под ним, над нами; 3. за столом, перед театром,[117] над землёй,[96] под стулом[91]; 4. с учителем,[115] с дядей,[118] перед музеем[102]; 5. вечером,[93] утром,[103] ночью[104]; 6. я писал[37] бы, он не продал[35] бы, купила[30] ли бы она? 7. мы не знали бы, не говорили ли бы вы? они не работали[121] бы.

1. with me, with them, with her; 2. before us, behind you, under him, over us; 3. behind *or* at the table, before the theatre, over (=above) the ground, under the chair; 4. with the teacher, with uncle, before the museum; 5. in the evening, in the morning, by night; 6. I should write, he would not sell, would she buy? 7. we would not know, would you not speak? they would not work.

24. Translate into English.

1. Я бы не говорил с ним. 2. Еслибы он знал что делать[31]! 3. Они не читали[33] бы этой книги. 4. Они были с ним вчера[74] у нас. 5. Я был бы очень[72] рад видеть их. 6. Мы бы вам писали,[37] но мы не знали вашего адреса. 7. Кто[60] был с ними вчера[74] вечером[67] перед театром?

1. I should not speak to *or* with him. 2. If he would know what to do... 3. They would not read this book. 4. They were with him yesterday at our place. 5. I should be very glad to see them. 6. We should have written (=should write) to you, but we did not know your address. 7. Who was with them yesterday evening before the theatre?

CONVERSATIONAL PRACTICE.

1. Где вы бы́ли вчера́ ве́чером ? 2. Мы не ви́дели вас в рестора́не. 3. Я был о́чень за́нят. 4. Что вы де́лали ? 5. Я рабо́тал.[121] 6. Где же* вы обе́дали[92] ? До́ма.   * emphatic = then.

1. Where were you yesterday evening ? 2. We did not see you at the restaurant. 3. I was very busy. 4. What were you doing ? 5. I was working. 6. Where then did you dine ? At home.

7. Чита́ли ли вы э́ту кни́гу ? 8. Да, она́ о́чень хорошо́ напи́сана.[122] 9. Зна́ете ли вы а́втора[89] ? 10. Коне́чно,[105] он мой друг. 11. Почему́[88] вы ему́ не ве́рите[77] ? 12. Он говори́т, что[61] зна́ет, но[90] не зна́ет, что говори́т. 13. Это моё де́ло.

7. Have you read this book ? 8. Yes, it is very well written. 9. Do you know the author ? 10. Of course, he is my friend. 11. Why do you not believe (to-) him ? 12. He says what he knows, but (he) does not know what he says. 13. That is my business.

14. Гото́вы ли вы ? 15. Да, но я не зна́ю, где моя́ шля́па. 16. Я ви́дел её под столо́м. 17. Это не ме́сто[58] для неё. 18. Я её то́лько вчера́ купи́л. 19. Вы пра́вы, коне́чно ; но э́то не моя́ вина́. 20. Кто э́тот господи́н ? 21. Это дире́ктор музе́я.

14. Are you ready ? 15. Yes, but I don't know where my hat is. 16. I saw it (=her) under the table. 17. That is not the place for it (=her). 18. I bought it (her) only yesterday. 19. You are right, of course ; but it is not my fault. 20. Who is this gentleman ? 21. It is the director of the museum.

VOCABULARY TO PAGES 35-40.

89. author а́втор
    ahf-torr
90. but но
    naw (short)
91. chair стул
    stool
92. to dine обе́дать
    ăh-b‚eh-dăht‚
93. evening ве́чер
    v‚eh-tcherr
94. fault вина́
    ve-nah
95. fork ви́лка
    veeL-kăh
96. ground земля́
    earth z‚em-l‚ah
97. if е́сли
    yeh-sle
98. knife нож
    noj
99. landlord хозя́ин
    khăh-z‚ah-een
100. lemon лимо́н
    le-mon
101. milk молоко́
    măh-wăh-kaw
102. museum музе́й
    moo-z‚ĕhˆe
103. morning у́тро
    oot-raw
104. night ночь
    notch
105. of-course коне́чно
    kăh-n‚etch-naw

106. or и́ли
    ee-le
107. paper бума́га
    boo-mah-găh
108. presently сейча́с
    now c‚ĕhᵏe-tchahss
109. pupil учени́к
    oo-tchĕh-neek
110. really? неуже́ли?
    n‚ĕh-oo-jeh-le?
111. so, thus так
    tăhk
112. spoon ло́жка
    woj-kăh
113. sugar са́хар
    sah-kharr
114. tea чай
    tchie or tchahˆe
115. teacher учи́тель
    oo-tchee-t‚el‚
116. train по́езд
    paw-yezd
117. theatre теа́тр
    t‚ĕh-ahtrr
118. uncle дя́дя
    d‚ah-d‚ăh
119. whole весь
    v‚ess‚
120. wife жена́
    jĕh-năh
121. to work рабо́тать
    răh-baw-tăht‚
122. written напи́сан
    nah-pee-săhn

SEVENTH LESSON.

123. army	а́рмия arr-me͡yăh	128. post-office	по́чта potch-tăh
124. dictionary	слова́рь swăh-varr,	129. school	шко́ла shkaw-wăh
125. factory	фа́брика fahb-re-kăh	130. station	ста́нция stahn-tse͡yăh
126. horse	ло́шадь (f.) waw-shăhd,	131. thing	вещь v͜esh͡tch
127. Peter	Пётр p-yottr	132. Tsar	Царь tsarr,

29. The PREPOSITIONAL CASE of practically all Nouns—soft and hard—ends in **e**.

about the doctor о до́кторе | on the ground на земле́
    ăh-dok-taw-r͜ĕh   năh-z͜em-l͜eh

near the house при до́ме | in business в де́ле
or at the house pre-daw-m͜ĕh   v'd͜eh-l͜ĕh

There are two exceptions: Feminine soft sign, and all Nouns ending in **ий, ия, ие,** which take **и**.

      on a horse на ло́шади | in the army в а́рмии

REMARK.—This case is called the 'Prepositional,' because it cannot be used without one of the Prepositions в, на, о, по, при.

30. The IMPERATIVE generally ends in **и́** or **и́те**; after a vowel it ends in **й** or **йте**.

INFINITIVE.	POLITE FORM. 2nd Person Plural.	FAMILIAR FORM. 2nd Person Sing.
to speak, говори́ть găh-văh-reet,	говори́те ! găh-văh-ree-t͜ĕh	говори́ ! găh-văh-ree
to buy, купи́ть koo-peet,	купи́те ! koo-pee-t͜ĕh	купи́ ! koo-pee
to give, дать daht,	да́йте ! die-t͜ĕh *or* dah͡e-t͜ĕh	да́й ! die *or* dah͡e
to read, чита́ть tche-taht,	чита́йте ! tche-tie-t͜ĕh	чита́й ! tche-tie

There are a few Verbs which end in **ь** and **ьте** which will be explained later on.

25. Translate into English.

1. о хозя́ине,[119] об офице́ре, о его́ жене́[120]; 2. на сту́ле, в музе́е, в словаре́[124]; 3. при её бра́те, при Царе́[132] Петре́,[127] при ста́нции[130]; 4. в на́шей а́рмии,[123] на ло́шади,[126] об э́той ве́щи[131]; 5. в э́том теа́тре, на ва́шей по́чте,[128] в мое́й шко́ле[129]; 6. о на́шем де́ле; 7. говори́те! не говори́те! 8. чита́йте! не чита́йте! 9. кури́те! не кури́те! 10. рабо́тайте! де́лайте э́то! 11. да́йте мне! 12. купи́те мне э́то!

1. about the landlord, of—about the officer, about his wife; 2. on the chair, in *or* at the museum, in the dictionary; 3. in-the-presence-of her brother, at-the-time of Tsar Peter, near the station; 4. in our army, on a horse, about this thing; 5. at this theatre, at your post-office, at my school; 6. about our business; 7. speak! don't speak! 8. read! don't read! 9. smoke! don't smoke! 10. work! do this! 11. give (to-) me! 12. buy this for me—to me!

26. Translate into English.

1. Мы говори́ли о ва́шем учи́теле.[115] 2. Бы́ли ли вы вчера́ ве́чером в теа́тре? 3. Кто кури́л в э́той ко́мнате? 4. Он чита́л э́то письмо́ при ва́шем дру́ге. 5. Да́йте ему́ газе́ту. 6. Не говори́те им об э́том. 7. Бы́ли ли они́ на ста́нции[130] и́ли на по́чте[128]?

1. We were speaking about your teacher. 2. Were you at the theatre yesterday evening? 3. Who has been smoking in this room? 4. He was reading this letter in-the-presence-of your friend. 5. Give (to-) him the newspaper. 6. Don't tell (to-) them about this. 7. Were they at the station or at the post-office?

31. PERSONAL PRONOUNS (continued from page 38)

The Prepositional Case.

(about) ME	(обо) мне ăh-băh-mn‚eh	(about) US	(о) нас ăh-nahss
,, thee	(о) тебé ăh-t‚eb-yeh	(in) YOU	(в) вас v'vahss
(on) HIM	(на) нём năh-n‚om	(upon) THEM	(на) них năh-neekh
(near) HER	(при) ней pre-n‚eh͡e (see remark, rule 29)		

PREPOSITIONS are joined to the following word when speaking or reading; their pronunciation is affected the same as if they formed part of the word: along the street по у́лице păh-oo-le-ts‚ĕh
in the room в ко́мнате f'kom-năh-t‚eh

32. э́то, meaning THIS IS or THAT IS, never changes.
    this is my brother   э́то мой брат
    is that his wife?   э́то ли его́ жена́?

But when it means THIS or THAT it agrees with the following Noun.
    that lady э́та да́ма   this wine э́то вино́
    this gentleman э́тот господи́н

33. HAD, when expressing possession, is also to be changed in Russian, as explained in paragraph 15, and был must agree with the Russian Subject.

I had a book	у меня́ была́ кни́га
=by me was a book	oo-m‚ĕh-n‚ah bɛ-wah knee-găh
had he a ticket?	был ли у него́ биле́т?
=was by him a ticket?	bɛɛl le oo-n‚ĕh-vaw be-l‚et?
we had no luggage	у нас не бы́ло багажа́
=by us not was luggage	oo-nahss n‚ĕh-bɛ-waw băh-găh-jah
had they no house?	не бы́ло ли у них до́ма?
=not was by them house?	n‚ĕh-bɛ-waw le oo-neekh daw-măh?

The Noun being in the Genitive after the negation, the Impersonal Form бы́ло (neuter) must be used.

27. Translate into English.

1. при нём, о них, на нас; 2. во мне, о ней, при вас; 3. на по́чте,[128] на у́лице,[11] на фа́брике[125]; 4. в теа́тре, в по́езде, в шко́ле[129]; 5. на ста́нции, в музе́е, в ко́мнате; 6. э́та ста́нция, э́то на́ша ста́нция; 7. э́тот офице́р, э́то офице́р; 8. э́то ли ваш по́езд[116]? 9. у меня́ был учи́тель[115]; 10. у них была́ фа́брика; 11. бы́ло ли у вас моё перо́? 12. у нас не бы́ло словаря́[124]; 13. не бы́ло ли у вас ло́шади[126]? 14. у неё был мой каранда́ш.

1. in-the-presence of him, about them, on *or* upon us; 2. in me, of=about her, near you; 3. at=on the post-office, in=on the street, at=on a factory; 4. at the theatre, in the train, at school; 5. at the station, at the museum, in the room; 6. this station, that is our station; 7. this officer, that is an officer; 8. is this your train? 9. I had a teacher; 10. they had a factory; 11. had you my pen? 12. we had no dictionary; 13. did you not have a horse? 14. she had my pencil.

28. Translate into English.

1. Не бы́ло ли у вас в шко́ле[129] словаря́[124]? 2. Не говори́те им обо мне́. 3. У нас на фа́брике не бы́ло бума́ги.[107] 4. На на́шей у́лице не бы́ло теа́тра. 5. Не говори́те об э́том де́ле. 6. Не кури́те э́той сига́ры.

1. Did you not have a dictionary at school? 2. Don't speak to them about me. 3. We did not have any paper in the factory = by us on the factory not was paper. 4. There was no theatre in = on our street. 5. Don't speak about this matter. 6. Don't smoke this cigar.

THE RUSSIAN VERBS.

Now that the various Tenses of the Verbs have been practised, it is necessary to give some further explanation on the working of the Russian Verbs.

Every Russian Verb has TWO forms, called the IMPERFECTIVE and the PERFECTIVE ASPECT.

<small>From these Forms, or Aspects as they are called in most grammars, the various Tenses are formed, as explained hereafter.</small>

The following is a simple explanation which will show in most cases whether the IMPERFECTIVE or the PERFECTIVE has to be used.

<small>Do not confuse these forms with the IMPERFECT and PERFECT TENSES.</small>

The IMPERFECTIVE is used:

(A) when the action is not finished. Examples:
<small>He is reading a book.   I was writing a letter.</small>
<small>In the second example, the action was not finished at the time referred to.</small>

(B) when the action is repeated several times, as:
<small>Take a spoonful three times a day.
I shall always buy this newspaper.</small>

The PERFECTIVE is used:

(A) when the action is finished. Examples:
<small>They paid me yesterday.   We have lost our money.</small>

(B) when the action takes place once only, as:
<small>Give him a sovereign.   I shall buy his house.</small>

THE PRESENT TENSE

can only be formed from IMPERFECTIVE VERBS.

Nearly all Verbs ending in ать and ять belong to the class taking ю, ешь, ет, ем, ете, ют.

<small>These terminations are added AFTER the Vowel before the ТЬ.</small>

I play   я игра́ю   he plays   он игра́ет
I take a walk, etc., я гуля́ю, он гуля́ет, etc.

Nearly all Verbs ending in ить and some in еть belong to the class taking ю, ишь, ит, им, ите, ят.

These terminations are added INSTEAD of the Vowel.

I believe	я ве́рю	she believes	она́ ве́рит
I am looking	я смотрю́		
she is looking	она́ смо́трит		

SOME REGULAR VERBS IN ать, ять, ить, еть.
(These words need not be learnt at once).

IMPERFECTIVE.	PERFECTIVE.	IMPERFECTIVE.	PERFECTIVE.
133.	to believe	142.	to print, publish
ве́рить	пове́рить	печа́тать	напеча́тать
134.	to boil	143.	to read
вари́ть	свари́ть	чита́ть	прочита́ть
135.	to count	144.	to smoke
счита́ть	сосчита́ть	кури́ть	вы́курить
136.	to do, make	145.	to teach
де́лать	сде́лать	учи́ть	научи́ть
137.	to dine	146.	to thank
обе́дать	пообе́дать	благодари́ть	поблагодари́ть
138.	to know	147.	to think
знать	узна́ть	ду́мать	поду́мать
139.	to look	148.	to wish
смотре́ть	посмотре́ть	жела́ть	пожела́ть
140.	to play	149.	to (take a) walk
игра́ть	поигра́ть	гуля́ть	погуля́ть
141.	to praise	150.	to work
хвали́ть	похвали́ть	рабо́тать	порабо́тать

IMITATED PRONUNCIATION.—133. păh-v‚eh-reet‚ ; 134. svăh-reet‚ ; 135. săh-sh͡tche-taht‚ ; 136. sd‚eh-waht‚ ; 137. păh-ăh-b‚eh-daht‚ ; 138. oo-znaht‚ ; 139. păh-smăht-r͡et‚ ; 140. păh-eeg-raht‚ ; 141. păh-khfăh-leet‚ ; 142. năh-p‚ĕh-tchah-tăht‚ ; 143. prăh-tche-taht‚ ; 144. vɛ-koo-reet‚ ; 145. năh-oo-tcheet‚ ; 146. păh-bwăh-găh-dăh-reet‚ ; 147. păh-doo-măht‚ ; 148. păh-jĕh-wăht‚ ; 149. păh-goo-l‚aht‚ ; 150. păh-răh-baw-taht‚.

4

THE FUTURE TENSE.

Perfective Verbs have no Present Tense, and therefore the endings in par. 17, when added to the Perfective Verbs, form the Future.

I shall think over*	я подумаю
thou wilt think over	ты подумаешь
he will think over	он подумает
we shall think over	мы подумаем
you will think over	вы подумаете
they will think over	они подумают

*or I shall think a little, etc.

Imitated Pronunciation: yăh păh-doo-măh-yoo, tE păh-doo-măh-yesh,, on păh-doo-măh-yet, mE păh-doo-măh-yem, vE păh-doo-măh-yĕh-t,ĕh, äh-ne păh-doo-măh-yoot.

he will not believe (to-) you   он не поверит вам
    on n,ĕh păh-v,eh-reet vähm
will you publish that ?   напечатаете ли вы это ?
    năh-pĕh-tchăh-tăh-yĕh-t,ĕh le vE a-taw ?
I shall think it over   я подумаю об этом
    yăh păh-doo-măh-yoo ăhb-a-tom
we shall read through   мы прочитаем эту
  this book   книгу
    mE prăh-tche-tăh-yem a-too k-nee-goo
they will do it for me   они сделают это для меня
    äh-nee sd,eh-wăh-yoot a-taw dläh-m,ĕh-n,ah

In all the above examples the action takes place once only.

But when the action is repeated frequently, the Future as shown in par. 25 must be used.

| I shall always think about you | я буду всегда думать о вас |
| we shall read every day | мы будем читать каждый день |

THE PAST TENSE
OF IMPERFECTIVE AND PERFECTIVE.

I knew him very well   я знал его очень хорошо
(IMPERFECTIVE, because I knew him = I used to know him).

I did not recognise him   я не узнал его
(PERFECTIVE, because I did not know him at the moment).

he was looking at you   он смотрел на вас
(IMPERFECTIVE, because the action was not finished at the time referred to)

he glanced at me   он посмотрел на меня
(PERFECTIVE, because he only looked once = glanced).

what were you doing at home ?   что вы делали дома ?
(IMPERFECTIVE, because the answer expected refers to an action or state going on then).

what have you done with your pen ?   что вы сделали с вашим пером ?
(PERFECTIVE, because it refers to a finished action or state).

IMPERATIVE
OF IMPERFECTIVE AND PERFECTIVE VERBS.

believe me !   поверьте мне !
do not believe him !   не верьте ему !
păh-v‚err‚-t‚ĕh mn‚eh !

think it over !   подумайте об этом !
do not think about it !   не думайте об этом !
păh-doo-mie-t‚ĕh ăhb-a-tom !

look at them !   посмотрите на них !
do not look at me !   не смотрите на меня !
păh-smaht-ree-t‚ĕh năh-neekh !

The above examples show that in the Imperative, the Perfective form is generally used ; but if the Imperative is NEGATIVE, the Imperfective is usually employed.

EIGHTH LESSON.

34. The Negation не must always come before the Verb in Russian.

  I do not know   я не знаю
  did you not see ? не видели ли вы ?

не comes immediately before the Verb, except when it negatives an Adverb or an adverbial phrase.

  he does not speak Russian он не очень хорошо
   very well   говорит по-русски

35. The particle ли, used in Questions in Russian, may come after any word in the sentence.

The word that is emphasized begins the sentence, followed by ли.

was your brother there ? был ли ваш брат там ?
was it your brother (that) was there ? ваш ли брат был там ?
was your brother there ? там ли был ваш брат ?
= was it there that your brother was ?

   ли has no special meaning of its own.

ли is not used if the sentence begins with an Adverb or Pronoun of Interrogation.

  where were they ? где они были ?
  why do you not work ? почему вы не работаете ?
  how are you getting on ? как вы поживаете ?

Notice that in these questions the Subject comes before the Verb in Russian ; therefore :

  how are you ? would be put in Russian : how you are ?

In conversation ли is very often omitted, the interrogation being merely indicated by raising the voice at the end.

  is he ready ?   он готов ?
  did you write to them ? вы писали им ?
  was Mr. K. here ?   господин К. был здесь ?

29. TRANSLATE INTO ENGLISH.
(See Verb List, page 47, and Rules on Future, page 48).

1. я прочитáю,¹ ты повéришь, он не посмóтрит²; 2. поблагодарит ли онá³? мы не напечáтаем,⁴ не сдéлаете ли вы э́того⁵? 3. они́ не пообéдают,⁶ я порабóтаю,⁷ они́ подýмают; 4. я дýмаю, я подýмаю; 5. он э́то дéлает, он э́то сдéлает; 6. мы бýдем читáть, мы прочитáем; 7. бýдут ли они́ рабóтать? порабóтают ли они́? 8. не бýдете ли вы курить? не вы́курите ли вы?

29. RE-TRANSLATE INTO RUSSIAN.

1. I shall read, thou wilt believe, he will not look; 2. will she thank? we shall not print, will you not do it? 3. they will not dine, I shall work, they will think over; 4. I am thinking, I shall think (it) over; 5. he is making it, he will make it; 6. we shall read, we shall read through; 7. will they work? will they work-for-a-certain-time? 8. will you not smoke? will you not smoke-to-the-end?

30. TRANSLATE INTO ENGLISH.

1. Что вы дéлаете? 2. Мы поо6éдаем зáвтра óчень рáно.⁸ 3. Благодарю́ вас. 4. Я поблагодарю́ их. 5. Порабóтаете ли вы час? 6. Они́ сдéлают э́то для нас.

1. What are you doing? 2. We shall dine tomorrow very early. 3. (I) thank you. 4. I shall thank them. 5. Will you work for an hour? 6. They will do it for us.

1 'read,' when translated by the PERFECTIVE, means 'read through' or 'finish reading'; 2 'look,' PERFECTIVE, means: to glance, to look once only, or for a moment; 3 once only; 4 or publish; 5 finish the task; 6 PERFECTIVE, generally used; 7 = for a short time; 8 see 153.

31. Translate into English.
(See Verb List, page 47, and Rules on Past and Imperative, page 49).

1. он ду́мал, они́ поду́мали; 2. что вы де́лали? кто э́то сде́лал? 3. мы кури́ли, он вы́курил[1] сига́ру; 4. зна́ли ли они́? узна́ли[2] ли они́? 5. сде́лайте э́то сейча́с, не де́лайте э́того; 6. поду́майте, не ду́майте; 7. поговори́те с[3] ним, не говори́те со[3] мной; 8. пове́рьте мне, не ве́рьте ему́; 9. сосчита́йте э́то, не счита́йте э́того.

1. he was thinking, they thought over; 2. what were you doing? who has done it? 3. we were smoking, he smoked a cigar; 4. did they know? have they known? 5. do it now, don't do it; 6. think (it) over, don't think; 7. speak to him, don't speak to me; 8. believe (to-) me, don't believe (to-) him; 9. count it, don't count it.

32. Translate into English.

1. О чём[4] вы ду́маете? 2. Кто научи́л вас говори́ть по-ру́сски? 3. Я напеча́таю э́то в газе́те. 4. Кто игра́ет на рояле? 5. Узна́ли ли вы его́ сра́зу[5]? 6. Не хвали́те его́ так мно́го.[5] 7. Когда́ вы обе́даете? 8. Не благодари́те меня́. 9. Вы узна́ете за́втра. 10. Погуля́ете ли вы с на́ми?

1. What are you thinking of? 2. Who has taught you to speak Russian? 3. I shall publish it in a newspaper. 4. Who is playing on the piano? 5. Did you recognize him at once? 6. Don't praise him so much. 7. When do you dine? 8. Don't thank me. 9. You will know to-morrow. 10. Will you take a walk with us?

1 = smoked to the end; 2 = heard *or* recognized; 3 = with; 4 = about what, ăh-tchom; 5 see Vocabulary, page 56.

CONVERSATIONAL PRACTICE.

(The English construction and wording is arranged according to the Russian when desirable; students can easily supply good English).

1. Говори́ли ли вы с до́ктором? 2. Нет ещё; он был о́чень за́нят сего́дня, но я поговорю́ с ним за́втра. 3. Если он узна́ет, что вы так мно́го ку́рите, он бу́дет о́чень недово́лен. 4. Я сего́дня вы́курил то́лько четы́ре сига́ры. 5. Вы, ка́жется, пло́хо сосчита́ли.

1. Have you spoken to (with) the doctor? 2. Not (no) yet; he has been very busy to-day, but I shall speak to him to-morrow. 3. If he will hear (know) that you smoke so much, he will be very dissatisfied. 4. I to-day have smoked only four cigars. 5. You, it seems, have counted badly.

6. Сосчита́йте ещё раз. 7. Как вы ду́маете: бу́дет ли он до́ма, и́ли нет? 8. Не зна́ю; ка́жется, бу́дет. 9. Я его́ ви́дел вчера́, но он меня́ не узна́л. 10. Где вы его́ встре́тили?

6. Count again=yet once. 7. What (=how) do you think: will he be at home, or not? 8. I don't know, I think (=it seems) he will be. 9. I saw him yesterday, but he did not recognize me. 10. Where did you meet him?

11. Почему́ вы с ним не поговори́ли? 12. У меня́ не́ было вре́мени. 13. Я ду́мал, что у вас всегда́ мно́го вре́мени. 14. Сде́лали ли они́ э́то для вас? 15. Да, но я их ещё не поблагодари́л.

11. Why didn't you speak to him (a little)? 12. I had no time. 13. I thought that you had (have) always plenty of (much) time. 14. Have they done it for you? 15. Yes, but I have not thanked them yet.

36. Many Russian Verbs change the last letter of the STEM, when a consonant, into a hissing sound.

The Stem is obtained by cutting off the ТЬ, and the vowel preceding it.

Infinitive : TO WORK, работать   STEM : работ...
    „   TO SPEAK, говорить   „   говор...
    „   TO LOOK, смотреть   „   смотр...

This change of consonant takes place when the terminations on pp. 46-47 are added to the Stem, according to the following table.

CONSONANTS CHANGING INTO HISSING SOUNDS.

| д and з change into ж | с and х change into ш |
| к „ т „ „ ч | ск „ ст „ „ щ |

37. Most Verbs ending in ать preceded by one of the above consonants change in this way.

TO WRITE, писа́ть (pe-saht,)   Perfective написа́ть

I write я пишу́	we write мы пи́шем
(ends in у instead of ю)	you write вы пи́шете
thou writest ты пи́шешь	they write они́ пи́шут
he writes он пи́шет	(ends in ут instead of ют)

IMITATED PRONUNCIATION : yăh pe-shoo, tE pee-shesh, on pee-shet ; mE pee-shem, vE pee-shĕh-t,eh, ăh-nee pee-shoot.

38. After the hissing sounds (ж, ш, ч, щ), the terminations are changed thus :

ю becomes у | ют becomes ут | ят becomes ат

For examples where ят becomes ат, see page 60.

TO CUT, ре́зать (r,eh-zăht)   Perf. поре́зать. Future :

I shall cut я поре́жу	we shall cut мы поре́жем
thou wilt „ ты поре́жешь	you will „ вы поре́жете
he will „ он поре́жет	they „ „ они́ поре́жут

IMITATED PRONUNCIATION : yăh păh-r,eh-joo, tE păh-r,eh-jesh, on păh-r,eh-jet ; mE păh-r,eh-jem, vE păh-r,eh-jĕh-t,ăh, ăh-nee păh-r,eh-joot.

33. Translate into English.
(For new words, see Vocabulary, page 56).

1. я пишу́, ты не пи́шешь, пи́шут ли они́? 2. мы не напи́шем, напи́шете ли вы? он не напи́шет; 3. мы ре́жем, он не ре́жет, ре́жут ли они́? 4. я не поре́жу, поре́жете ли вы? она́ поре́жет; 5. вы не пря́чете, не пря́чет ли он? спря́чете ли вы? 6. она́ и́щет, и́щут ли они́? я поищу́; 7. он не пла́чет, она́ попла́чет.

1. I am writing, thou dost not write, do they write? 2. we shall not write, will you write? he will not write; 3. we are cutting, he does not cut, are they cutting? 4. I shall not cut, will you cut? she will cut; 5. you are not hiding, does he not hide? will you hide? 6. she looks for, are they looking for? I shall look for; 7. he does not cry, she will cry (Perfective, unless she keeps on crying).

34. Translate into English.

1. Он вам напи́шет за́втра. 2. Почему́ она́ пла́чет? 3. Они́ пи́шут мне о ва́шем дру́ге. 4. Что вы и́щете? 5. Я ищу́ моего́ бра́та. 6. Этот нож о́чень пло́хо ре́жет. 7. Что он пря́чет в руке́? 8. Куда́ вы спря́чете ключ? 9. Поищи́те у вас в ко́мнате.

1. He will write (to-) you to-morrow. 2. Why does she cry? 3. They are writing to-me about your friend. 4. What are you looking-for? 5. I am looking-for my brother. 6. This knife very badly cuts.[1] 7. What does he hide in (his) hand? 8. Where-to will you hide the key? 9. Look-for (it) in your room (= by you in room).

[1] this is the usual Russian order of the words.

VOCABULARY TO PAGES 50-55.

151. at once   сразу
 (all at once)   srah-zoo
152. badly   плохо
 pwaw-khaw
153. early   рано
 rah-näh
154. how, like   как
 kăhk
155. hand   рука
 roo-kah
156. key   ключ
 kl͵ootch

157. much   много
 mnaw-gaw
158. once   раз
 rahz
159. piano   рояль (m. & f.)
 răh-yahl͵
160. satisfied   доволен
 dăh-vaw-l͵en
161. it-seems   кажется
 kah-jet-s͵ăh
162. where to?   куда?
 koo-dah?

IMPERFECTIVE.	PERFECTIVE.
163. to cry, weep	
плакать	поплакать
164. to cut	
резать	порезать
165. to hide	
прятать	спрятать
166. to look for	
искать	поискать

IMPERFECTIVE.	PERFECTIVE.
167. to say, tell	
(говорить)	сказать
168. to show	
показывать	показать
169. to tie, bind	
вязать	связать
170. to write	
писать	написать

IMITATED PRONUNCIATION.—163. păh-pwah-käht͵; ; 164. păh-r͵eh-zäht͵; ; 165. spr͵ah-täht͵; ; 166. păh-ee-skaht͵; ; 167. skăh-zaht͵; ; 168. păh-käh-zaht͵; ; 169. sf͵äh-zaht͵; ; 170. näh-pe-saht͵,.

IMPERFECTIVE.	PERFECTIVE.
171. to answer	
отвечать	ответить
172. to ask	
спрашивать	спросить
173. to invite	
приглашать	пригласить

IMPERFECTIVE.	PERFECTIVE.
174. to meet	
встречать	встретить
175. to pay	
платить	заплатить
176. to see	
видеть	увидеть
177. to wear, carry	
носить	поносить

IMITATED PRONUNCIATION.—171. äht-f͵eh-teet͵; ; 172. sprăh-ceet͵; ; 173. pre-gwăh-ceet͵; ; 174. fstr͵eh-teet͵; ; 175. zah-pwăh-teet͵; ; 176. oo-vee d͵et͵; ; 177. păh-näh-ceet͵,.

COLLOQUIAL IDIOMATIC EXPRESSIONS.

When two Russians meet they both say здра́вствуйте!
zdrah-stfoo^e-t‚ĕh! or, when rapidly speaking, zdrahss-t‚ĕh!

It is the Imperative of the verb здра́вствовать, to be in good health, and means literally: be in good health!

This expression corresponds to the English: Good morning! Good day! Good evening! etc., which expressions are seldom rendered literally in Russian.

How do you do? How are you getting on?	Как вы поживаете? kăhk vᴇ păh-je-vah-yĕh-t‚ĕh! literally: how you live?
How is your health? =are you quite well?	Как ва́ше здоро́вье? kăhk vah-shĕh zdăh-rov-yĕh!
Thanks, very well. (familiar, in Russian)	Спаси́бо, о́чень хорошо́. spăh-cee-băh, aw-tchen, hăh-răh-shaw
Thank you. (more polite in Russian)	Благодарю́ вас. bwăh-găh-dăh-r‚oo văhss,
so, so ... (literally, so to one's self)	так себе́. tăhk c‚ĕh-b‚eh
And how (are) you?	А как вы?
What is the news? Is there anything new?	Что но́вого? shtaw naw-văh-vaw? literally: what of-new?
How is business?	Как дела́ (Plural)? kăhk d‚ĕh-wah?
What (how) is your Christian name?	Как ва́ше и́мя (Neut.)? kăhk vah-shĕh eem-yăh?
What is your surname?	Как ва́ша фами́лия? kăhk vah-shăh făh-me-le^yăh
What is the name? (referring to a thing)	Как назва́ние? kăhk năh-zvah-ne-yĕh?
Good-bye; till we meet again. =the French 'au revoir'	До свида́ния. dăh-sfe-dah-ne^yăh
I beg your pardon. I am sorry.	Винова́т. ve-năh-vaht (literally: am-guilty)

NINTH LESSON.

39. The Nominative Plural of Russian Nouns has the following endings:

Masc. and Fem. ы (soft и); Neut. a (soft я)

These terminations are added instead of the last letter of the Nominative Singular if the last letter is a vowel or a soft sign.

Masculine: ticket билéт   tickets билéты
Feminine: room кóмната   rooms кóмнаты
Neuter: business дéло   businesses делá

In the Soft Declension ы becomes и, and a becomes я, according to rule 2, page 32.

night ночь opinion мнéние dictionary словáрь
Plural: нóчи   Plur. мнéния   Plur. словарú

The Accusative Plural is the same as the Nominative Plural as regards terminations.

In the case of living beings, the Accusative terminations are the same as those of the Genitive in all words.

40. After guttural (г, к, х) and hissing (ж, ч, ш, щ) letters, ы becomes и, ю becomes у, я becomes а.

books кнúги spoons лóжки pencils карандашú

Plural: my мой   these, those э́ти
   ,,   our нáши   your вáши

41. Many Verbs in ить and еть change the consonant of the Stem according to the table in par. 36, BUT ONLY IN THE FIRST PERSON SINGULAR.

to pay платúть   I pay я плачý pwăh-tchoo
to see вúдеть   I see я вúжу vee-joo
BUT: he pays он плáтит   he sees он вúдит
          pwah-teet   vee-deet

(see List on page 56, Nos. 171 to 177).

35. Translate into English.
(For new Verbs, see Vocabulary, page 56).

1. ваша газета, ваши газеты; 2. этот автор, эти авторы; 3. наши сёстры, ваши письма, мой словари; 4. мои карандаши, наши книги, ножи и вилки; 5. я вижу, видите ли вы? 6. я спрошу, он не спросит; 7. я не заплачу, мы заплатим; 8. я ношу, не носят ли они? 9. я не приглашу его, я встречу их; 10. я не отвечу им, ответит ли он вам?

1. your newspaper, your newspapers; 2. this author, these authors; 3. our sisters, your letters, my dictionaries; 4. my pencils, our books, knives and forks; 5. I see, do you see? 6. I shall ask,* he will not ask; 7. I shall not pay, we shall pay; 8. I wear, do they not carry? 9. I shall not invite him, I shall meet them; 10. I shall not answer (to-) them, will he answer (to-) you?

* In the Future Tense the Perfective is to be used, unless the contrary is indicated by an (I.).

36. Translate into English.

1. Я всегда⁷⁵ ношу шляпу.⁵⁴ 2. Я встречу вас у музея.¹⁰² 3. Я не вижу, где касса.⁷ 4. Я отвечу завтра⁸⁷ на ваше письмо. 5. Я не спрошу их. 6. Вот наши ученики.¹⁰⁹ 7. Я знаю его ошибки.* 8. У них были билеты. 9. Есть ли у вас наши книги? 10. Кто эти дамы?

1. I always wear a hat. 2. I shall meet you at the museum. 3. I do not see where the booking-office is. 4. I shall answer to-morrow (on) your letter. 5. I shall not ask them. 6. Here are our pupils. 7. I know his faults.* 8. They had the tickets. 9. Have you our books? 10. Who are these ladies?

* fault = mistake, ошибка ăh-sheep-kăh

42. The GENITIVE PLURAL of Nouns is formed in the following manner :

    HARD MASCULINE NOUNS add ов.
    „   FEM. & NEUT. „ drop a and o.

MASC.	a pound	фунт	GENITIVE PLUR.	фу́нтов
FEM.	a street	у́лица	„ „	у́лиц
NEUT.	a place	ме́сто	„ „	мест

    All Soft Nouns change their last letter into ей.

	a teacher	учи́тель	GEN. PLUR.	учителе́й
	a horse	ло́шадь	„	лошаде́й
	the field	по́ле	„	поле́й

Except Feminines in я which take ь, and Masculines in й which take ев ; but there are very few of these Nouns.

GENITIVE PLURAL	OF MY	мои́х	OF YOUR	ва́ших
	OF OUR	на́ших	OF THESE	э́тих

43. Many Verbs in ать preceded by a hissing letter take the и endings instead of e endings :

    TO HEAR, слы́шать   Perfective : услы́шать

I hear	я слы́шу		we hear	мы слы́шим
thou hearest	ты слы́шишь		you hear	вы слы́шите
he hears	он слы́шит		they hear	они́ слы́шат

    a instead of я after hisser.

44. The GENITIVE PLURAL must be used after all numbers from 5 upwards (except compounds with 1-4).

    5 пять.   6 шесть.   7 семь.   8 во́семь.
    p‚äht‚   shest‚   c‚em‚   vaw-c‚em‚

    9 де́вять.   10 де́сять.   (See par. 11, for Nos. 2, 3, 4)
    d‚ĕh-v‚ĕht‚   d‚ĕh-s‚ĕht‚

ONE   Masc. оди́н   Fem. одна́   Neut. одно́
                 ăh-deen   ăh-dnah   ăh-dnaw

37. Translate into English.
(For Verbs, see Vocabulary, page 64).

1. ученик, учеников, книга, книг, место, мест; 2. домов, квартир, вин; 3. наших гостиниц, ваших ресторанов, этих дел; 4. моих лошадей, этих словарей, морей; 5. музеев, пуль, наших учителей; 6. я молчу, ты молчишь, молчит ли он? 7. мы не молчим, молчите ли вы? не молчат ли они? 8. я не держу, держит ли он? не держат ли они?

1. a pupil, of the pupils, a book, of books, a place, of places; 2. of houses, of flats, of wines; 3. of our hotels, of your restaurants, of these businesses; 4. of my horses, of these dictionaries, of the seas; 5. of the museums, of bullets, of our teachers; 6. I am silent, thou art silent, is he silent? 7. we are not silent, are you silent? are they not silent? 8. I do not hold, does he keep? are they not holding?

38. Translate into English.

1. Не видели ли вы наших газет? 2. Нет ли у него моих билетов? 3. У нас пять домов в Лондоне. 4. Знаете ли вы этих офицеров? 5. Почему они молчат? 6. Не слышите ли вы, что я вам говорю? 7. Молчите, когда вас не спрашивают.[45] 8. Что он держит в руке? 9. Есть ли у вас десять рублей?

1. Did you not see our newspapers? 2. Has he not got my tickets? 3. We have five houses in London. 4. Do you know these officers? 5. Why are they silent? 6. Do you not hear what I am telling (to-) you? 7. Be silent, when they do not ask you (= when you are not asked). 8. What is he holding in (his) hand? 9. Have you got ten roubles?

45. The Dative Plural of Nouns is very simple:
Hard Nouns end in ам. | Soft Nouns end in ям.

до́ктор,	doctor	Dative Plural :		доктора́м
рука́,	hand	,,	,,	рука́м
Царь,	Tsar	,,	,,	Царя́м

Imitated Pronunciation.—dok-tăhr, dăhk-tăh-rahm ; roo-kah, roo-kahm ; tsarr,, tsăh-r,ahm.

Dative Plural	TO MY	мои́м	TO THESE	э́тим
	TO OUR	на́шим	TO YOUR	ва́шим

46. The Dative must be used after the Prepositions по and к.

по is used when there is a movement ALONG a surface.

(walking along) in the streets	по у́лицам
through (=along) the town	по го́роду
on (=along) the way	по доро́ге
by the side of (=along) the river	по реке́

по also means ACCORDING TO.

according to his words	по его́ слова́м
according to this book	по э́той кни́ге

к means TO (indicating movement) or TOWARDS.

(I went) to him	к нему́
(they went) to the doctor	к до́ктору
(he is very good) towards your brother	к ва́шему бра́ту

47. Nearly all Verbs in ить and еть, preceded by б, п, в or м, insert an л before the termination ю, but only in the First Person Singular.

TO BUY (Perfect), купи́ть

I shall buy, я куплю́ BUT : he will buy, он ку́пит

39. Translate into English.

1. семь учеников, восемь комнат, девять рублей; 2. нашим армиям, моим сёстрам, этим мальчикам; 3. по этим улицам, к нашим учителям, к этим дамам; 4. по вашим словам, по моим письмам, к солдатам; 5. я люблю, любит ли он? 6. я не сплю, не спят ли они? 7. я стерплю, мы не стерпим; 8. я давлю, давите ли вы?

1. seven pupils, eight rooms, nine roubles; 2. to-our armies, to-my sisters, to-these boys; 3. along these streets, to *or* towards our teachers, towards *or* to these ladies; 4. according-to your words, according-to my letters, towards the soldiers; 5. I like *or* love, does he like? 6. I do not sleep, do they not sleep? 7. I shall bear* *or* suffer,* we shall not suffer; 8. I press,† do you press?

* to stand, endure, tolerate. † to squeeze, crush, pinch.

40. Translate into English.

1. Дайте это вашим сёстрам. 2. Сколько вы заплатили этим шофёрам[85]? 3. Мы гуляли вчера по этому парку. 4. Я не люблю его. 5. Почему вы их не любите? 6. Она любит читать романы. 7. Я сплю очень плохо в этой комнате. 8. Хорошо ли вы спите? 9. Я не стерплю этого у меня в доме. 10. Они не терпят шума.

1. Give this to your sisters. 2. How much did you pay to these taxi drivers? 3. We were walking yesterday through (along) this park. 4. I do not like him. 5. Why don't you like them? 6. She loves to read novels. 7. I sleep very badly in this room. 8. Do you sleep well? 9. I shall not stand this in my house.[1] 10. They do not tolerate the noise.

[1] =by me in house.

VOCABULARY TO PAGES 58-65.

178.	at once	сейча́с	186.	novel	рома́н
	now, presently	c͡ĕh͡e-tchahss		story	răh-mahn
179.	bag	чемода́н	187.	now	тепе́рь
		tchĕh-măh-dahn		at the present time	t͜ĕh-p͜err͜,
180.	boy	ма́льчик	188.	park	парк
		mahl͜,-tcheek			parrk
181.	box	коро́бка	189.	question	вопро́с
		kăh-rop-kăh			văh-pross
182.	bread	хлеб	190.	rouble	рубль (m.)
		khl͜ep			roobl͜,
183.	bullet	пу́ля	191.	shop	магази́н
		poo-l͜ăh			măh-găh-zeen
184.	cigarette	папиро́са	191a.	soldier	солда́т
		păh-pe-raw-săh			săhʟ-daht
185.	noise	шум	192.	well	хорошо́
		shoom		=all right	hăh-răh-shaw

Imperfective.	Perfective.	Imperfective.	Perfective.
193. to ask=beg, request		199. to like, love	
проси́ть	попроси́ть	люби́ть	полюби́ть
194. to buy		200. to press, crush	
покупа́ть	купи́ть	дави́ть	подави́ть
195. to fly		201. to sleep	
лете́ть	полете́ть	спать*	поспа́ть
196. to hear		202. to sit	
слы́шать	услы́шать	сиде́ть	посиде́ть
197. to keep, hold		203. to be silent	
держа́ть	подержа́ть	молча́ть	помолча́ть
198. to lie		204. to suffer, tolerate	
лежа́ть	полежа́ть	терпе́ть	стерпе́ть

Imitated Pronunciation.—193. păh-präh-ceet͜,; 194. păh-koo-paht͜,; 195. păh-l͜,ĕh-t͜,et͜,; 196. oo-swe-shaht͜,; 197. păh-d͜,err-jaht͜,; 198. păh-l͜,eh-jaht͜,; 199. păh-l͜,oo-beet͜,; 200. păh-dăh-veet͜,; 201. păh-spaht͜,; 202. păh-ce-d͜,et͜,; 203. păh-măhʟ-tchaht͜,; 204. st͜,err-p͜,et͜,.

* follows rule 47 although ending in ать.

CONVERSATIONAL PRACTICE.

1. Я ищу́[166] ва́шего дру́га.—Где он? 2. Он пи́шет[170] письмо́. 3. Я его́ не ви́жу.[176] 4. Я его́ сейча́с[178] попрошу́.[193] 5. Хорошо́,[192] я посижу́[202] здесь. 6. Слы́шите[196] ли вы э́тот шум[185]? 7. Почему́ она́ всегда́[75] молчи́т[203]?

1. I am looking-for your friend.—Where is he? 2. He is writing a letter. 3. I don't see him. 4. I shall ask him at once. 5. All right (=well), I shall sit here. 6. Do you hear this noise? 7. Why is she always silent?

8. Где вы их встре́тите[174]? — В рестора́не. 9. Я не заплачу́[175] за э́то. 10. Что вы пря́чете[165] в руке́? 11. Я вам э́то сейча́с покажу́.[168] 12. Почему́ вы не ре́жете[164] хле́ба[182]? 13. Кто вас у́чит[145] по-ру́сски? 14. Я не люблю́ ва́шего учи́теля. 15. Почему́ вы его́ не лю́бите[199]?

8. Where will you meet them?—At the restaurant. 9. I shall not pay for this. 10. What are you hiding in (your) hand? 11. I shall show it to you presently. 12. Why don't you cut the bread? 13. Who is teaching you Russian? 14. I don't like your teacher. 15. Why don't you like him?

16. Я всегда́ покупа́ю[194] сига́ры в э́том магази́не.[191] 17. Я вам куплю́ коро́бку[181] папиро́с.[184] 18. Я не отве́чу[171] сего́дня на ва́ши вопро́сы.[189] 19. Почему́ вы всегда́ но́сите[177] чемода́н[179]? 20. Я не сплю,[201] не зна́ю почему́.

16. I always buy cigars in this shop. 17. I shall buy (to-) you a box of cigarettes. 18. I shall not answer (on) your questions to-day. 19. Why do you always carry a bag? 20. I can't (=do not) sleep, I do not know why.

TENTH LESSON.

48. The INSTRUMENTAL and PREPOSITIONAL Cases of the PLURAL OF NOUNS are very simple:
INSTRUMENTAL, Hard Nouns ами | Soft Nouns ями
PREPOSITIONAL,   „   „   ах | „   „   ях

   with-his-hands   руками   roo-kah-me
   by-the-bullets   пулями   poo-l‚äh-me
   about the soldiers   о солдатах   ăh-săhl-dah-tăhkh
   in (=on) the fields   на полях   năh-păh-l‚ahkh

INSTRUMENTAL { WITH-MY, МОИ́МИ   BY-YOUR, ВА́ШИМИ
PLURAL   { WITH-OUR, НА́ШИМИ   BY-THESE, Э́ТИМИ

   In the INSTRUMENTAL 'with' or 'by' are not translated separately, see paragraphs 23 and 27.

PREPOSITIONAL { MY, МОИ́Х   YOUR, ВА́ШИХ
PLURAL   { OUR, НА́ШИХ   THESE, Э́ТИХ

   The PREPOSITIONAL cannot be used without one of the five Prepositions, see paragraph 29.

49. In Russian, REFLECTIVE VERBS add ся or сь to the ordinary terminations, throughout the Verb:

   ся (pronounced: s‚ah *or* sah) is a contraction of себя́, one's self; if the termination ends in a vowel сь is used instead of ся. When adding ся, ь is retained.

TO LAUGH, СМЕЯ́ТЬСЯ.   Perfect: ПОСМЕЯ́ТЬСЯ.

I laugh   я смею́сь | we laugh   мы смеёмся
thou laughest ты смеёшься | you laugh   вы смеётесь
he laughs   он смеётся | they laugh   они́ смею́тся

   IMITATED PRON.: sm‚ĕh-yaht‚-săh; sm‚ĕh-yooss‚; sm‚ĕh-yosh-s‚ăh; sm‚ĕh-yot-s‚ăh; sm‚ĕh-yom-s‚ăh; sm‚ĕh-yaw-t‚ess‚; sm‚ĕh-yoot-s‚ăh.

to learn (=to teach one's self), учи́ться. Perf. поучи́ться. I learn, я учу́сь; does he learn? у́чится ли он? she does not learn, она́ не у́чится; we learn, мы у́чимся; do you learn? у́читесь ли вы? they do not learn, они́ не у́чатся.

41. Translate into English.

(For Vocabulary, see page 70; for Prepositions, see pars. 27 and 29).

1. за этими гостиницами, с нашими солдатами,[191a] вашими телеграммами; 2. перед моими учителями, над нашими полями,[222] под этими машинами; 3. о моих учениках,[109] об этих мнениях,* на наших фабриках[125]; 4. в этих музеях,[102] при ваших сёстрах*; 5. я греюсь,[219] он не греется, греетесь ли вы? 6. мы не греемся, греется ли она? они не греются.

1. behind these hotels, with our soldiers, by-your telegrams; 2. in front of *or* before my teachers, above our fields, under these machines; 3. about my pupils, of *or* about these opinions, at=on our factories; 4. in these museums, in-the-presence-of your sisters; 5. I warm myself, he does not warm himself, do you warm yourself *or* yourselves? 6. we do not warm ourselves, does she warm herself? they do not warm themselves.   * see page 33, last two lines.

42. Translate into English.

1. Почему он смеётся[a] над вами? 2. Где вы учитесь по-русски? 3. Я учусь теперь[187] по-английски.[51] 4. Не смейтесь над ним. 5. Кто будет обедать[137] за этими столами? 6. Ваша ли[b] шляпа лежит под столом? 7. Аэроплан[220] летел[195] над нашими улицами.

1. Why is he laughing at (=over) you? 2. Where are you learning Russian? 3. I am learning English now. 4. Don't laugh at him. 5. Who will dine at (=behind) these tables? 6. Is your hat lying under the table? 7. An aeroplane was flying above our streets.

  a. ё is always stressed.
  b. the emphasized 'your' is followed by ЛИ.

IMITATED PRONUNCIATION of 'to learn' (see par. 49).

oo-tcheet,-s,ăh, păh-oo-tcheet,-s,ăh, yăh oo-tchoos, oo-tcheet-s,ăh le on? ăh-nah n,ĕh oo-tcheet-s,ăh, mE oo-tcheem·s,ăh, oo-tche-t,es le vE? ăh-ne n,ĕh oo-tchăht-s,ăh. E=oo˜e or we.

50. The PAST TENSE and the FUTURE of the Reflective Verbs are formed in exactly the same way, as shown in par. 49.

they did not laugh   они не смеялись
                 ăh-ne n,ĕh sm,ĕh-yah-liss,

I shall learn (for a definite time)   я поучусь
                 yăh păh-oo-tchooss,

51. The English REFLECTIVE or REFLEXIVE PRONOUNS are rendered in Russian by ся or сь. But many Verbs are REFLECTIVE in Russian without being so in English. TO LEARN or TO TEACH ONE'S SELF:

I learn or I teach myself, thou learnest or thou teachest thyself, he learns or he teaches himself, she learns or she teaches herself; we learn or we teach ourselves, you learn or you teach yourself (or selves), they learn or they teach themselves.

52. Verbs ending in овать change this ending into ую (уешь, ует, уем, уете, уют).

This is done in the Present Tense, the Future Perfective, and the Imperative.

205. to advise   советовать   посоветовать
206. „ feel   чувствовать   почувствовать
207. „ try, sample   пробовать   попробовать

IMITATED PRONUNCIATION.—205. păh-săh-v,eh-tăh-văht,; 206. păh-tchoof-stfăh-văht,; 207. păh-**praw**-băh-văht,.

I advise   я советую   yăh săh-v,eh-too-yoo
I felt   я чувствовал   yăh tchoof-stfăh-văhL
try!   попробуйте!   păh-praw-boo˜e-t,ĕh!
    he does not feel   он не чувствует
                on n,ĕh tchoof-stfoo-yet
   will you try?   попробуете ли вы?
              păh-praw-boo-yĕh-t,ĕh le vE?

43. Translate into English.
(For Vocabulary, see page 70).

1. я одеваюсь, не одеваетесь ли вы? 2. он извиняется, не извинились ли они? 3. она не жалуется, мы пожалуемся; 4. почему они прячутся? я бы не спрятался; 5. он занимается, занимаетесь ли вы этим? 6. я надеюсь, надеялись ли они? 7. он купается, выкупайтесь; 8. я ручаюсь вам, они поручились за* меня; 9. не жалуйтесь, пожалуйтесь мне; 10. погрейтесь, не смейтесь; 11. я учусь по-французски, учились ли вы по-английски[51]?

1. I am dressing myself, do you not dress[a] yourself? 2. he apologizes, did they not apologize[b] (P.)? 3. she is not complaining, we shall complain; 4. why are they hiding themselves? I should not hide[b] myself; 5. he occupies[a] himself, do you occupy yourself with-this? 6. I hope, did they hope? 7. he is taking a bath, take a bath; 8. I guarantee (to-) you, they guaranteed for me; 9. don't complain, complain to me; 10. warm yourself, don't laugh; 11. I am learning French, have you been learning English?

44. Translate into English.

1. Чем вы занимаетесь? 2. Она очень медленно одевается. 3. Он спрятался в нашем парке[188] за деревом. 4. Ручаетесь ли вы за* него? 5. Купаетесь ли вы каждый день?

1. What is your profession or business = with what do you busy yourself? 2. She is dressing very slowly. 3. He hid in our park behind a tree. 4. Do you guarantee for him? 5. Do you take a bath every day? * за = for, when followed by Accusative.

a. the Imperfective is quite regular; b. the Imperfective must be used if the apologizing or hiding is being repeated.

LIST OF SOME VERBS ENDING IN СЯ.
(They follow the rules given, except when marked IRR).

208.	to apologize	извиня́ться	извини́ться
209.	„ bath(e)	купа́ться	вы́купаться
210.	„ complain	жа́ловаться	пожа́ловаться
211.	„ dress one's self	одева́ться	оде́ться (irr.)
212.	„ guarantee	руча́ться	поручи́ться
213.	„ hide one's self	пря́таться	спря́таться
214.	„ hold „	держа́ться	удержа́ться
215.	„ hope	наде́яться	понаде́яться
216.	„ laugh	смея́ться	посмея́ться
217.	„ learn	учи́ться	научи́ться
218.	„ occupy one's self*	занима́ться	заня́ться (irr.)
219.	„ warm „	гре́ться	погре́ться

IMITATED PRONUNCIATION.—208. eez-ve-n‚aht‚-s‚äh, eez-ve-neet‚s‚äh; 209. vE-koo-päht‚-s‚äh; 210. päh-jah-waw-väht‚-s‚äh; 211. äh-d‚ĕh-vaht‚-s‚äh, äh-d‚et‚-s‚äh; 212. roo-tchaht‚-s‚äh, päh-roo-tcheet‚-s‚äh; 213. spr‚ah-täht‚-s‚äh; 214. oo-d‚err-jaht‚-s‚äh; 215. päh-näh-d‚eh-yäht‚-s‚äh; 216. päh-sm‚ĕh-yaht‚-s‚äh; 217. näh-oo-tcheet‚-s‚äh; 218. zäh-ne-maht‚-s‚äh, zäh-n‚aht‚-s‚äh; 219. päh-gr‚et‚-s‚äh. *or to busy one's self

VOCABULARY TO PAGES 66-71.

220. aeroplane аэропла́н
ăh-a-raw-pwahn

221. every day ка́ждый день
kahj-dEˆe d‚en‚

222. field по́ле
paw-l‚ĕh

223. in French по-францу́зски
päh-frähn-tsoos-ke

224. machine маши́на
mäh-she-näh

225. mistake оши́бка
ăh-sheep-käh

226. school шко́ла
shkaw-wäh

227. slowly ме́дленно
m‚ed-l‚en-naw

228. tree, wood де́рево
d‚eh-r‚ĕh-vaw

229. with what? чем?
(Instr. of что) tchem?

CONVERSATIONAL PRACTICE.

1. Здравствуйте, наконец,[a] мы вас встретили[174]! 2. Мы вас искали[166] каждый день. 3. Я не был в городе.[b] 4. Где же[c] вы были? 5. Мой дядя[118] пригласил[173] меня в деревню.[d] 6. Жалко,[e] что у нас нет дяди! 7. Довольны[160] ли вы вашей поездкой[f]? Очень доволен.

    1. How-do-you-do? At-last, we have met you! 2. We were looking-for you every day. 3. I was not in town. 4. Where then have you been=were you? 5. My uncle invited me to the country. 6. It-is-a-pity that we have no uncle! 7. Are you satisfied with your trip? Very satisfied.

8. Что вы делали у вашего дяди? 9. Ничего[g]; поэтому[h] я и[i] доволен. 10. Чем же вы занимались[218]? 11. Кушал[j] хорошо, гулял[149] по парку,[188] спал,[201] курил сигары (конечно,[105] не мой, а дяди), играл[140] в футбол. 12. Словом, не желал[148] домой[k] ехать.[l] 13. Как вы чувствуете[206] себя теперь[187]?

    8. What were you doing at your uncle's? 9. Nothing; that is why I am satisfied. 10. With-what then did you occupy yourself? 11. (I) ate well, walked through the park, slept, smoked cigars (of course, not mine, but uncle's), played (at) football. 12. In-one-word, I did not wish to go home. 13. How do you feel yourself now?

    IMITATED PRONUNCIATION.—*a.* năh-kăh-n‚ets; *b.* gaw-rod; *d.* d‚ĕhr‚ev-n‚ăh; *e.* jahʟ-kaw; *f.* păh-yest-kăh; *g.* ne-tchĕh-vaw; *h.* păh-a-taw-moo; *j.* koo-shăht‚; *k.* dăh-moy; *l.* yĕh-khăht‚.

    b. town, **город**; *c.* **же** emphatic 'then'; *d.* country, village, **деревня**; *f.* trip, excursion, **поездка**; *h.* therefore; *i.* emphatic, no equivalent in English; *j.* to eat, **ку́шать**, **поку́шать**; *k.* used only with movement, otherwise **дома** is used; *l.* to go.

ELEVENTH LESSON.

53. Most Russian Adjectives end in ый.

clever у́мный   stupid глу́пый   difficult тру́дный
   oom-nēˆe   gwoo-pēˆe   trood-nēˆe

This is the form in which the Adjectives are given in dictionaries, etc. It is called the Nominative Masculine Singular in grammar.

There are also Adjectives ending in о́й.

    dear, expensive дорого́й   young молодо́й
                  dăh-răh-goy   măh-wăh-doy

These Adjectives end in о́й because the stress is on the termination.

54. This ый or о́й is changed in the Feminine into ая and in the Neuter into ое.

    a clever teacher   у́мный учи́тель
    a clever lady   у́мная да́ма
    a clever word   у́мное сло́во
   oom-nēˆe oo-tchee-t‚el‚,   oom-năh-yăh dah-măh,
         oom-naw-yĕh swaw-vaw

    an expensive dentist   дорого́й данти́ст
    an expensive hotel   дорога́я гости́ница
    an expensive wine   дорого́е вино́
   dăh-răh-goy dăhn-teest, dăh-răh-gah-yăh gah-ste-ne-tsăh,
         dăh-răh-gaw-yĕh ve-naw

55. The termination of the Plural for Masculine, Feminine and Neuter is: ые.

    stupid questions   глу́пые вопро́сы
                      gwoo-pe-yĕh văh-praw-ce
    difficult words   тру́дные слова́
                      trood-ne-yĕh swăh-vah

According to Rule 40, ы is changed into и after к.

    high, tall высо́кий   easy лёгкий
           vē-saw-keˆe   l‚okh-keˆe

45. Translate into English.

(For Vocabulary, see page 76).

1. кра́сный каранда́ш, бе́лая бума́га,[107] чёрное перо́; 2. чёрные шля́пы, кра́сные конве́рты,[52] бе́лые поля́[222]; 3. молодо́й офице́р, дешёвое вино́, бога́тая да́ма; 4. дешёвые кварти́ры,[18] молоды́е солда́ты; 5. ру́сский го́род, ру́сская дере́вня, ру́сское сло́во; 6. ру́сские словари́,[124] ру́сские газе́ты; 7. англи́йский дом, англи́йская гости́ница, англи́йское пи́во; 8. англи́йские ло́шади,[126] англи́йские пи́сьма; 9. францу́зское вино́, францу́зская а́рмия, францу́зский а́втор[89]; 10. францу́зские кни́ги, францу́зские шофёры.[85]

1. a red pencil, white paper, a black pen; 2. black hats, red envelopes, white fields; 3. the young officer, cheap wine, a rich lady; 4. cheap flats *or* apartments, young soldiers; 5. a Russian town, a Russian village, a Russian word; 6. Russian dictionaries, Russian newspapers; 7. an English house, the English hotel, English beer; 8. English horses, English letters; 9. French wine, the French army, a French author; 10. French books, French taxi drivers.

46. Translate into English.

1. Лю́бите ли вы францу́зское вино́? 2. Мы чита́ли сего́дня[71] ру́сские газе́ты. 3. В э́той гости́нице о́чень дороги́е ко́мнаты, но дешёвый стол. 4. Они́ всегда́[75] но́сят[177] бе́лые пла́тья.

1. Do you like French wine? 2. We have read to-day the Russian papers. 3. In this hotel (there are) very expensive rooms, but the board (=table) is cheap. 4. They always wear white dresses.

56. ы, in the endings ый, etc., is changed into и when coming after a guttural (г, к, х).

strict стро́гий	quiet ти́хий	low ни́зкий
straw-ghe͡e	tee-khe͡e	nees-ke͡e

ADJECTIVES are generally in the Long Form as given in Rules 53 to 56, but when the Adjective is the PREDICATE, the SHORT FORM must be used (see rule 57).

An ADJECTIVE is the PREDICATE, when it follows the SUBJECT (Noun or Pronoun) in English, with which it is joined by TO BE: This man is RICH; he was too OLD; were they SATISFIED? your friends are not FORTUNATE.

An ADJECTIVE coming before the NOUN is the ATTRIBUTE.

57. The SHORT or PREDICATE Form is obtained by dropping the ый or ой (see rule 6).

a young doctor	молодо́й до́ктор
this doctor is young	э́тот до́ктор мо́лод
măh-wăh-doy doc-torr,	a-tot doc-torr maw-wod
a rich lady	бога́тая да́ма
this lady is very rich	э́та да́ма о́чень бога́та
băh-gah-tăh-yăh dah-măh,	a-tăh dah-măh aw-tchen, băh-gah-tăh
these are difficult words	э́то тру́дные слова́
these words are too difficult	э́ти слова́ сли́шком тру́дны
a-taw trood-nE-yĕh swăh-vah,	a-te swăh-vah sleesh-kom trood-nE

58. There are not many ADJECTIVES with SOFT TERMINATIONS, and they end of course in ий instead of ый.

It is important not to confuse these with the Adjectives in ий, where the и is used after г, к, or х,—see par. 56.

	Fem.	Neut.	Plur. Masc., Fem. & Neut.
blue: си́ний	си́няя	си́нее	си́ние
cee-ne͡e	cee-n‚ăh-yăh	cee-n‚ĕh-yĕh	cee-ne-yĕh

Feminine, Neuter and Plural are formed according to rule 2, on page 3**2**.

47. Translate into English.
(For Vocabulary, see page 76).

1. тихий дом, лёгкая задача, высокое окно; 2. лёгкие вопросы, тихие ночи; 3. строгий учитель, наш учитель очень строг; 4. дорогая сигара, эта шляпа слишком дорога; 5. умные мальчики,[180] эти мальчики очень умны; 6. он ещё[84] молод, они не глупы; 7. раннее лето, поздний гость, передняя дверь; 8. они русские,* этот город английский,* эти ключи золотые.*

* Adjectives of nationality, materials, and soft endings, have no short form.

1. a quiet house, an easy problem, a high window; 2. easy questions, quiet nights; 3. a strict teacher, our teacher is very strict; 4. an expensive cigar, this hat is too expensive; 5. clever boys, these boys are very clever; 6. he is still young, they are not stupid; 7. an early summer, a late guest, the front door; 8. they are Russians, this town is English, these keys are golden.

48. Translate into English.

1. Есть ли у вас синие карандаши? 2. Как вы бы это сказали по-русски? 3. Я не знаю, я не русская. 4. Вот коробка[181] сигар для вас.—Благодарю[146] вас. 5. Сколько вы за них заплатили[175]? 6. Посмотрите[139] в словаре.[124] 7. Этого слова нет в словаре. Неужели.[110]

1. Have you (got any) blue pencils? 2. How would you say that in Russian? 3. I don't know, I (f.) am not Russian. 4. Here-is a box of cigars for you.—Thank you. 5. How much did you pay for them? 6. Look in the dictionary. 7. This word is not in the dictionary. Really.

VOCABULARY TO PAGES 72-77.

230. because потому́ что
   păh-tăh-moo shtaw
231. beer пи́во
   pee-vaw
232. black чёрный
   tchorr-nᴇ̂e
233. blue си́ний
   cee-nê e
234. cheap дешёвый
   d,ĕh-sh,aw-vᴇ̂e
235. clever у́мный
   oom-nᴇ̂e
236. country дере́вня
   village d,ĕh-r,ev-n,äh
237. dear дорого́й
   expensive dăh-ráh-goy
238. difficult тру́дный
   trood-nᴇ̂e
239. door (f.) дверь
   dv,err,
240. dress пла́тье
   pwaht,-yĕh
241. early ра́нний
   (Adjective) rahn-ne^e
242. easy лёгкий
   l,okh-ke^e
243. English англи́йский
   ăhn-glee^e-ske^e
244. enough дово́льно
   fairly dăh-vol,-naw
245. French францу́зский
   frăhn-tsoo-ske^e
246. front(al) пере́дний
   p,ĕh-r,ed-ne^e

247. good хоро́ший
   hăh-raw-she^e
248. high высо́кий
   tall vᴇ-saw-ke^e
249. late по́здний
   (Adjective) pozd-ne^e
250. opinion мне́ние
   mn,eh-ne-yĕh
251. problem зада́ча
   zăd-dah-tchäh
252. quiet ти́хий
   tee-khe^e
253. red кра́сный
   krahs-nᴇ^e
254. rich бога́тый
   băh-gah-tᴇ^e
255. Russian ру́сский
   roo-ske^e
256. strict стро́гий
   straw-ghe^e
257. stupid глу́пый
   gwoo-pᴇ^e
258. summer ле́то
   l,eh-taw
259. town го́род
   gaw-rod
260. visitor (m.) гость
   guest gosst,
261. white бе́лый
   b,eh-wᴇ^e
262. window окно́
   ăhk-naw
263. young молодо́й
   măh-wăh-doy

CONVERSATIONAL SENTENCES.

1. Как вы поживаете? 2. Виноват, я вас не узнал.[138] 3. Мы думали, что вы в деревне. 4. Что вы делаете в городе? 5. Я здесь по делу.[13] 6. Где я вас завтра увижу[176]? 7. Я завтра буду очень занят, но я вам напишу.[170]

1. How are you getting on? 2. Sorry, I did not recognize you. 3. We thought that you (were) in the country. 4. What are you doing in town? 5. I am here on (because of) business. 6. Where shall I see you to-morrow? 7. I shall be very busy to-morrow, but I shall write to you.

8. Где вы купили эту шляпу?—На Ф— улице. 9. Сколько вы за неё заплатили?—Девятнадцать* рублей. 10. Это очень дорого. 11. Я за мою заплатил только[69] пятнадцать* рублей.

8. Where did you buy this hat?—In (on) F— street. 9. How much did you pay for it?—Nineteen roubles. 10. This is very dear. 11. I paid for mine only fifteen roubles.

12. Где вы будете сегодня вечером? 13. Дома. Моя жена пригласила гостей. 14. Жалко†!—Почему? 15. Потому что у меня (есть) для вас билеты в театр. 16. Довольны ли вы квартирой и столом? 17. Комната у меня довольно[244] хорошая, но кушать дают очень плохо.[152]

* see par. 220.   †jahl-kaw.

12. Where will you be this evening? 13. At home. My wife invited guests. 14. It-is-a-pity!—Why? 15. Because I have tickets for the theatre for you. 16. Are you satisfied with (your) apartments and (with the) food (=table)? 17. I have a fairly good room, but the food is rather poor (=they-give very badly to eat).

TWELFTH LESSON.

59. CAN, MAY, TO BE ABLE TO, МОЧЬ.   Perf. СМОЧЬ
motch,   smotch,

PRESENT : I can, etc., я могу́, ты мо́жешь, он мо́жет, мы мо́жем, вы мо́жете, они́ мо́гут.

PAST : I could, я мог ;   she was able, она́ могла́ ; we could, мы могли́, etc.

FUTURE (Perfective only) : я смогу́, etc.
(conjugated exactly like the Present).

CONDITIONAL : I should be able to, etc., я мог бы, or я бы мог ; Fem., могла́ бы ; Plur., могли́ бы.
(Conditional is formed from the Past).

IMITATED PRONUNCIATION.—Present : yăh măh-goo, tE maw-jesh, on maw-jet, mE maw-jem, vE maw-jĕh-t‚ĕh, ăh-nee maw-goot. Past : yăh mokh, ăh-năh măh-gwah, mE măh-glee. Future : yăh smăh-goo. Conditional : yăh mokh bE *or* yăh bE mokh ; măh-gwah bE ; măh-glee bE.   kh represents a guttural sound.

---

60. { TO WANT TO
TO BE WILLING to } хоте́ть   Perf. захоте́ть
hăh-t‚et,   zăh-hăh-t‚et,

PRESENT : I want to, etc., я хочу́, ты хо́чешь, он хо́чет, мы хоти́м, вы хоти́те, они́ хотя́т.

PAST and CONDITIONAL (regular) : я хоте́л, Fem. хоте́ла, Plur. хоте́ли ; я хоте́л бы, etc.

FUTURE (Perfective only) : я захочу́, etc.
(Conjugated exactly like the Present).

IMITATED PRONUNCIATION.—Present : yăh hăh-tchoo, tE haw-tchesh. on haw-tchet, mE hăh-teem, vE hăh-tee-t‚ĕh, ăh-nee hăh-t‚aht. Past & Cond. : yăh hăh-t‚eL, yăh hăh-t‚eL bE.   Future : yăh zăh-hăh-tchoo.

---

61. When CAN means TO KNOW HOW TO it is translated by уме́ть, Perf. суме́ть (both like ать Verbs).

can he write ?
=does he know how to write ?
can you swim ?
=do you know how to swim ? уме́ет ли он писа́ть ?
oo-m‚eh-yet le on pe-saht‚ ?
уме́ете ли вы пла́вать ?
oo-m‚eh-yĕh-t‚ĕh le vE pwah-văht‚ ?

49. Translate into English.

1. я не могу́, смо́жете ли вы? мы не могли́; 2. не мо́жет ли он? они́ не смо́гут, я не мог; 3. он не хо́чет, не захотя́т ли они́? она́ не хоте́ла бы; 4. не хоти́те ли вы? мы не захоти́м, хоте́ли бы вы? 5. уме́ете ли вы? я не суме́ю, он не уме́л; 6. кто хо́чет? кто смо́жет? кто уме́л бы?

1. I cannot, will you be-able-to? we were not able-to; 2. may he not? they will not be-able-to, I could not; 3. he does not want-to, will they not want-to? she would not be-willing-to; 4. are you not willing-to? we shall not want-to, would you like (=want)-to? 5. can you *or* do you know-how-to? I shall not know-how-to, he could not; 6. who wants? who will be-able-to? who would-know-how-to?

50. Translate into English.

1. Могу́ ли я дать ему́ э́то? 2. Не хоти́те ли вы погуля́ть[149] со мной? 3. Э́тот ма́льчик не уме́ет ни* писа́ть ни* чита́ть. 4. Что они́ хотя́т сказа́ть? 5. Мы не мо́жем ви́деть их. 6. Говори́т ли ваш друг по-англи́йски? 7. Смо́жете ли вы сде́лать э́то для меня́? 8. Я бы хоте́л стака́н пи́ва[231] и́ли вина́. 9. Он не захо́чет э́того прода́ть.[35]   * ни...ни, neither...nor.

1. May I give (to-) him this? 2. Do you not want to take-a-walk with me? 3. This boy can(not) neither write nor read. 4. What do they want to say? 5. We cannot see them. 6. Does your friend speak English? 7. Will you be able to do it for me? 8. I should like (want) a glass of beer or wine. 9. He will not want to sell this.

62. MUST, TO BE OBLIGED TO, TO HAVE TO, are rendered by the Adjective до́лжен (Fem. должна́, Neut. должно́, Plur. должны́) and the Verb TO BE.

(TO BE is not expressed in the Present Tense).

 I must go-away я до́лжен уйти́
  yăh doL-jen (j like s in 'measure') oo˘e-tee

 she was obliged to она́ должна́ была́
  ăh-nah dăhL-jnah bE-wah

 they will have to они́ должны́ бу́дут
  ăh-nee dahL-jnE boo-doot

 he would be obliged to он до́лжен был бы
  on doL-jen bEEL bE

Notice that the Verb TO BE is put AFTER до́лжен.

63. When the Verb 'to be' PRECEDES до́лжен, then the meaning is TO OWE.

 I owed him five я был ему́ до́лжен пять
  roubles рубле́й
  yăh bEEL yĕh-moo doL-jen p‚ăht, roo-blĕh˘e

64. Adjectives used impersonally are considered Adverbs in Russian; they are then in the Neuter Singular of the Short Form, which ends in o.

 it is easy, легко́ it is difficult, тру́дно
  l‚ekh-kaw   trood-naw
  (IT IS is not translated).

it was hot, бы́ло жа́рко; it will be cold, бу́дет хо́лодно
  bE-waw jarr-kaw   boo-d‚et haw-wod-naw

65. The English Subject is in the DATIVE in Russian in Impersonal Expressions.

 I was cold мне бы́ло хо́лодно
  =to me (it) was cold mn‚ĕh bE-waw haw-wod-naw

 he was very jolly ему́ бы́ло о́чень ве́село
  yĕh-moo bE-waw aw-tchen‚ v‚eh-c‚ĕh-waw

 this lady feels dull э́той да́ме ску́чно
  =to this lady (it) is dull a-toy dah-m‚ĕh skootch-naw

51. Translate into English.
(For Vocabulary, see page 83).

1. она́ должна́, не должны́ ли вы? он не до́лжен; 2. мы не должны́ бы́ли, не́ были ли вы должны́? 3. он бу́дет вам до́лжен, должна́ ли она́ бу́дет? 4. они́ бы должны́ бы́ли, ско́лько он был до́лжен? 5. мне бы́ло о́чень легко́[242]; 6. не жа́рко ли вам? 7. нам о́чень прия́тно; 8. э́то о́чень глу́по[257]; 9. он нездоро́в сего́дня; 10. винова́т; 11. в э́том до́ме о́чень ти́хо; 12. гото́во.

1. she must, are you not obliged-to? he must not; 2. we had not to, did you not owe? 3. he will owe (to-) you, will she be obliged-to? 4. they would have-to, how much did he owe? 5. it was very easy for me; 6. are you not very warm (=hot)? 7. we are very pleased=to us is very pleasant; 8. this is very stupid; 9. he is not well to-day; 10. I am sorry=guilty; 11. it is very quiet in this house; 12. it is ready.

52. Translate into English.

1. Ско́лько вы ему́ должны́? 2. Вы должны́ погуля́ть с на́ми. 3. Я не могу́, я сли́шком за́нят. 4. Хоти́те ли вы кури́ть? 5. Нет, спаси́бо; я не курю́ днём. 6. Не хо́лодно ли вам здесь? 7. Я бы хоте́л поговори́ть с хозя́ином.[99]

1. How much do you owe (to-) him? 2. You must take a walk with us. 3. I can't, I am too busy. 4. Do you want to smoke? 5. No, thanks; I don't smoke in-daytime. 6. Are you not cold here? 7. I should like to speak to the landlord.

53. Translate into English.
(For Vocabulary, see page 83).

1. красивый мальчик,[180] удобная квартира, жаркое лето[258]; 2. эта комната очень неудобна[266]; 3. красивы ли её платья[240]? 4. им было очень жарко, это возможно; 5. мне скучно! ваша книга очень полезна; 6. не жалко ли? 7. почему вы так грустны? 8. неприятная вещь,[131] нам очень приятно; 9. странное слово, это очень странно! 10. вам смешно,[276] ей грустно.

1. a good-looking boy, a convenient flat, a hot summer; 2. this room is very uncomfortable; 3. are her dresses nice? 4. they were very warm (=hot), this is possible; 5. I feel dull! your book is very useful; 6. is it not a pity? 7. why are you so sad? 8. an unpleasant thing, we are very pleased; 9. a strange word, this is very strange! 10. it is funny to you, she is sad *or* depressed.

54. Translate into English.

1. Подарите мне ваш новый роман. 2. Ваши слова безполезны; он сделает всё, что захочет. 3. Я бы не дал ни* гроша за† эту бумагу. 4. На ней писать невозможно. 5. В комнате жарко, а мне холодно. Почему это? 6. Это странно! Не больны ли вы?

1. Give (present) (to-) me your new novel 2. Your words are useless; he will-do all (that) he will-want-to. 3. I should not give not-even* a farthing for this paper. 4. It is impossible to write on it. 5. It is hot in the room, but I am cold. Why is that? 6. This is strange! Are you not ill?

* ни = not even.

† за meaning FOR is followed by the Accusative.

VOCABULARY TO PAGES 78-82.

By adding or omitting не the opposite meaning is conveyed; see 274 & 281.

264. at last наконец
    năh-kăh-n,ets
265. cold холодный
    hăh-wod-nE^e
266. convenient удобный
    comfortable   oo-dob-nE^e
267. dull скучный
    bored skootch-nE^e
268. farthing грош
    grosh
269. hot жаркий
    jarr-ke^e
270. ill, sick больной
    băhl-noy
271. jolly весёлый
    v,ĕh-s,aw-wE^e
272. nice красивый
    good-looking krăh-cee-vE^e
273. it is pity! жалко!
    jahL-kaw!

274. pleasant приятный
    pleased pre-yaht-nE^e
275. possible возможный
    văhz-moj-nE^e
276. ridiculous смешной
    funny sm,esh-noy
277. strange странный
    strahn-nE^e
278. sad грустный
    depressed groost-nE^e
279. trip поездка
    excursion păh-yest-kăh
280. umbrella зонтик
    zon-teek
281. unpleasant
    неприятный
    n,ĕh-pre-yaht-nE^e
282. useful полезный
    păh-l,ez-nE^e
283. useless бесполезный
    b,ez-păh-l,ez-nE^e

Adjectives used impersonally are translated by the adverbial form.

284. CAN, MAY see par. 59
    to be able to
285. MUST see par. 62
    to be obliged to, to have to
286. WANT see par. 60
    to be willing to

IMPERFECTIVE.   PERFECTIVE.
    (to) present
287. дарить подарить
    dăh-reet, păh-dăh-reet,
    (to) receive
288. получать получить
    păh-woo-tchaht, păh-woo-tcheet,

In the above Vocabulary, the Adjectives given in the long form can all be used impersonally, as explained in pars. 64 and 65.

it is strange!   странно!   strahn-naw!
this is impossible!   это невозможно!
    a-taw n,ĕh-văhz-moj-naw!

CONVERSATIONAL PRACTICE.
(For Vocabulary, see page 83).

1. Где моя газе́та?— Не зна́ю; здесь её нет. 2. Есть ли у вас мой зо́нтик?—Нет, у меня́ нет ва́шего зо́нтика. 3. Получи́ли ли вы на́ше письмо́?—Нет, я его́ ещё[84] не получи́л. 4. Бу́дут ли у вас го́сти[260] сего́дня ве́чером?—Бу́дут.

1. Where is my newspaper?—(I) don't know; it is-not here. 2. Have you (got) my umbrella?— No, I haven't got your umbrella. 3. Did you receive our letter?—No, I have not received it yet. 4. Will (there) be visitors at your place this evening?—There will be.

5. Есть ли у них ру́сский[255] слова́рь? — Есть. 6. Понима́ете ли вы, что он хо́чет сказа́ть[167]?— Понима́ю, но не о́чень хорошо́. 7. Ско́лько он вам до́лжен?—Де́сять фу́нтов.[80]

5. Have they got a Russian dictionary? — They have. 6. Do you understand what he wants to say?—I do, but not very well. 7. How much does he owe (to-) you?— Ten pounds.

8. Я ему́ до́лжен заплати́ть[175] сего́дня, а у меня́ нет ни гроша́. 9. Бы́ли ли у вас францу́зские[245] кни́ги?—Да, но я их подари́л моему́ ученику́.[109] 10. Я бы хоте́ла поговори́ть с ней. 11. Ва́ша жена́ и́щет[166] вас. 12. Скажи́те ей, что я тепе́рь[187] о́чень за́нят.

8. I must pay (to-) him to-day, and I have not got (not) a farthing. 9. Did you have (any) French books?—Yes, but I presented them to my pupil. 10. I (f.) should like to speak to her. 11. Your wife is looking-for you. 12. Tell (to-) her that I am very busy at present.

COLLOQUIAL IDIOMATIC EXPRESSIONS.

What time is it?   Который час?
=which hour?   käh-taw-rEˆe tchähss?

It is one o'clock, 2 o'clock.   Час, два часа́.
   tchähss, dvah tchäh-**sah**

It is five o'clock.   Пять часо́въ.
   p‚äht, tchäh-**sof**

What is the matter?   В чёмъ де́ло?
=in what is business?   f'tchom d‚eh-waw?

What is the matter with you?   Что съ ва́ми?
=what with you?   shtaw s'**vah**-me?

Really, indeed.   В са́момъ де́ле.
=in same affair   f'**sah**-mom d‚eh-l‚ĕh

I am much obliged to you.   Я вамъ о́чень благода́ренъ.
=I am very grateful to you   yäh vahm aw-tchen‚ bwäh-gäh-**dah**-r‚en

Don't mention it.   Не́ за что.
=not for what   n‚eh-zäh-shtaw

Is that so?   Really?   Неуже́ли? or Ра́зве?
   n‚ĕh-oo-jeh-le *or* rahz-v‚eh?

It does not matter. }   Ничего́!
That's all right. }   = nothing   ne-tchĕh-**vaw**!

All right! Very good!   Хорошо́!
Very well! =well!   häh-räh-**shaw**!

Excuse (me), please.   Извини́те, пожа́луйста.
   eez-ve-nee-t‚eh, päh-**jah**-wooss-täh

Is that you?   Это вы?

Pleasant journey!   Счастли́вого пути́!
=happy way!   sh-tchäh-stlee-väh-vaw poo-tee!

Farewell!   Проща́йте!
   präh-shtchahˆe-t‚ĕh!

I wish you every happiness.*   (жела́ю вамъ) всего́ хоро́шего!
=all good!   (jĕh-**wah**-yoo vähm) fc‚ĕh-vaw häh-raw-shĕh-vaw!

* The last two words are often used instead of 'Good-bye.'

THIRTEENTH LESSON.

The NOMINATIVE of the ADJECTIVES is fully explained in paragraphs 53-58.

The DECLENSION of the other Cases of the ADJECTIVES is quite simple, the endings being nearly the same as those of э́тот. Compare tables on pp. 88-89.

These Cases are: Genitive, Dative, Accusative, Instrumental, and Prepositional, in fact all Cases except the Nominative.

66. The GENITIVE of the MASCULINE and NEUTER ends in ого; FEMININE, ой; PLURAL, ых.

red, кра́сный. GENITIVE: Masc. & Neut. кра́сного.
   Feminine, кра́сной. Plural, кра́сных.
    krahss-nE͡e, krahss-năh-vaw, krahss-noy, krahss-nE-kh

67. The Soft Endings do not require learning. They are derived from the hard ones by changing the first letter of the ending according to rule 2, page 32.

late, по́здний. GENITIVE: Masculine and Neuter, по́зднего; Fem., по́здней; Plur., по́здних.
    pozd-ne͡e, pozd-n͵ĕh-vaw, pozd-n͵ĕh͡e, pozd-neekh

289. ally	сою́зник		294. portion	по́рция
	săh-yoo-zneek			porr-tse͡yăh
290. meat	мя́со		295. price	цена́
	m͵ah-saw			ts͵ĕh-nah
291. name	фами́лия		296. ship	кора́бль (m.)
surname	făh-me-le͡yăh			kăh-rahbl͵
292. new	но́вый		297. tie	га́лстук
	naw-vE͡e			gahL-stook
293. old	ста́рый		298. water	вода́
	stah-rE͡e			văh-dah

For Prepositions, see paragraph 14.

55. Translate into English.
(For Adjectives, see Vocabularies, pages 76, 83 and 86).

1. для стáрого солдáта,[191a] от богáтой дáмы, у сńнего мóря; 2. из рýсской газéты, без безполéзных слов, у стáрого дéрева[228]; 3. без бéлого гáлстука, стакáн[20] крáсного винá, áдрес хорóшего дóктора; 4. от нáшего богáтого дя́ди, цéнá э́той сńней бумáги; 5. кораблń нáших англńйских сою́зников, офицéры францýзской áрмии; 6. для рáнних гостéй,[260] фамńлия э́того молодóго офицéра.

1. for an old soldier, from the rich lady, at the blue sea; 2. out of a Russian newspaper, without useless words, at *or* by an old tree; 3. without a white tie, a glass of red wine, the address of a good doctor; 4. from our rich uncle, the price of this blue paper; 5. the ships of our English allies, the officers of the French army; 6. for early visitors, the name of this young officer.

56. Translate into English.

1. Знáете ли вы ценý э́той нóвой кнńги? 2. Дáйте мне, пожáлуйста, два фýнта[80] бéлого хлéба.[182] 3. Я бы хотéл пóрцию холóдного мя́са. 4. Как фамńлия э́того высóкого господńна? 5. Это óчень стрáнно, что егó ещё нет дóма. 6. Это óчень трýдный вопрóс.[189]

1. Do you know the price of this new book? 2. Give me, please, two pounds of white bread. 3. I should like (=want) a portion of cold meat. 4. What (=how) is the name of this tall gentleman? 5. It is very strange that he is not yet at home (=that of-him yet there-is-not at-home). 6. This is a very difficult question.

TABLE of DECLENSION of the PRONOUNS (previously practised in the Grammar).

PRONOUN STEM.

NOMINATIVE TERMINATIONS.

	STEM.		MASCULINE.	FEMININE.	NEUTER.	PLURAL.
THIS	эт...	also THAT unless meaning 'yonder'	от	а	о	и
OUR	наш...	YOUR ваш...		а	е	и
MY	мо...	THY тво... †сво...	й	я́	ё	й

† свой, one's own, is also used for: my, thy, his, her, our, your, their, when referring to the Subject of the Sentence.

When the NOMINATIVE of these Pronouns has been mastered, the endings of the other cases are easy, as they have great similarity to one another. They are also very much like the Terminations of the Adjectives given opposite.

STEM.	MASC. & NEUT.	FEM.		STEM.	MASC. & NEUT.	FEM.	PLURAL.
	ого	ой	GEN.	MY, мо... ⎫	его́	е́й	и́х
THIS эт... ⎧	ому	ой	DAT.	THY, тво... ⎬	ему́	е́й	и́м
or THAT ⎨	от	у	ACC.	ONE'S OWN, сво... ⎭	й	ю́	й
	им	ой	INSTR.	OUR, наш... ⎫	и́м	е́й	и́ми
	ом	ой	PREP.	YOUR, ваш... ⎭	ём	е́й	и́х

1. The accents on the PRONOUN TERMINATIONS must be omitted when the STEM is stressed; consequently ё becomes е if not stressed.
2. The TERMINATIONS OF ADJECTIVES are practically the same as those of these PRONOUNS;

the hard declension being like э'тот, and the soft one like наш. Plural the same for all. The и of the Pronoun terminations becomes ы throughout the hard Adjective declension. The NOMINATIVE must be learnt,—see page 72.

In the TABLES on the opposite page the Soft Terminations are in parentheses.

They are formed by changing the first vowel of the hard ending thus: а=я, о=е, у=ю, ы=и.

TERMINATIONS OF NOUNS.

	MASCULINE.	NEUTER.	FEMININE.
	consonant (й) ь	О (е) МЯ see rule 74	А (я) ь
		А (я)	Ы (и) и
		У (ю)	Ē и
like Nominative, or Genitive for living beings			У (ю) ь
	ОМ (ем)		ОЙ*(ей) ью
		Ē	и

	MASCULINE.	NEUTER.	FEMININE.
	Ы (и) и	А (я)	Ы (и) и
	ОВ (ев) ей	consonant (ей)	consonant (ь) ей
		АМ (ям)	
like Nominative, or Genitive for living beings			
	АМИ (ями)		
	АХ (ях)		

*ою and ею are another, but less usual, form for ой and ей.

TERMINATIONS OF ADJECTIVES.

SINGULAR.

	MASCULINE.	NEUTER.	FEMININE.
NOMINATIVE.	ЫЙ (ий)	ОЕ (ее)	АЯ (яя)
GENITIVE.	ОГО (его)		ОЙ (ей)
DATIVE.	ОМУ (ему)		ОЙ (ей)
ACCUSATIVE.	like N. or G.		УЮ (юю)
INSTRUMENTAL.	ЫМ (им)		ОЙ*(ей)
PREPOSITIONAL.	ОМ (ем)		ОЙ (ей)

PLURAL.

	MASCULINE.	NEUTER.	FEMININE.
NOMINATIVE.		ЫЕ (ие)	
GENITIVE.		ЫХ (их)	
DATIVE.		ЫМ (им)	
ACCUSATIVE.	like Nominative, or Genitive for living beings		
INSTRUMENTAL.		ЫМИ (ими)	
PREPOSITIONAL.		ЫХ (их)	

*ою and ею are another, but less usual, form for ой and ей.

299. broad широкий
large she-raw-keˆe
300. company общество
society op-shˆtchĕh-stfaw
301. day день (m.)
d,en,
302. dentist дантист
dăhn-teest
303. frequent частый
often tchah-stEˆe
304. home домой
= homewards dăh-moy
305. little маленький
mah-l,en,-keˆe
306. please пожалуйста
păh-jah-woo-stăh

307. motor car автомобиль (m.)
ahf-tăh-măh-beel,
308. poor бедный
b,ed-nEˆe
309. quick скорый
skaw-rEˆe
310. regiment полк
poLk
311. slow медленный
m,ed-l,en-nEˆe
312. stamp марка
(postage) marr-kăh
313. woman женщина
jen-shˆtche-năh

57. TRANSLATE INTO ENGLISH.

(For Vocabulary, see pages 76, 83, 86, 90; Preposition rules 27, 29, 46).

1. старому солдату, бедной женщине, маленьким мальчикам; 2. красным карандашом, этими смешными вопросами,[189] с молодой женой; 3. в синем платье, о французской армии, на английских кораблях; 4. к своему* богатому дяде; 5. в маленьком, старом доме; 6. по этой широкой улице; 7. за этим красивым[272] парком[188]; 8. в весёлом обществе; 9. в жаркий день.

1. DATIVE: to-an-old soldier, to-a-poor woman, to-the-little boys; 2. INSTRUMENTAL: with-a-red pencil, by-these-ridiculous questions, with a young wife; 3. PREPOSITIONAL: in a blue dress, about the French army, on English ships; 4. to (D.) his rich uncle; 5. in (P.) a little old house; 6. along (D.) this broad street; 7. on-the-other-side-of = beyond (I.) this beautiful park; 8. in (P.) a jolly company; 9. on=in (A.) a hot day. * see table, page 88.

CONVERSATIONAL PRACTICE.

1. Что он вам сказа́л?—Ничего́. 2. Ви́дели ли вы его́ автомоби́ль? 3. У него́ нет автомоби́ля. — Как нет! 4. Я был бы о́чень рад[27] ви́деть их сего́дня. 5. Как ва́ше здоро́вье*?— Спаси́бо,* о́чень хорошо́.

1. What did he tell (to-) you?—Nothing. 2. Did you see his motor car? 3. He has not got a motor car.—Of course, he has = how not? 4. I should be very glad to see them to-day. 5. How is your health?—Thanks, very well.

6. Я был вчера́ ве́чером у ва́шего дру́га. 7. Бы́ло о́чень прия́тно.[274] 8. Его́ жена́ игра́ла на роя́ле.[159] 9. Она́ о́чень хорошо́ игра́ет, непра́вда-ли? 10. Да, она́ у́чится мно́го лет.

6. I was at your friend's yesterday evening. 7. It was very pleasant. 8. His wife played (on) the piano. 9. She plays very well, does she not (=not-truth)? 10. Yes, she has been studying (=learns) many years (=many of-summers).

11. Почему́ вы им не отве́тили[171]?—У нас не́ было ма́рки. 12. Он всегда́ за́нят. 13. Ве́рите ли вы мне, и́ли нет? 14. Это стра́нный вопро́с[189]; коне́чно,[105] нет. 15. Да́йте мне, пожа́луйста, три фу́нта мя́са. 16. Ско́лько вы да́ли шофёру[85]? 17. Я ему́ дал два рубля́. 18. Это сли́шком мно́го.

11. Why did you not answer (to-) them?—We had no stamp. 12. He is always busy. 13. Do you believe (to-) me, or not? 14. This is a strange question; of course not. 15. Give (to-) me, please, three pounds of meat. 16. How much did you give to the taxi driver? 17. I gave (to-) him two roubles. 18. This is too much.

* for pronunciation and explanation, see page 57.

FOURTEENTH LESSON.

The RUSSIAN IRREGULAR VERBS are conjugated on the same principle as the REGULAR VERBS.

68.   TO GO, TO WALK, ИТТИ́, ПОЙТИ́.

ИТТИ́ is often spelt ИДТИ́.   eet-tee, päh^e-tee

The first form is the Imperfective, and the second the Perfective.

PRESENT : I go, etc., я иду́, ты идёшь, он идёт ;
мы идём, вы идёте, они́ иду́т.

PRESENT : yăh ee-doo, tE ee-d‚osh, on ee-d‚ot ; mE ee-d‚om, vE ee-d‚aw-t‚ĕh, ăh-nee ee-doot.

Except the FIRST PERSON SINGULAR the Terminations of the PRESENT TENSE are quite regular (with a very few exceptions).

FUTURE :   I shall go, etc., я пойду́, он пойдёт ;
мы пойдём, вы пойдёте, они́ пойду́т.

yăh päh^e-doo, on päh^e-d‚ot, ăh-nee päh^e-doot.

The FUTURE terminations are the same as those of the PRESENT, but added to the PERFECTIVE. For explanation of the FUTURE, see page 48.

Therefore to conjugate these Tenses it is only necessary to know the FIRST PERSON SINGULAR, and ONE of the other persons from which the rest is formed regularly. (See explanation on opposite page).

PAST :   I or he was going or walking, я or он шёл ;
Fem.: I or she   „   „   я or она́ шла ;
Plur.: we, you, they „   „   мы, вы, они́ шли.
   Perfective : I went, I have gone, etc., пошёл ;
   Feminine : пошла́ ;   Plural : пошли́.

yăh or on shol ; shwăh ; shlee.   päh-shol‚ ; päh-shwah ; päh-shlee.

CONDITIONAL : I should go, etc., я шёл бы, etc.
   Perfective : я пошёл бы, etc.
      yăh shol-bE ;   päh-shol-bE.

IMPERATIVE: go ! Imperf.: иди́те ! Perf.: пойди́те !
   IMPERATIVE : e-dee-t‚ĕh !   päh^e-dee-t‚ĕh !

To enable students to conjugate the PRESENT or FUTURE, the SECOND PERSON SINGULAR is generally given, but this Person being almost useless for Englishmen, the THIRD PERSON SINGULAR is given here. The other Persons are formed from it by changing the endings in the usual way.

Whenever there can be a doubt about the Third Person Plural, it is shown.

'TO-COME' is rendered in Russian by 'TO-GO,' except when it means 'TO-ARRIVE.' Come with me=Go with me.
  but : I shall come to you=I shall arrive at your place.
  The train is coming=The train arrives.
  (This Verb is explained on the next page).

58. TRANSLATE INTO ENGLISH.

1. я иду́, мы не пойдём, он шёл; 2. пойдёте ли вы? она́ не идёт, они́ пошли́; 3. не идёте ли вы? она́ не пошла́, я не пойду́; 4. пойди́те с ним, не иди́те домо́й.†

1. I go, we shall not go, he was walking; 2. will you go? she is not going, they went (P.); 3. are you not going? she did not go (P.), I shall not go; 4. go with him, don't go home.† † see page 71, note к.

59. TRANSLATE INTO ENGLISH.

1. Мы идём сего́дня в теа́тр. 2. Пойдёте ли вы с на́ми? 3. Почему́ он пошёл домо́й так ра́но[153]? 4. Мы шли по* э́той у́лице. 5. Я не пошёл бы с ни́ми. 6. Кто идёт? 7. Пойдёте погуля́ть[149] со мной? 8. Они́ иду́т к* до́ктору. 9. Скажи́те[167] им, что я пошёл домо́й.

1. We are going to-day to the theatre. 2. Will you come (=go) with us? 3. Why did he go home so early? 4. We walked along* this street. 5. I should not come (=go) with them. 6. Who comes (=goes)? 7. Will you go to-walk (for a walk) with me? 8. They are going to* the doctor. 9. Tell (to-) them that I went home.   * see rule 46.

69. The Verb TO GO is always to be translated итти́, пойти́, unless the meaning expresses frequency or repetition. In that case, ходи́ть (hăh-deet,) is used.

he goes to the theatre   он хо́дит в теа́тр
every day   ка́ждый день

ходи́ть is also used in sentences where no definite action is referred to, like :

they walk very quickly, she does not like to walk, etc.

---

70. TO WALK, TO GO, ходи́ть (Perfective, not usual) is conjugated according to rule 41, д=ж in 1st Pers.

PRESENT : I am walking or going, etc., я хожу́, хо́дишь, хо́дит ; хо́дим, хо́дите, хо́дят.

IMITATED PRONUNCIATION : hăh-joo, haw-deesh, haw-deet ; haw-deem, haw-de-t‚ĕh, haw-d‚ăht. Notice the change of stress.

FUTURE : я бу́ду ходи́ть, etc.

This form is used because the Perfective is not usual.

PAST : ходи́л, etc.   IMPERATIVE : ходи́те !
CONDITIONAL : я ходи́л бы, etc.

---

71. TO COME, TO ARRIVE, приходи́ть, прийти́
or придти́   pre-khăh-deet,   preˆe-tee

All Verbs in rules 68 to 71 are used only when meaning 'on foot.'

The IMPERFECTIVE is conjugated exactly like ходи́ть, and the PERFECTIVE like пойти́ (see rule 68).

PRESENT : I am coming, etc., я прихожу́, etc.
FUTURE : I shall arrive, etc., я прийду́, etc.
PAST : I was coming, etc., я приходи́л, etc.
   Perfective : I arrived (on foot), я пришёл.
IMPERATIVE : come ! приходи́те ! Perf. прийди́те !

The Perfective form of the Imperative is not used with a Negation.

IMITATED PRONUNCIATION : pre-khăh-joo, preˆe-doo, pre-khăh-deeL, pre-shoL, pre-khăh-dee-t‚ĕh, preˆe-dee-t‚ĕh.

60. Translate into English.

1. он прихо́дит, не прихо́дят ли они́? 2. мы прийдём, она́ не прийдёт; 3. не приходи́ли ли вы? кто пришёл? 4. прийди́те ра́но,[153] не приходи́те по́здно[249]; 5. когда́ пришёл по́езд[116]? 6. мой полк прихо́дит за́втра; 7. лю́бите[199] ли вы ходи́ть? 8. я не люблю́ мно́го[157] ходи́ть; 9. мы ходи́ли к ним ка́ждый день; 10. я хожу́ о́чень ме́дленно.

1. he is coming, are they not coming? 2. we shall arrive, she will not come; 3. were you not coming? who has-come? 4. come early, don't come late; 5. when did the train arrive? 6. my regiment is arriving to-morrow; 7. do you like to walk? 8. I do not like to walk much; 9. we were going to them every day; 10. I walk very slowly.

61. Translate into English.

1. Прийди́те к нам сего́дня ве́чером. 2. Го́сти[260] пришли́. 3. Он не мо́жет прийти́ за́втра. 4. Не ходи́те так ско́ро. 5. Он идёт домо́й. 6. Почему́ вы хо́дите так ча́сто к данти́сту? 7. Пойдёте ли вы со мной в теа́тр? 8. Я пойду́ ему́ сказа́ть.[167] 9. Когда́ по́чта[128] прийдёт? 10. Пришёл ли ваш друг?

1. Come to us this (= to-day) evening. 2. Visitors have-come. 3. He cannot come to-morrow. 4. Don't walk so quickly. 5. He goes home. 6. Why are you going so often to the dentist? 7. Will you come (= go) with me to the theatre? 8. I shall go to tell (to-) him. 9. When will the post arrive? 10. Has your friend come?

72. There are a good many Nouns in Russian which omit the o or e of the NOMINATIVE in the other Cases ; some of the most important are :

church	цéрковь (f.)	father	отéц
coal	ýголь (m.)	mouth	рот
corner	ýгол	piece	кусóк
day	день (m.)	stone	кáмень (m.)

Examples : in daytime, днём (I.)
at the father's, у отцá   in a church, в цéркви

<small>Strictly speaking, this o and e are added in the Nominative to the Stem to facilitate the pronunciation, as otherwise too many consonants would meet. The other Cases can easily be sounded without o or e.</small>

73. In forming the PREDICATE FORM of ADJECTIVES o or e are often inserted in the Masculine (mostly where the Adjective ends in ный).

clever	ýмный	Short Form :	умён
difficult	трýдный	,,	трýден
full	пóлный	,,	пóлон
sick, ill	больнóй	,,	бóлен

Feminine, Neuter and Plural are formed without o or e.
Feminine : умнá   Plural : умны́

74. There are nine NEUTER NOUNS in мя that insert ен before the termination, and are declined as follows :

	PLURAL.			PLURAL.
N. врéмя time	временá	A.	like N.	
G. врéмени	времён	I. врéменем	временáми	
D. врéмени	временáм	P. о врéмени	временáх	

The following are the most important :

burden	брéмя	Christian name	и́мя
flame	плáмя	flag, banner	знáмя

75. мать (mother) and дочь (daughter) insert ер before the termination.
Singular: N. A. мать, G.D.P. мáтери, I. мáтерью;
Plur.: N. мáтери, G.A. матерéй, D. матеря́м, etc.

76. The GENITIVE SINGULAR MASCULINE often ends in y instead of a, when used in a Partitive Sense.
sugar, сáхар сáхару | people, нарóд нарóду
a pound of tea (чай) фунт чáю (ю=у)
_{soft ending}

77. Examples where the Prepositional Singular Masculine ends idiomatically in ý instead of e.

in the forest	в лесý	in the garden	в садý
on the floor	на полý	in view	в видý
in the year	в годý	at a ball	на балý

78. Many MASCULINE NOUNS end in the Nominative Plural in accented á (я́) instead of ы (и).

addresses	адресá	professors	профессорá
doctors	докторá	towns	городá
houses	домá	teachers	учителя́

79. The following are some of the most important IRREGULAR PLURALS:

NOMINATIVE.		GENITIVE.	
brothers	брáтья	of the brothers	брáтьев
friends	друзья́	of the friends	друзéй
sons	сыновья́	of the sons	сыновéй
husbands	мужья́	of the husbands	мужéй
gentlemen	господá	of the gentlemen	госпóд
landlords	хозя́ева	of the landlords	хозя́ев
chairs	стýлья	of the chairs	стýльев
pens	пéрья	of the pens	пéрьев

The Dative, Instrumental, and Prepositional are formed regularly from the Nominative Plural.

80. Nouns ending in ин, referring to persons, change this termination in the Plural into **e**.

Englishman	Англича́нин	GEN. PLUR.
Englishmen	Англича́не	Англича́н
peasant, countryman	крестья́нин	
peasants, countrymen	крестья́не	крестья́н

The other Cases are formed regularly from the Nominative plural.

81. Examples of Nouns having two forms for Nominative Plural, each form having a different meaning.

colour, flower, цвет	flowers, цветы́	colours, цвета́
bread, хлеб	loaves, хле́бы	crops, хлеба́
fur, мех	bellows, мехи́	furs, меха́

82. There are many MASCULINE NOUNS which have Genitive Plural and Nominative Singular alike.

boot сапо́г	eye глаз	soldier солда́т
of the boots	of the eyes	of the soldiers

Most denote measures, or the various kinds of soldiers.

lancer ула́н	yard арши́н
of the lancers	of the yards

83. Nouns ending with a consonant, preceded by a hissing letter (ж, ч, ш, щ), end in the Genitive Plural in **ей** instead of **ов**.

knife	нож	Genitive Plural :	ноже́й
key	ключ	„ „	ключе́й

84. SUCH NOUNS end in the INSTRUMENTAL SINGULAR in **ем** instead of **о́м** if the termination is not accented.

with the husband	с му́жем
BUT : with a knife	ножо́м

Similarly, Feminines in **a** after a hisser end in the Instrumental in **ей** instead of **о́й**, if the termination is not accented.

CONVERSATIONAL SENTENCES.
(See Vocabulary page 104, and refer to Idioms page 85).

1. Где вы были сегодня ?—Дома. 2. Готовы ли вы ?—Готов. 3. Кому вы писали ? 4. Это моё дело. 5. Вы правы, извините. 6. Не за что ; я же шутил. 7. Который час ?—Два часа, кажется.[161] 8. Я бы никогда не сказал, что уже так поздно.[249]

1. Where have you been to-day ?—At home. 2. Are you ready ?—I am. 3. To whom did you write ? 4. This is my business. 5. You are right, excuse (me). 6. Do not mention it; I was joking. 7. What time is it ?—Two o'clock, it-seems. 8. I should never have thought—I should never say, that (it is) already so late.

9. Как название этой книги ?—Белые[261] Ночи. 10. Когда вы идёте домой[304]?—Сейчас.[178] 11. Я пойду с вами.—Хорошо. 12. Есть ли у вас красное вино ? 13. Нет, у нас есть только белое.[261] 14. Сколько стоит бутылка ?—Десять рублей. 15. Почему[88] так[111] дорого[237] ? 16. Это очень старое французское вино.

9. What is the name of this book ? — White Nights. 10. When are you going home ?—Presently. 11. I shall go with you.—(Very) well. 12. Have you got (any) red wine ? 13. No, we have only white-one. 14. How much does a bottle cost ? — Ten roubles. 15. Why so dear ? 16. This is a very old French wine.

17. Куда он пошёл ?—К дантисту.[302] 18. Когда я пришёл, его не было дома. 19. Виноват, это моё место. 20. Он не мог ответить на мой вопрос.[189]

17. Where did he go-to ?—To the dentist. 18. When I came, he (of-him) was not at home. 19. Sorry, this is my place. 20. He could not answer (on) my question.

FIFTEENTH LESSON.

85. The following are a few examples of Nouns used only in the Plural in Russian:

ink, чернúла (n.)   scissors, нóжницы (f.)
tcherr-nee-wăh   noj-ne-tsE

clock, watch, часы́ (m.) tchăh-oE

money, дéньги (f.); Genitive Plural: дéнег
d‚en‚-ghe   d‚eh-n‚ekh

лю́ди is the only Plural for человéк, man, person.
l‚oo-de (men, people)   tchĕh-wăh-v‚ek (human being)

86. child, дитя́ (n.) de-t‚ah, is irregular, but it is not much used in the Singular, ребёнок r‚ĕh-b‚aw-nok being generally used instead. ребёнок is declined according to rule 72 (Gen. ребёнка, etc.)

In the Plural, 'children' is rendered by дéти (n.) d‚eh-te.

G. & A. детéй. D. дéтям. I. детьми́. P. дéтях.

---

87.   TO GIVE, дава́ть dăh-vaht,   дать dăht,

PRESENT: I give, etc., я даю́, ты даёшь, он даёт; мы даём, вы даёте, они́ даю́т.
dăh-yoo, dăh-yosh, dăh-yot; dăh-yom, dăh-yot-yĕh, dăh-yoot.

FUTURE: I shall give, etc., я дам, ты дашь, он даст; мы дади́м, вы дади́те, они́ даду́т.
dăhm, dăhsh, dăhst; dăh-deem, dăh-dee-t‚ĕh, dăh-doot.
The Future of the Imperfective is rarely used.

PAST: I was giving, я дава́л; Feminine: дава́ла; Plural: дава́ли. Perfective: I gave or I have given, я дал; Fem. дала́; Plur. да́ли.
dăh-vahL, dăh-vah-wăh, dăh-vah-le; dăhL, dăh-wah, dah-le.

CONDITIONAL: I should give, я дава́л бы.
Perfective: я дал бы.

IMPERATIVE: give! дава́йте! Perfective: да́йте!
dăh-vah^e-t‚ĕh! or dăh-vie-t‚ĕh! dah^e-t‚ĕh!

62. Translate into English.

1. он не даёт, дади́те ли вы? я не дал; 2. не даю́т ли они́? мы дади́м, да́ли бы вы? 3. он не даст, не даёте ли вы? мы дава́ли; 4. они́ нам даду́т, я ему́ э́того не дам; 5. да́ли ли они́ вам? не дава́йте ему́!

1. he does not give, will you give? I did not give; 2. are they not giving? we shall give, would you give? 3. he will not give, do you not give? we were giving; 4. they will give (to-) us, I shall not give (to-) him that; 5. did they give (to-) you? do not give (to-) him!

63. Translate into English.

1. Кто ему́ э́то дал? 2. Я говори́л с ва́шим отцо́м. 3. Он ва́ми о́чень недово́лен.[160] 4. Да́йте мне, пожа́луйста,[306] стака́н ча́ю. 5. Кто э́ти господа́?—Э́то мои́ бра́тья. 6. Ва́ша шля́па на полу́. 7. В э́той ко́мнате нет сту́льев. 8. Зна́ете ли вы мно́го англича́н? 9. Я э́то дам мое́й до́чери. 10. Кото́рый час*? Не зна́ю, у меня́ нет часо́в. 11. Да́йте мне, пожа́луйста, кра́сные черни́ла. 12. Лю́бите ли вы дете́й?

* see page 85.

1. Who gave (to-) him this? 2. I spoke to your father. 3. He is very dissatisfied with you. 4. Give (to-) me, please, a cup (glass) of tea. 5. Who are these gentlemen?—These are my brothers. 6. Your hat is on the floor. 7. There are no chairs in this room. 8. Do you know many Englishmen? 9. I shall give it (=this) to my daughter. 10. What is the time?—I do not know, I have not got a watch. 11. Give (to-) me the red ink, please. 12. Do you like children?

88. Declension of WHO? and WHAT?

	NOM.	GEN.	DAT.	ACC.	INSTR.	PREP.
WHO	кто ktaw	кого́ kăh-vaw	кому́ kăh-moo	кого́ kăh-vaw	кем k͵em	ком kom
WHAT	что shtaw	чего́ tchĕh-vaw	чему́ tchĕh-moo	что shtaw	чем tchem	чём tchom

89.   TO LIVE, RESIDE, жить, прожи́ть.
                   DWELL, STAY   jeet,   prăh-jeet,

Present : I live, etc., я живу́, ты живёшь, он живёт ; мы живём, вы живёте, они́ живу́т.
    je-voo, je-v͵osh, je-v͵ot ; je-v͵om, je-v͵aw-t͵ĕh, je-voot

Future : I shall reside, etc., я бу́ду жить, он бу́дет жить, etc.

<small>The Future of this Verb is mostly formed from the IMPERFECTIVE.</small>

    Perfective : I shall live, etc., я проживу́, etc.
                                       yăh prăh-je-voo
<small>Conjugated exactly like the Present ; see examples below.</small>

Past : I was living, I used to live, etc., я жил, etc.
    Feminine : жила́.   Plural : жи́ли.

    Perfective : I lived, I have lived, я прожи́л.
<small>   Exactly like the Imperfective Past ; see examples below.</small>

Conditional : I should live, etc., я жил бы, etc.
Imperative : live ! живи́те !

The Perfective Form of this Verb is not much used, except when a definite period is stated.

| he lived for a year in Paris | он прожи́л год в Пари́же |
| we shall live (stay) there (for) six weeks | мы проживём там шесть неде́ль |

прийду́т is now generally spelt приду́т. The й is omitted throughout the Future,—see sent. 1, par. 65.

64. Translate into English.

1. я живу́, он не живёт, живёте ли вы? 2. они́ не живу́т, она́ жила́, жи́ли ли они́? 3. я бу́ду жить, где вы бу́дете жить? 4. кто живёт здесь? с кем вы живёте? 5. не живи́те там, я проживу́ здесь два дня[174]; 6. о чём вы говори́те? кого́ вы встре́тили? 7. кому́ она́ э́то дала́? чем вы э́то сде́лали? 8. о ком они́ спра́шивали? для чего́ вы э́то купи́ли?

1. I am living, he does not live, do you live? 2. they do not live, she was living, were they living? 3. I shall live, where will you live? 4. who is living here? with whom are you living? 5. don't live there, I shall live (P.) here (for) two days (rule 72); 6. of what are you speaking? whom did you meet? 7. to whom did she give it? what did you do it with? 8. about whom did they ask? what did you buy it for?

65. Translate into English.

1. Приду́т ли они́ сего́дня? — Приду́т. 2. Живу́т ли они́ в э́том до́ме? — Не живу́т. 3. Могу́ ли я прочита́ть э́то письмо́? — Мо́жете or Пожа́луйста. 4. Кому́ вы э́то дади́те? 5. Мы э́то дади́м ва́шему ребёнку. 6. У меня́ нет вре́мени сего́дня. 7. Ско́лько у вас де́нег? 8. Как ва́ше и́мя? (rule 74.)

1. Will they come to-day? — They will. 2. Are they living in this house? — They are not. 3. May I read this letter? — You may, or please. 4. To whom will you give it? 5. We shall give it to your child (rule 86). 6. I have no time (rule 74) to-day. 7. How much money (rule 85) have you got? 8. What (= how) is your Christian-name?

VOCABULARY TO PAGES 99-103.

314. bottle   бутылка
       boo-TEEL-käh
315. brothers   братья
   see rule 79   braht,-yäh
316. to cost   стоить
       staw-eet,
317. chairs   стулья
   see rule 79   stool-yäh
318. children   дети
   see rule 86   d,eh-te
319. cup*   чашка
       tchahsh-käh
320. daughter   дочь
   see rule 75   dotch
321. Englishman
       англичанин
   see rule 80   ähn-gle-tchah-neen
322. father   отец
   see rule 72   äh-t,ets
323. floor   пол
   see rule 77   poL

324. gentlemen господа
   see rule 79   gäh-späh-dah
325. ink   чернила
   see rule 85   tcherr-nee-wäh
326. to joke   шутить
   see rule 41   shoo-teet,
327. many   много
(or much), followed by Genitive
       mnaw-gaw
328. name   название
(of a thing) näh-zvah-ne-yĕh
329. never   никогда
       ne-käh-gdah
330. sorry   виноват
(my fault)   ve-näh-vaht
only used for excusing or accusing
331. tea   чай
   see rule 76   tchäh^e
332. watch   часы
clock (see rule 85) tchäh-ce
333. week   неделя
       n,ĕh-d,eh-l,äh

* CUP is translated by GLASS in Russian when referring to tea.

COMPARE THE RUSSIAN AND ENGLISH ANSWERS.

Are you ready ?	I am.
Готовы ли вы ?	Готов (ready).
Were you there ?	I was not.
Были ли вы там ?	Не был.
Do you understand ?	I do ; I do not.
Понимаете ли вы ?	Понимаю ; не понимаю.
Is Mr. K— at home ?	He is.
Дома ли господин К— ?	Дома (at home).

66. Translate into English.
(Repetition of Verbs, pages 78, 80, 92, 94).

1. мо́жете ли мне сказа́ть? я не мог э́того сде́лать; 2. что вы хоти́те? я ничего́ не хочу́; 3. хоте́ли бы вы пойти́ с на́ми? он не суме́ет э́того написа́ть; 4. ско́лько он вам до́лжен? они́ должны́ бы́ли пойти́ домо́й; 5. куда́[162] вы идёте? я иду́ в теа́тр; 6. они́ шли по э́той у́лице, я пошёл к нему́ и сказа́л; 7. иди́те домо́й, не ходи́те* с ни́ми; 8. он хо́дит о́чень ско́ро, я хожу́ в шко́лу ка́ждый день.

* иди́те if referring to a definite action.

1. can you* tell (to-) me? I could not *or* I was not able to do it; 2. what do you want? I do not want anything†; 3. would you like (want) to come (go) with us? he will not know-how-to write it; 4. how much does he owe (to-) you? they were obliged to go home; 5. where are you going to? I am going to the theatre; 6. they were going along this street, I went to him and said; 7. go‡ home, don't go with them; 8. he walks very quickly, I go every day to school.

67. Translate into English.

1. Он прийдёт сего́дня ве́чером. 2. Кто пришёл? 3. Они́ всегда́ по́здно[249] прихо́дят. 4. Когда́ прихо́дит по́езд? 5. Не приходи́те сли́шком по́здно. 6. Пойдёте ли вы с на́ми? 7. Когда́ вы пришли́? 8. Она́ не лю́бит ходи́ть.

1. He will come this evening. 2. Who has come? 3. They always come late. 4. When does the train arrive? 5. Don't come too late. 6. Will you come with us? 7. When did you come? 8. She does not like to walk.

* The Pronoun is usually omitted, and ЛИ can also be left off colloquially.
† =nothing, see page 85. ‡ here the IMPERFECTIVE is preferable.

SIXTEENTH LESSON.

90.   TO GO, TRAVEL   ехать, поéхать.
                DRIVE, RIDE   yeh-khäht, păh-yeh-käht,
This Verb can only be used when TO GO does not mean : to go on foot.

PRESENT : I am going, etc., я éду, ты éдешь, он éдет ; мы éдем, вы éдете, они́ éдут.

FUTURE : I shall go, or travel, etc., я поéду, etc.
         The Future is conjugated exactly like the Present.
   PRESENT : yeh-doo, yeh-d‚esh, yeh-d‚et ; yeh-d‚em, yeh-d‚ĕh-t‚ĕh, yeh-doot.   FUTURE : păh-yeh-doo.

PAST : I was going, я éхал ;   Feminine, éхала ; Plural, éхали.   PERFECTIVE : I travelled, I have gone, etc., я поéхал, etc.
PAST : yeh-khähL, yeh-khäh-wăh, yeh-khäh-le.   PERF. păh-yeh-khähL.

CONDITIONAL : I should travel, etc., я бы éхал, etc.
   Perfective : I should have travelled, я бы поéхал.
   CONDITIONAL : yah bE yeh-khähL ; yah bE păh-yeh-khähL.

IMPERATIVE (Perfective only) : go ! поезжáйте !
păh-yehz-jah͡e-t‚ĕh !   For the Imperfective Imperative, see page 108.

---

91. The PERSONAL PRONOUNS, when OBJECT, may be put before or after the Verb in Russian, but usually they come before the Verb.

   I saw HIM   я егó ви́дел
   we bought IT   мы э́то купи́ли
where will he meet THEM ? гдe он их встрéтит ?
IT is generally rendered by э́то, which also comes before the Verb.

92. If ли is used, the OBJECT PRONOUN must come at the end of the sentence.
   will they write to us ? напи́шут ли они́ нам ?
   has he not told you ? не сказáл ли он вам ?
   did she give it to you ? далá ли онá вам э́то ?

68. Translate into English.
(For Vocabulary, see page 110).

1. куда́ вы е́дете? она́ е́хала на автомоби́ле[307]; 2. я пое́ду в дере́вню,[236] пое́дете ли вы со мной? 3. мы бы пое́хали по́ездом,[116] поезжа́йте на автомоби́ле; 4. они́ е́хали по го́роду,[259] я е́ду в Ленингра́д[344]; 5. кто э́то сде́лал? мы вам не ска́жем; 6. почему́ вы э́то купи́ли? я э́того не покупа́л; 7. написа́ли ли вы им? они́ нам не отве́тили; 8. она́ мне э́того не сказа́ла, не дал ли он вам э́того?

1. where are you driving to? she was riding in a motor car; 2. I shall go to the country, will you come (travel) with me? 3. we should have gone by-train, go by (on) motor car; 4. they were driving through (along) the town, I am going to Leningrad; 5. who has done that? we shall not tell (to-) you; 6. why did you buy it? I used not to buy it; 7. did you write to them? they did not answer (to-) us; 8. she did not tell (to-) me this, did he not give it to you?

69. Translate into English.

1. Куда́ вы е́дете?—Я е́ду в Пари́ж. 2. Как до́лго вы там бу́дете жить?—Три неде́ли. 3. Почему́ так до́лго?—Мои́ сыновья́ живу́т в Пари́же. 4. Чем они́ занима́ются[218]? 5. Они́ у́чатся[217] по-францу́зски. 6. (Я) жела́ю* вам счастли́вого пути́.   * Genitive after 'to wish'.

1. Where are you travelling to?—I am travelling to Paris. 2. How long will you stay there?—Three weeks. 3. Why so long?—My sons are living in Paris. 4. What are they doing* (there)? 5. They are learning French. 6. I wish (to-) you a happy journey.
  * =with what do they occupy themselves?

The Verb TO GO, meaning TO TRAVEL, DRIVE, or RIDE, is to be translated by ѣхать, поѣхать, par. 90.

93. But if the Verb expresses repetition or frequency, ѣздить (yez-deet,) must be used, see par. 94.

  he travels very often   онъ ѣздитъ очень часто
  to Paris   въ Парижъ

This Verb is also used when making an abstract statement, without referring to a definite action, thus :

  they like to travel   они любятъ ѣздить

---

94.   TO GO, TO TRAVEL, ѣздить ($\substack{\text{Perfective not}\\\text{much used}}$)
  DRIVE, RIDE (frequently)   yez-deet,
conjugated according to rule 41 (д=ж in 1st Person Present).

PRESENT : I am travelling, etc., я ѣзжу, ѣздишь, ѣздитъ ; ѣздимъ, ѣздите, ѣздятъ.
  yez-joo, yez-deesh, yez-deet ; yez-deem, yez-dee-t,ĕh, yez-d,äht.

FUTURE : I shall go, etc., я буду ѣздить, etc.
  The Imperfective Future is used, as the Perfective Form is not usual.

PAST : я ѣздилъ, etc.   IMPERATIVE : не ѣздите !

CONDITIONAL : I should travel, etc., я бы ѣздилъ, etc.

---

95. TO COME, TO ARRIVE, пріѣзжать, пріѣхать
           pre-yez-jaht,   pre-yeh-khäht,

The Verbs in pars. 90, 94, 95, can only be used when not meaning 'on foot.'

The Imperfective Form of this Verb is quite regular ; the Perfective is conjugated exactly like ѣхать in par. 90, thus :

PRESENT : I am arriving, я пріѣзжаю, -аешь, etc.

FUTURE : I shall come, etc., я пріѣду, -ешь, etc.

PAST : I was arriving, etc., я пріѣзжалъ, etc.

  Perfective : I arrived *or* have arrived, я пріѣхалъ.

IMPERATIVE (Imperfective only): пріѣзжайте !

  PRONUNCIATION.—Present : pre-yez-jah-yoo. Future : pre-yeh-doo.
Past : pre-yez-jahl, pre-yeh-khähl. Imperative : pre-yez-jah^e-t,ĕh !

70. Translate into English.
(For Vocabulary, see page 110).

1. я езжу каждый день в город; 2. он ездит очень часто в Париж; 3. любите ли вы ездить? 4. он всегда ездит на автомобиле; 5. мы ездили этим поездом; 6. я буду всегда ездить на автомобиле; 7. кто приехал к вам? 8. мои братья³¹⁵ приехали из Парижа; 9. он приезжает сегодня; 10. когда они приедут? 11. не ездите так скоро! 12. приезжайте сейчас!

1. I am driving to town every day; 2. he is travelling to Paris very often; 3. do you like to drive? 4. he always rides in a motor car; 5. we used to go by-this train; 6. I shall always travel in a motor car; 7. who has come* to your place—to you? 8. my brothers arrived from Paris; 9. he is arriving* to-day; 10. when will they come*? 11. don't drive so quickly! 12. come* at once!

71. Translate into English.

1. Поедете ли вы поездом? 2. Нет, я пойду пешком. 3. Мой друг приезжает сегодня из Ленинграда. 4. Гость пришёл. 5. Хотели бы вы поехать на автомобиле? 6. Нет, спасибо, я люблю ходить. 7. Вы не должны ходить так много. 8. Мои сыновья приедут завтра из Франции (Nom. Франция).

1. Will you go by-train? 2. No, I shall go on foot. 3. My friend arrives to-day from Leningrad. 4. A visitor has come. 5. Would you like to go-for-a-ride in a motor car? 6. No, thanks, I like to walk. 7. You must not walk so much. 8. My sons will arrive to-morrow from France.   *not on foot.

VOCABULARY TO PAGES 105-109.

334. already   ужé or уж
     oo-jeh *or* ooj
335. brothers   брáтья
     see par. 79   braht,-yäh
336. club   клуб
     kwoob
337. happy   счастлúвый
     sh'tchäh-stlee-vEˆe
338. journey   путь (m.)
     voyage   poot,
339. long   дóлгий
     referring to time   doL-gheˆe
340. long   длúнный
     dleen-nEˆe
341. often   чáсто
     tchah-staw
342. on foot*   пешкóм
     p'esh-kom

343. Paris   Парúж
     päh-reej
344. Leningrad   Ленингрáд
     lĕh-neen-graht
345. sons   сыновья́
     see par. 79   cE-năhv-yah
346. too   слúшком
     sleesh-kom

           see par.
347. to arrive   71
     on foot
348. to arrive   95
     not on foot
349. to go = walk   68
350.   ,, frequently   69
351. to go = travel   90
352.   ,, frequently   93

353. nothing, ничегó ; Genitive of ничтó.
     ne-tchĕh-vaw, ne-tchtaw   For idiomatic use, see page 85.

*generally not translated, but sometimes used for emphasis after Verbs in pars. 68, 70, 71.

96. YEAR is translated by год ; Plural : гóды.
                               god   gaw-dE

two years, два гóда   four years, четы́ре гóда
in our time (= years), в нáши гóды

But after Numbers from 5 upwards, and after Adverbs of Quantity, YEARS is translated by лет (Gen. Plur. of лéто, summer).   (l,et)

five years, пять лет   many years, мнóго лет
how old are you ? скóлько вам лет ?
⎯how many to-you years?   skol,-kaw vähm Let?

COLLOQUIAL IDIOMATIC EXPRESSIONS.

By the way!
=the French: *à propos*
Кста́ти!
kstah-te!

Before I forget...
=in order not to forget
Чтобы не забы́ть...
shtaw-bE n,ĕh zăh-bEet,

With pleasure!
С удово́льствием!
s'oo-dăh-vol,-stfe͡yem!

Unfortunately.
=to (my) regret
К сожале́нию.
k'săh-jăh-l,eh-ne͡yoo

(I) congratulate you.
Поздравля́ю вас.
păh-zdrăh-vl,ah-yoo văhs

In such a case.
В тако́м слу́чае.
f'tăh-kom swoo-tchăh-yĕh

Consequently.
=it means
Зна́чит.
znah-tcheet

Impossible!
=cannot be!
Не мо́жет быть!
n,ĕh maw-jet bEet,!

Leave off! That will do!
=enough! *or* will-be!
Дово́льно! *or* Бу́дет!
dăh-vol,-naw! *or* boh-d,et!

Do not trouble!
Не безпоко́йтесь!
n,ĕh b,ez-păh-koy-t,ess!

This place is engaged.
(ENGAGED is also used for BUSY)
Это ме́сто за́нято.
eh-taw m,eh-staw zah-n,ăh-taw

I have the honour.
Честь име́ю.
tchest, e-m,eh-yoo

Allow me to introduce to-you.
Позво́льте предста́вить вам.
păhz-vol,-t,ĕh pr,ed-stah-veet, văhm

Pleased to meet you.
=very pleasant
О́чень прия́тно.
aw-tchen, pre-yaht-naw

It is time to go!
=to me, to him time!
Пора́! Мне, ему́ пора́!
păh-rah! mn,ĕh, yĕh-moo păh-rah!

I am very sorry.
I regret very (much). }
Я о́чень сожале́ю.
yah aw-tchen, săh-jăh-l,eh-yoo

Wait a second.
Подожди́те секу́нду.
păh-dăh-jde-t,ĕh c,ĕh-koon-doo

SEVENTEENTH LESSON.

TABLE OF PERSONAL PRONOUNS.
(previously practised in the Grammar).

SINGULAR.

	I	THOU	HE	IT	SHE
Nom.	я	ты	он	оно́	она́
Gen.	меня́	тебя́	его́		её
Dat.	мне	тебе́	ему́		ей
Acc.	exactly like the Genitive				её
Instr.	мной*	тобо́й*	им		ей*
Prep.	мне	тебе́	нём		ней

* ою is another form for ой, and ею for ей.

PLURAL.

	WE	YOU	THEY
Nom.	мы	вы	они́
Gen.	нас	вас	их
Dat.	нам	вам	им
Acc.	exactly like the Genitive		
Instr.	на́ми	ва́ми	и́ми
Prep.	нас	вас	них

Notice the similarity in the terminations of the Third Person (he, they), with the terminations of мой, on page 88.

for him, для него́   for his brother, для его́ бра́та
    from them   от них
    from their friend   от их дру́га

These examples show that Pronouns beginning with е or и prefix an н after a Preposition, except when followed by a Noun.

CONVERSATIONAL PRACTICE.

For Position of the Object Pronouns, ME, HIM, YOU, THEM, etc., see paragraphs 91 and 92.

1. Понима́ете ли вы меня́? 2. Я его́ встре́чу[174] в рестора́не. 3. О чём он вас спра́шивал[172]? 4. Где вы её уви́дите[176]? 5. Я её не уви́жу сего́дня. 6. Мы ему́ напи́шем за́втра. 7. Покажи́те[168] нам ва́шу кварти́ру.

1. Do you understand me? 2. I shall meet him in the restaurant. 3. What did he ask you about? 4. Where will you see her? 5. I shall not see her to-day. 6. We shall write (to-) him to-morrow. 7. Show (to-) us your flat.

8. Они́ мне ничего́ не сказа́ли.[167] 9. Дади́те ли вы им э́то? 10. Пойдёте[349] ли вы со мной? 11. Я с ни́ми не пое́ду.[351] 12. Они́ живу́т над на́ми. 13. Кто прие́хал[348] с ней? 14. Мы говори́ли о вас. 15. Он э́то сказа́л при мне.

8. They did not tell (to-) me anything — nothing.* 9. Will you give (to-) them that? 10. Will you go with me? 11. I shall not travel with them. 12. They live above us. 13. Who came with her? 14. We were speaking about you. 15. He said this in my presence (=near me).

16. Кто пришёл[347] к вам? 17. Я вас не слы́шу.[196] 18. Дово́лен ли он ва́ми? 19. Они́ меня́ пригласи́ли. 20. Почему́ вы мне ещё не заплати́ли? 21. Хоти́те ли вы погуля́ть со мной? 22. Я его́ не люблю́.[199]

16. Who has come to you? 17. I do not hear you. 18. Is he satisfied with-you? 19. They invited me. 20. Why have you not paid (to-) me yet? 21. Do you want to take-a-walk with me? 22. I do not like him.

* Notice the double negation in the Russian.

	MASC.	FEM.	NEUT.	PLUR.
THAT	тот	та	то	те
(opposed to THIS)	tot	tăh	taw	t,ĕh
SELF	сам	самá	самó	сáми
(emphatic)	săhm	săh-mah	săh-maw	sah-me
ONE, ALONE	одúн	однá	однó	однú
	ăh-deen	ăhd-nah	ăhd-naw	ăhd-ne

The above words take the same endings as этот,—see page 88.

	MASC.	FEM.	NEUT.	PLUR.
ALL, WHOLE	весь	вся	всё	все
	v,es,	fs,ăh	fs,aw	fc,ĕh
WHOSE	чей	чья	чьё	чьи
	tchĕh˘e	tch-yăh	tch-yaw	tch-ye

The above words take the same endings as мой,—see page 88.

ENDINGS LIKE этот.				ENDINGS LIKE мой.	
MASC. & NEUT.	FEM.	SINGULAR.		MASC. & NEUT.	FEM.
огó	óй	GEN.		егó	éй
т ⎱ омý	óй	DAT.	вс ⎱	емý	éй
сам ⎬ —	ý	ACC.	чь ⎬	—	ю́
одн ⎰ úм	óй	INSTR.		úм	éй
óм	óй	PREP.		ём	éй

The Instrumental of тот is тем, and of весь — всем (instead of тим and всим).

The Accusative Feminine of сам is самоё.

	PLURAL.	
úх	GEN.	éх
сам ⎱ úм	DAT.	т ⎱ éм
чь ⎬ —	ACC.	вс ⎬ —
одн ⎰ úми	INSTR.	éми
úх	PREP.	éх

97. The FIVE words given on the opposite page are the remaining ones that take the terminations as shown on page 88.

1. тот is used when THAT is in opposition to THIS.

    in this street, or in that ?   на этой улице, или на той ?

2. тот is used for THE, THIS or THAT, when followed by a sentence beginning with что, кто, где, etc.

    is that true, what he says ?   правда ли то, что он говорит ?

    the house, where we live ...   тот дом, где мы живём ...

    those, who can ...   те, кто могут ...

тот ... этот also are used for 'the former ... the latter.'

3. сам (SELF) is used for the EMPHATIC 'myself, thyself, himself,' etc.; it FOLLOWS IMMEDIATELY after the Pronoun, but it usually PRECEDES the Noun.

    he himself, он сам   she herself, она сама

we ourselves, мы сами   they themselves, они сами

    BUT : the king himself, сам король

4. один, etc., when meaning A, ONE, A CERTAIN, is put before the Noun ; but when meaning ALONE it comes after the Noun or Pronoun.

    one lady *or* a certain lady,   одна дама

BUT : she was at home alone, она была дома одна

5. всё (Neuter Singular) means also EVERYTHING, and все (Plural) EVERYBODY.

    he knows everything   он всё знает
    everybody likes him   все его любят

72. Translate into English.
(For new words, see page 117).

1. мы сáми, емý самомý, о них самих; 2. чья книга? чьи билéты? в чьём дóме? 3. одномý господину, об однóй дáме, одним слóвом; 4. весь гóрод, все дéньги, всéми спóсобами; 5. с ним одним, ей однóй; 6. все в дóме, всё в порядке; 7. то, о чём вы говорили; 8. то, что вы мне дáли; 9. этот мáльчик рабóтает, а тот ничегó не дéлает; 10. он говорил с самим дирéктором.

1. we ourselves, to-him himself, about them themselves; 2. whose book? whose tickets? in whose house? 3. to-one gentleman, about a certain lady, with-one word; 4. the whole town, all the money, by-all means; 5. with him alone, to-her alone; 6. everybody in the house, everything is in order; 7. that about what you were speaking; 8. (that) what you gave me; 9. this boy works, but (and) that-one does nothing; 10. he spoke to (with) the director himself.

73. Translate into English.

1. На чьей шляпе вы сидите? 2. Они весь день ничегó не дéлают. 3. Могý ли я поговорить с самим хозяином? 4. Мы сáми емý скáжем. 5. Я бы хотéла видеть её однý. 6. Один офицéр спрáшивал меня про вас. 7. Это всё, что вы хотите сказáть?—Всё.

1. On whose hat are you sitting? 2. They do not do anything the whole day. 3. Can I speak to the landlord himself? 4. We shall tell (to-) him ourselves. 5. I (fem.) should like (want) to see her alone. 6. A-certain officer asked me about you. 7. Is that all (that) you want to-say?—(That is) all.

VOCABULARY TO PAGES 114, 115, 118.

354.	alone	одѝн ăh-deen	358.	self (emphatic)	сам săhm
355.	all	весь v‚es‚	359.	that	тот tot
356.	a certain	одѝн ăh-deen	360.	the whole	весь v‚es‚
357.	one	одѝн ăh-deen	361.	whose	чей tchĕh˄e
362.	each	кàждый kahj-dE˄e	366.	such	такòй tăh-koy
363.	every	всякий fs‚ah-ke˄e	367.	what ? what kind of ?	какòй ? kăh-koy ?
364.	other another	другòй droo-goy	368.	which ?	котòрый ? kăh-taw-rE˄e ?
365.	same	сàмый sah-mE˄e		who, which, that (Relative) also translated by	котòрый
369.	about followed by the Accusative	про praw	372.	order (NOT command or decoration) see par. 72	порядок păh-r‚ah-dok
370.	idiot	идиòт e-de-ot	373.	page	странѝца străh-ne-tsăh
371.	means expedience	спòсоб spaw-sob	374.	window	окнò ăhk-naw

98. Words Nos. 362-368 in Vocabulary take the same terminations as the ADJECTIVES in the FULL FORM.
(see paragraphs 53 and 66, also Table on page 89).

These words are used adjectively (that is, followed by a Noun), or pronominally (that is, not followed by a Noun).

  each boy   каждый мàльчик
  a rouble to each one рубль каждому
  every newspaper   всякая газèта
  everyone will tell you всякий вам скàжет

каждый and всякий can be used almost indifferently. In the advanced part of this grammar numerous examples will be given to illustrate the difference.

99. ANY, and EVERY meaning ANY, must be translated by всякій.

        any minute (Acc.)   всякую минуту

100. WHO, WHICH, and THAT, when RELATIVE, are translated by который, etc.

        the lady, who ...   дама, которая ...
        the letter, that ...   письмо, которое ...
        the tickets, which ...   билеты, которые ...

WHOM, WHICH, and THAT, when OBJECT, cannot be omitted in Russian.

        the telegram (that) we   телеграмма, которую
             received   мы получили

The Preposition must come before the Noun or Pronoun in Russian.

        the gentleman, whom you were speaking about
        господин, о котором вы говорили

101. WHICH ? is also translated by который ?

        which place ?   которое место ?
which of these books ?   которая из этих книг ?

102. WHAT ? meaning WHAT KIND OF ? is translated by какой ? (declined like Adjectives in ой pars. 53 & 40).

        what (kind of) room ?   какая комната ?
        what (kind of) people ?   какие люди (Plur.) ?

103. There are, however, many expressions where какой and который are interchangeable.

        On what floor do you live ?
На котором *or* На каком этаже вы живёте ?

    It is useless for comparative beginners to trouble about such niceties. Ample examples will be given in the advanced part of the Grammar.

74. TRANSLATE INTO ENGLISH.

1. каждый день, всякая минута; 2. каждое письмо, всякая страница; 3. другой дом, другое время*; 4. в другой комнате, на другой день; 5. такой идиот, такое дело; 6. такие времена, такая улица; 7. какой день? какая гостиница? какое письмо? 8. который час? которая дама? которое окно? 9. всякую минуту, в другую гостиницу; 10. на каждом столе, под каждым стулом; 11. из другой улицы, для других детей†; 12. на такой улице, в такой день.

* see par. 74. † see par. 86.

1. each day, every minute; 2. each letter, every page; 3. the other house, another time; 4. in the other room, on another day; 5. such an idiot, such a business; 6. such times, such a street; 7. what day? what hotel? what letter? 8. what (=which) hour? which lady? which window? 9. any minute (Acc.), into another hotel; 10. on each table, under each chair; 11. from the other street, for the other children; 12. in (on) such a street, on (in) such a day.

75. TRANSLATE INTO ENGLISH.

1. Во всяком случае, он не прав. 2. Сколько стоят эти вещи[131]? — Четыре рубля каждая. 3. Я бы не говорил с таким как[154] он. 4. Про которого вы думаете? 5. Скажите, пожалуйста,[206] который час.

1. In any case, he is not right. 2. How much do these things cost?—Four roubles each. 3. I should not speak to such one as (like[154]) he. 4. (About) which one do you mean (think)? 5. Tell (me), please, what time (which hour) it is.

EIGHTEENTH LESSON.

104. In Russian, TO CARRY is translated by носи́ть, поноси́ть, when NO SINGLE DEFINITE ACTION is referred to.   (see Vocabulary, No. 177 and Rule 41).

<small>The above words are used: (a) when a GENERAL STATEMENT is made: Carrying coal is hard work; (b) when frequency or repetition is expressed: He always carries an umbrella. They carried the parcels every day.</small>

<small>(To WEAR is always translated by the above Verbs).</small>

105. But нести́, понести́, must be used when the CARRYING refers to A DEFINITE ACTION, like the following:

<small>He carried his bag to the station.   I will carry it for you.</small>

---

106.   TO CARRY, нести́, понести́.
<small>n‚ĕh-ste   păh-n‚ĕh-ste</small>

PRESENT: I carry, etc., я несу́, ты несёшь, он несёт; мы несём, вы несёте, они́ несу́т.
<small>n‚ĕh-soo, n‚ĕh-s‚osh, n‚ĕh-s‚ot; n‚ĕh-s‚om, n‚ĕh-s‚aw-t‚ĕh, n‚ĕh-soot.</small>

FUTURE: I shall carry, etc., я понесу́, etc.
<small>Conjugated exactly like the Present.   păh-n‚ĕh-soo</small>

PAST: I was carrying, etc., я нёс;   Fem. несла́; Plur. несли́.   <small>n‚oss, n‚ĕh-swah, n‚ĕh-sle.</small>

Perfective: I carried, I have carried, я понёс.
<small>Exactly like the Imperfective Past.   păh-n‚oss.</small>

CONDITIONAL: I should carry, etc., я нёс бы, etc.
Perfective: я понёс бы, etc.
<small>Conditional: yăh n‚oss bE.   Perfective: yăh păh-n‚oss bE.</small>
<small>бы can come before or after the Verb, see rule 28.</small>

IMPERATIVE: carry! неси́те! Perf. понеси́те!
<small>Imperative: n‚ĕh-ce-t‚ĕh!   Perfective: păh-n‚ĕh-ce-t‚ĕh!</small>

76. Translate into English.
(For Vocabulary, see page 126).

1. я ношу́, носи́ли ли вы? он бу́дет носи́ть*;
2. он не но́сит, она́ носи́ла, не бу́дут ли они́ носи́ть? 3. я не несу́, несёте ли вы? они́ не несли́; 4. понесёт ли он? понеси́те! я понёс; 5. он не но́сит шля́пы, како́е пла́тье[240] она́ носи́ла? 6. он не бу́дет э́того носи́ть, почему́ вы не но́сите зо́нтика[280]? 7. кто несёт ваш чемода́н[179]? 8. они́ понесу́т э́то на ста́нцию.

To RULE 104: 1. I am wearing, did you wear? he will wear; 2. he does not carry, she carried, will they not carry? To RULE 106: 3. I am not carrying, are you carrying? they were not carrying; 4. will he carry? carry! I have carried; 5. he does not wear a hat, what dress did she wear? 6. he will not wear this, why don't you carry an umbrella? 7. who is carrying your bag? 8. they will carry this to the station.

*In this Verb the FUTURE is generally formed from the IMPERFECTIVE.

77. Translate into English.

1. Ка́ждый нёс сам свой бага́ж.† 2. Куда́ вы э́то несёте?—В другу́ю ко́мнату. 3. Почему́ вы но́сите таки́е перча́тки? 4. Не вся́кий мог бы носи́ть тако́е бре́мя. 5. Прочита́ли ли вы всю страни́цу? 6. Чей э́тот автомоби́ль?

1. Each one carried his own luggage. 2. Where do you carry this to?—Into another room. 3. Why do you wear such gloves? 4. Not every one would be able to carry such a burden. 5. Have you read the whole page? 6. Whose (is) this motor car?

†=each carried himself (emphatic) his-own (see page 88) luggage.

107. TO BRING, приноси́ть, принести́.
   pre-näh-ceet,   pre-n‚ĕh-ste

The IMPERFECTIVE FORM is quite regular according to rule 41, and the PERFECTIVE is conjugated exactly like TO CARRY (rule 106).

PRESENT : я приношу́, прино́сит ; прино́сят.
FUTURE : я принесу́, принесёт ; принесу́т.
PAST : Imperfective quite regular.
   Perfective : принёс, принесла́, принесли́.
CONDITIONAL : formed in the regular way.
IMPERATIVE : приноси́те ! принеси́те !

108. THE SAME is rendered in Russian by тот-же.*
   тот takes the usual endings, but же is invariable.
   the same room   та же ко́мната
   the same people   те же лю́ди
   they are always the same   они́ всегда́ те же

*The stress is on the first of these two words; they may be joined by a hyphen.

To render THE SAME still more emphatic, са́мый is sometimes added after тот-же equalling THE VERY SAME.
   at the very same   в† тот же са́мый
   moment   моме́нт

са́мый is seldom used by itself; its principal use is in the formation of the SUPERLATIVE, as will be shown. — Do not confuse this word with the emphatic сам, explained in par. 3, page 115.

109. JUST (AS), SIMILAR (TO) are rendered тако́й же.
   I have a similar one (to) ; у меня́ тако́й же (как) ;
   this pen is just as good   э́то перо́ тако́е же хо-
      as that one.   ро́шее, как то.

са́мый may also be added to render тако́й же more emphatic:
   тако́й же са́мый   a very similar one
   в тако́м же са́мом до́ме   in a very similar house

† в mostly requires the ACCUSATIVE in Expressions of Time.

78. Translate into English.
(For Vocabulary, see page 126).

1. я приношу́, принесёте ли вы? он не принёс; 2. не прино́сят ли они́? мы не принесём, они́ приноси́ли; 3. принеси́те, не приноси́те, я бы принесла́; 4. в том же до́ме, о той же да́ме; 5. в* тот же са́мый день, тому́ же са́мому господи́ну; 6. у меня́ таки́е же перча́тки; 7. он тако́й же, как был; 8. он мне принёс тако́й же зо́нтик; 9. они́ всем принесли́ то-же са́мое.   * see page 122.

1. I am bringing, will you bring? he did not bring; 2. do they not bring? we shall not bring, they were bringing; 3. bring, do not bring, I (f.) should bring; 4. in the same house, about the same lady; 5. on the very same day, to-the very same gentleman; 6. I have the same (=similar) gloves; 7. he is just (*or* the same) as he was; 8. he brought (to-) me the same (=similar) umbrella; 9. they brought to-all the very same.

79. Translate into English.

1. Принеси́те мне стака́н воды́.[298] 2. Не приноси́те э́того сюда́. 3. Почему́ вы не принесли́ моего́ словаря́? 4. Мы живём в той же гости́нице. 5. Я вам принесу́ за́втра таку́ю же вещь. 6. Он всегда́ говори́т то-же са́мое. 7. Она́ э́то сейча́с принесёт. 8. Что вы принесли́?

1. Bring (to-) me a glass of water. 2. Don't bring it here (hither). 3. Why did you not bring my dictionary? 4. We are living in the same hotel. 5. I shall bring (to-) you the same (=similar) thing to-morrow. 6. He always says the same (=very same). 7. She will bring it presently. 8. What did you bring?

INDEFINITE PRONOUNS

(not followed by a Noun; for Imitated Pronunciation see page 126).

NOBODY, никто́   1.   NOTHING, ничто́

SOMEBODY, кто́ то   2.   SOMETHING, что́ то
SOMEONE
 ,,   ко́е кто   3.   ,,   ко́е что

The words marked 2 are more usual than those marked 3.

ANYBODY, кто́ нибудь   4.   ANYTHING, что́ нибудь
ANYONE
 ,,   кто ли́бо   5.   ,,   что ли́бо

Either 4 or 5 can be employed, but 4 is the more usual.

The words written in two parts may be connected by a hyphen, but in modern books this is generally omitted.

SOMEONE, не́кто   6.   SOMETHING, не́что

The words numbered 6 are very indefinite, and not often used.

110. The above words do not change, except кто and что which are declined as usual (par. 88).

    to-nobody, никому́; about something, о чём то
        with anybody, с ке́м нибудь
        of-anything, чего́ ли́бо

111. If a PREPOSITION is used with the words numbered 1 and 3, it is placed in the middle, the whole forming three separate words:

    for nobody, ни для кого́; to nothing, ни к чему́
        with someone, ко́е с кем
        about something, ко́е о чём

112. Verbs used with никто́ or ничто́ (No. 1) must be preceded by не.

    he knows nothing, он ничего́ не зна́ет

NOT ANYBODY must be translated by NOT NOBODY.
NOT ANYTHING   ,,   ,,   NOT NOTHING.

    I did not see anybody, я никого́ не ви́дел.

80. Translate into English.

1. никому́, ничему́, о чём то; 2. с ке́м нибудь, для чего́ нибудь; 3. кого́ ли́бо, чем ли́бо; 4. ни о чём, ко́е с кем; 5. ни от кого́, ко́е о чём; 6. кто́-то пришёл[347]; 7. был ли кто́-нибудь здесь? 8. он никого́ не зна́ет; 9. напиши́те ему́ что ли́бо; 10. они́ что́ то принесли́; 11. я хочу́ с ва́ми ко́е о чём поговори́ть*; 12. встре́тили ли вы кого́ нибудь?

1. to-nobody, to-nothing, about something; 2. with anybody, for anything; 3. of-anyone, with-anything; 4. about nothing, with someone; 5. from nobody, about something; 6. someone has-come; 7. was anybody here? 8. he does not know anybody; 9. write (to-) him anything; 10. they brought something; 11. I want to speak to (with) you about something; 12. did you meet anybody?

81. Translate into English.

1. Ви́дели ли вы что́ нибудь? 2. Нет, я ничего́ не ви́дел. 3. Говори́л ли он с кем ли́бо? 4. Да, он говори́л ко́е с кем. 5. Понима́ет ли здесь кто́ нибудь по-ру́сски? 6. Спра́шивали ли они́ вас о чём ли́бо? 7. Мы никому́ э́того не дади́м. 8. Я вам принёс ко́е что. 9. Никому́ э́того не говори́те!

1. Did you see anything? 2. No, I did not see anything. 3. Did he speak to anyone? 4. Yes, he spoke to someone. 5. Does anybody understand Russian here? 6. Did they ask you about anything? 7. We shall not give it to anybody. 8. I have brought (to-) you something. 9. Do not tell this to anybody!

* The PERFECTIVE FORM is generally used after TO WANT, etc.

VOCABULARY TO PAGES 120-127.

375. after   после
    paw-sl,ĕh
376. anybody кто нибудь
    anyone ktaw-ne-bood,
    see page 124.
377. anyone   кто либо
    anybody ktaw-le-baw
    see page 124.
378. anything   что либо
    shtaw-le-baw see page 124.
379.   „   что нибудь
    shtaw-ne-bood, see page 124.
380. breakfast   завтрак
    or lunch   zahf-trähk
381. burden   бремя
    br,eh-m,äh   see rule 74.
382. butter   масло
    mah-swaw
383. coffee   кофе
    the same in all cases   kaw-f,ĕh
384. dining-room
    stäh-waw-väh-yäh столовая
    declined like an Adjective
385. egg   яйцо
    yäh^e-tsaw
386. glove   перчатка
    p,err-tchaht-käh
387. hither   сюда
    =here   s,oo-dah

388. hungry   голодный
    gäh-wod-nᴇ^e   see rule 73.
389. little   мало
    Adverb   mah-waw
390. more   больше
    bol,-shĕh
391. mustard   горчица
    garr-tche-tsäh
392. nobody   никто
    ne-ktaw   see page 124.
393. nothing   ничто
    ne-tchtaw   see page 124.
394. piece   кусок
    koo-sok   see rule 72.
395. (it is) possible можно
    =one may   moj-naw
396. pleasure   удоволь-
    oo-däh-vol,-stfe^yĕh   ствие
397. salt   соль
    sol,
398. somebody   кто то
    =someone ktaw-taw see p. 124.
399. someone   кое кто
    =somebody kaw-yĕh-ktaw
    see page 124.
400. something что то
    shtaw-taw see p. 124.
401. something кое что
    kaw-yĕh-shtaw see p. 124.

402. to bring, see par. 107 | 403. to carry, see par. 106
404. to come—kindly   жаловать   пожаловать
    see rule 52.   jah-waw-väht,   päh-jah-waw-väht,
405. to eat   кушать   покушать
    koo-shäht,   päh-koo-shäht,
406. to pass, stretch, hand подавать   подать
    conjugated like 'to give,' par.87.   päh-däh-vaht,   päh-daht,

CONVERSATIONAL PRACTICE.
(For new words, see Vocabulary on the opposite page).

1. Завтрак готов. 2. Хорошо, мы сейчас придём.[347] 3. Господа, пожалуйте в столовую. 4. Вы* хотите яйцо, или холодное[265] мясо[290]?— Яйцо, пожалуйста. 5. Я вам дам ещё кусок хлеба[182] с маслом. 6. Нет, спасибо, я не могу больше. 7. Почему вы так мало кушаете?— Я не голоден сегодня.

    1. Breakfast (or lunch) is ready. 2. All right, we shall come presently. 3. Gentlemen, come-kindly into the-dining-room. 4. Do you want an-egg, or cold meat ? — An-egg, please. 5. I shall give you another (=yet) piece of-bread and (=with) butter. 6. No, thanks (I cannot more). 7. Why do you eat so little ?—I am not hungry to-day.

8. Сейчас принесут кофе. 9. Хотите* чашку[319] кофе ? 10. Нет, благодарю вас ; я бы хотел стакан чаю с лимоном, если можно. 11. Могу ли вас попросить подать мне соль и горчицу ? —С удовольствием.

    8. They will presently bring the coffee. 9. Do you want a cup of coffee ? 10. No, thank you ; I should like a cup (=glass) of-tea with lemon, if possible. 11. May I ask you to pass (to-) me the salt and the mustard ?—With pleasure.

12. Не слишком холоден ли ваш чай ?—Нет, он очень хорош. 13. Вы любите чай с сахаром[113] ?—Сколько кусков сахару ? 14. Что вы хотите делать после завтрака ?

    12. Is not your tea too cold ?—No, it is very good. 13. Do you like tea with sugar ? — How many pieces of sugar ? 14. What are you going (=want) to do after breakfast ?

* Questions are frequently formed by merely raising the voice—see p. 50.

113.   TO LEAD, вести́, повести́.
          CONDUCT, GUIDE v‚ĕh-ste păh-v‚ĕh-ste

PRESENT : я веду́,   он ведёт,   они́ веду́т.
           v‚ĕh-doo   v‚ĕh-d‚ot   v‚ĕh-doot

FUTURE : поведу́, поведёшь, поведу́т.

PAST : вёл.   Feminine : вела́.   Plural : вели́.
       v‚ol   v‚ĕh-wah   v‚ĕh-le

Perfective : повёл, повела́, повели́.

IMPERATIVE : веди́те !   Perfective : поведи́те !
             v‚ĕh-de-t‚ĕh !

114. The above Verb is generally the translation for TO LEAD, but when FREQUENCY IS EXPRESSED 'TO LEAD' is rendered by води́ть (văh-deet‚)

This is exactly the same as explained in paragraphs 69 and 93.

води́ть is quite regular according to rule 41, and is conjugated exactly like ходи́ть (see par. 70).

115.   TO LEAD TO, приводи́ть, привести́.
           TO BRING   pre-văh-deet‚ pre-v‚ĕh-ste

The Imperfective is quite regular according to rule 41 ; the Perfective is conjugated exactly like вести́.

PRESENT : я привожу́, etc.   FUTURE : я приведу́.
PAST : я приводи́л, etc.   Perfective : я привёл.
IMPERATIVE : приводи́те !   „   приведи́те !

To BRING is translated as in Rule 115 when referring to a person or animal (when not actually carried), but when TO BRING means TO CARRY the Verb in Rule 107 must be used.

116. MYSELF, HIMSELF, OURSELVES, etc., when not emphatic, are translated by : Gen. себя́, Instr. собо́й, Dat. and Prep'. себе́.   This word has no Nominative.

IMITATED PRONUNCIATION : c‚ĕh-b‚ah, săh-boy, c‚ĕh-b‚eh.

he thinks only about him-   он ду́мает то́лько о
  self   себе́

82. Translate into English.

1. мы ведём, поведёте ли вы? они́ повели́; 2. поведи́те нас, он вёл; 3. во́дите ли вы? мы не бу́дем води́ть; 4. она́ приво́дит, приведёте ли вы? 5. я привёл, они́ не приводи́ли; 6. куда́ он нас ведёт? кто их повёл? 7. кого́ вы привели́? мы его́ приведём; 8. не води́те его́ по го́роду, приведи́те ва́шего бра́та; 9. они́ приво́дят друзе́й; 10. куда́ ведёт э́та у́лица?

1. to par. 113: we lead, will you lead? they led; 2. lead us, he was leading; 3. to par. 114: are you leading? we shall not lead; 4. to par. 115: she leads-to, will you bring? 5. I led-to, they were not bringing; 6. where (whither) does he lead us to? who has-led them? 7. whom did you bring? we shall bring him; 8. do not lead him about (=along) the town, bring your brother; 9. they are bringing friends; 10. where does this street lead to?

83. Translate into English.

1. Поведи́те меня́, пожа́луйста, на ста́нцию. 2. Он нас вёл по той же са́мой у́лице. 3. Я вас поведу́ в музе́й, е́сли хоти́те. 4. Не ходи́те с ни́ми; они́ вас бу́дут води́ть весь день. 5. Я вам привёл моего́ дру́га. 6. Приведу́т ли они́ свою́ сестру́?

1. Conduct me to the station, please.* 2. He was leading us along the very same street. 3. I will take (=lead) you to the museum if you wish. 4. Don't go with them; they will drag you about (=lead you) the whole day. 5. I brought you my friend. 6. Will they bring their sister?

* the Russian for PLEASE is generally put after the Verb, or after the Object if it is a Pronoun.

117. Russian ADVERBS requiring the following word in the GENITIVE.

407.	MUCH, MANY	мно́го	mnaw-gaw
408.	A LITTLE, NOT MUCH, NOT MANY	немно́го	n͵ĕh-mnaw-gaw
409.	(diminutive form for A LITTLE)	немно́жко	n͵ĕh-mnoj-kaw

This diminutive form is much used instead of немно́го.

410.	SO MUCH, SO MANY	сто́лько	stol͵-kaw
411.	HOW „ HOW „	ско́лько	skol͵-kaw
412.	SOME, A FEW	не́сколько	n͵eh-skol͵-kaw
413.	LITTLE, FEW	ма́ло	mah-waw
414.	MORE	бо́льше	bol͵-shĕh
415.	LESS, FEWER	ме́ньше	m͵en͵-shĕh
416.	ENOUGH	дово́льно	dăh-vol͵-naw
417.	SUFFICIENT	доста́точно	dăh-stah-totch-naw

EXAMPLES.

he has very little money	у него́ о́чень ма́ло де́нег[1]
bring (to-) me a little water	принеси́те мне немно́жко воды́
there-were very few people at the theatre	в теа́тре бы́ло о́чень ма́ло наро́ду[2]
I should like to tell (to-) you a few words	я бы хоте́л сказа́ть вам не́сколько слов
they have too many friends	у них сли́шком мно́го друзе́й[3]
the less work, the more trouble(s)	чем[4] ме́ньше рабо́ты, тем[4] бо́льше забо́т

1 see rule 85; 2 see rule 76; 3 see rule 79; 4 the... the.

118. The GENITIVE is used after Nouns like:

a glass of wine	стака́н вина́
a pound of butter	фунт ма́сла

84. Translate into English.

1. мно́го де́нег, ско́лько фу́нтов? 2. ма́ло наро́ду, бо́льше вре́мени; 3. не́сколько слов, сли́шком мно́го рабо́ты; 4. немно́жко со́ли,[397] дово́льно горчи́цы[391]; 5. сто́лько дете́й, ме́ньше удово́льствия[396]; 6. пять арши́н сукна́, буты́лка пи́ва[231]; 7. ча́шка[319] ко́фе, стака́н вина́; 8. у нас сли́шком ма́ло вре́мени для э́того; 9. вы должны́ бо́льше рабо́тать и ме́ньше говори́ть; 10. здесь сли́шком мно́го хозя́ев[99]; 11. заче́м вам так мно́го (or сто́лько) сту́льев? 12. я чита́ю по-ру́сски и говорю́ немно́го.

(The small numbers after the English refer to the Rules).

1. much money,[85] how-many pounds? 2. few people,[76] more time[74]; 3. a few words, too much work; 4. a little salt, enough mustard; 5. so-many children,[96] less pleasure; 6. five yards[82] of cloth, a bottle of beer; 7. a cup of coffee,* a glass of wine; 8. we have too little time[74] for that; 9. you must work more and speak less; 10. (there-are) too many masters (landlords[79]) here; 11. why do you want (=what for to you) so many chairs[79]? 12. I read Russian, and speak a little. * COFFEE is indeclinable in Russian, see Vocab. 383.

85. Translate into English.

1. Почему́ вы привели́ сто́лько госте́й? 2. Принеси́те мне немно́жко горя́чей воды́. 3. Он жил у нас не́сколько дней. 4. Ско́лько вы ему́ заплати́ли?—Три рубля́. 5. Приведёте ли вы кого́ нибу́дь[376]?

1. Why did you bring[115] so-many guests? 2. Bring (to-) me a little hot water. 3. He was staying[89] with us for-a-few days.[72] 4. How-much did you pay (to-) him?—Three roubles. 5. Will you bring[115] anybody?

NINETEENTH LESSON.

The letters in brackets indicate the 'CASE' required by the PREPOSITION. Where there is no letter, the Genitive must be used.

Prepositions are pronounced as if they were a part of the next word.

418. about   о[1] (P.)
concerning   ăh
419. about   про (A.)
concerning   prăh
(418 is the more usual)
420. above   над[2] (I.)
over   năhd
421. along   по (D.)
according to   păh
422. after   после
   paw-sl‚ĕh
423. at, by, near   у
at the place of   oo
424. before   перед[2] (I.)
in front of   p‚eh-r‚ed
425. behind   за (I.)
beyond, on the other side of   zăh
426. between   между (I.)
among   m‚ej-doo
427. beside   кроме
besides, except   kraw-m‚ĕh
428. for   для
   dl‚ăh
429. for in exchange of   за (A.)
instead of   zăh
430. from, out of   из[2]
   iz

431. from, off   с[2]
(= from the top of)   ss
432. from   от
   ăht
433. in, at   в[2] (P.)
(rest or state)   v' or f'
434. into, to   в[2] (A.)
(movement)   v' or f'
435. near, about   около
   aw-kaw-waw
436. near   при (P.)
in the time of, in the presence of
435 is the more usual   pre
437. on, upon, at   на (P.)
(rest or state)   năh
438. on, on to   на (A.)
(movement)   năh
439. to, towards   к[2] (D.)
(with Verbs of movement only)   k'
440. under   под (I.)
(Acc. if movement)   păhd
441. up to, till   до
   daw or dăh
442. with   с (I.)
meaning together with   ss
443. without   без
   b‚ez

1.—о is changed into об before a vowel, and into обо in the following expressions: about me, обо мне; about everything, обо всём; about all, обо всех.

2.—о is added before a word beginning with several consonants together: with me, со мной; but there are a few exceptions.   424-425.—Acc. if movement.

86. Translate into English.
(For new words, see pages 132 and 140).

1. к портно́му,* к го́роду, ко мне; 2. по у́лице, по ру́сским газе́там; 3. о ком? об э́том господи́не, обо всём; 4. о́коло на́шей шко́лы, при ва́шей сестре́, при Царе́ Петре́; 5. ме́жду на́ми, с мои́м учи́телем, со мной; 6. над его́ до́мом, на́до все́ми; 7. пе́редо мной, перед Рождество́м; 8. у нас, у[423] теа́тра, у него́ кни́га; 9. из Росси́и, с[431] по́лки, от бра́та, со стола́.

*See Vocabulary, page 140, No. 469.

1. to the tailor, towards the town, to me; 2. along the street, according to Russian papers; 3. about whom? about this gentleman, about everything; 4. near our school, in-the-presence-of your sister, in-the-time of the Tzar Peter; 5. between us, with my teacher, with me; 6. over his house, above everybody; 7. in-front-of me, before Christmas; 8. at our-place, by the theatre, he has a book; 9. from Russia, from the shelf, from my-brother, from the table.

87. Translate into English.

1. Они́ пошли́ к ва́шему дру́гу. 2. Кто вам э́то принёс? 3. О чём вы ду́маете? 4. Где каранда́ш?— Он в мое́й ко́мнате, на столе́. 5. Мы пойдём за́втра в теа́тр. 6. Пое́дете ли вы на ста́нцию? 7. Ва́ша шля́па под столо́м. 8. Кто её положи́л под стол?

1. They went to your friend. 2. Who brought this to-you? 3. What are you thinking about? 4. Where is the pencil?—It is in my room, on the table. 5. We shall go to-morrow to the theatre. 6. Will you drive[90] to the station? 7. Your hat is under the table. 8. Who put[119] it under the table?

119. TO PUT, TO LAY   класть, положи́ть.
    (IN A LYING POSITION)   kwahst,   păh-wăh-jeet,

PRESENT : я кладу́, он кладёт, они́ кладу́т.
            kwăh-doo   kwăh-d‚ot   kwăh-doot

FUTURE : я положу́, он поло́жит, они́ поло́жат.
         păh-wăw-joo   păh-waw-jeet   păh-waw-jăht

PAST : клал.   Perfective : положи́л.
       kwahl   păh-wăh-jeel

IMPERATIVE : клади́те !   Perfective : положи́те !
           kwăh-de-t‚ĕh !   păh-wăh-je-t‚ĕh !

120. The following remarks on the use of PREPOSITIONS are very important :

(A) OF is not translated by a separate word, but rendered by the GENITIVE (see pages 12-13).

(B) TO is generally not translated by a separate word, but is rendered by the DATIVE (see pages 28-31).

(C) But if TO indicates a movement towards a person or place, it is rendered by к (ко) (see par. 46).

(D) WITH and BY (= by means of) are simply rendered by the INSTRUMENTAL ; but when WITH means TOGETHER WITH it is translated by с (par. 23).

(E) The Prepositions в, на, за, о (against), под, require the ACCUSATIVE when movement is expressed or implied.

    The Accusative answers to the question " whither ? "

121. PUT is generally translated as in par. 119, except when meaning to put in an upright position.

         TO PUT, STAND   ста́вить, поста́вить.
   (IN AN UPRIGHT POSITION)   stah-veet,   păh-stah-veet,
        Conjugated quite regularly according to par. 47.

he put the umbrella in the corner	он поста́вил зо́нтик в у́гол
put the bottle on the table	поста́вьте буты́лку на стол

88. Translate into English.

(For Vocabulary, see page 140; for Prepositions, see page 132).

1. положи́те э́то в карма́н—в я́щик; 2. они́ кладу́т э́то на роя́ль[159]—на стол; 3. он был в музе́е—на по́чте[128]—за де́ревом[228]; 4. мы жи́ли под ни́ми, она́ положи́ла письмо́ под кни́гу; 5. да́йте э́то ма́льчику—шофёру[85]—сестре́—им; 6. они́ гуля́ют с учи́телем[115]—с да́мами—с ни́ми; 7. ку́шайте ножо́м[98] и ви́лкой[95]; 8. мы принесли́ э́то для ва́шего ребёнка—для вас; 9. за биле́т—за обе́д; 10. из Росси́и—из ко́мнаты; 11. с по́лки—со стола́; 12. от э́того господи́на—от нас; 13. о́коло на́шего до́ма—о́коло шести́* рубле́й.

1. put this in your-pocket—in the drawer; 2. they are putting it on the piano—on the table; 3. he was at the museum—at (on) the post-office—behind the tree; 4. we were living under them, she has put the letter under the book; 5. give it to the boy—to the taxi driver—to the sister—to them; 6. they are walking with the teacher—with ladies—with them; 7. eat with-knife and fork; 8. we brought it for your child[86]—for you; 9. for the ticket—for the dinner; 10. from Russia—from the room; 11. from the shelf—from the table; 12. from this gentleman—from us; 13. near *or* about our house—about six* roubles.

89. Translate into English.

1. Вы из Росси́и?—Когда́ вы е́дете в Росси́ю? 2. Мои́ бра́тья живу́т в Пари́же. 3. Приведи́те его́ к нам сего́дня ве́чером.

1. Are you from Russia?—When are you going to Russia? 2. My brothers[79] live in Paris. 3. Bring[115] him to us this evening.

*Gen. of шесть.

122. Adverbs can be formed in Russian from Adjectives by changing the ending ый, etc., into **o**.

    nice, краси́вый   nicely, краси́во
        krăh-ce-vĕ͡e   krăh-ce-vaw
    bad, плохо́й   badly, пло́хо
        pwăh-hoy   pwaw-haw
    good, хоро́ший   well, хорошо́
        hăh-raw-she͡e   hăh-răh-shaw

123. Adverbs generally come BEFORE THE VERB.

they came very late	они́ о́чень по́здно пришли́
he speaks Russian well	он хорошо́ говори́т по-ру́сски

    The idiomatic use of Russian Adverbs is very important. It was fully explained in pars. 64-65, and at the foot of page 83.

we are sorry for them	нам их жа́лко
=to-us of-them it-is-pity	năhm eekh jahL-kaw

124.   TO SEND   посыла́ть, посла́ть.
                           păh-ce-waht,   păh-swaht,

    In the Perfective the **c** changes into **ш**. The Perfective only is given here, as the Imperfective Form is quite regular.

FUTURE : я пошлю́, он пошлёт, они́ пошлю́т.
            păh-shl,oo   păh-shl,ot   păh-shl,oot

PAST : посла́л.   IMPERATIVE : пошли́те !
     păh-swahL   păh-shle-t,ĕh !

    Very fine shades of meaning are shown in Russian by changing the Preposition prefixed to the Verb, but only advanced students should trouble about this :

they sent (to-) me the money	мне присла́ли де́ньги
	mn,ĕh pre-swah-le d,en,-ghe
they sent (to-) me money from home	мне вы́слали де́ньги из дому
(notice stress on Preposition)	mn,ĕh vE-swăh-le d,en,-ghe iz-daw-moo

    The first of these examples means that I have received the money ; the second, that the money has been sent off, but not received by me.

    For beginners, it is simplest to always use the Verb in par. 124.

90. Translate into English.
(For Vocabularies, see pages 76, 83, and 140).

1. у́мный, умно́; дорого́й, до́рого; 2. тру́дный, тру́дно; высо́кий, высоко́; 3. безполе́зно, смешно́; 4. он пло́хо пи́шет, она́ бога́то одева́ется[211]; 5. мы по́здно пришли́, вы э́то дёшево купи́ли; 6. пошлёте ли вы? мы посла́ли, не посыла́ют ли они́? 7. пошли́те! я посыла́л, не посыла́йте! 8. я э́то пошлю́ за́втра; 9. когда́ они́ вам э́то посла́ли *or* присла́ли? 10. не посыла́йте э́того сего́дня!

1. clever, cleverly; dear, dearly; 2. difficult (Adj.), difficult (Adv.); high, highly *or* high-up; 3. it is useless, it is ridiculous; 4. he writes badly, she dresses richly; 5. we came late, you bought this cheap(ly); 6. will you send? we have sent, are they not sending? 7. send! I was sending, do not send! 8. I shall send it to-morrow; 9. when did they send it to you? 10. don't send it to-day!

91. Translate into English.

1. Вы за э́то о́чень до́рого заплати́ли. 2. Мне его́ жа́лко.[273] 3. Он о́чень гру́стно[278] смо́трит. 4. Легко́ говори́ть, но тру́дно де́лать. 5. Далеко́ ли они́ живу́т отсю́да? 6. Нет, о́чень бли́зко; пять мину́т пешко́м.[342] 7. Мы вам посыла́ем това́р сего́дня. 8. Мы вам бу́дем посыла́ть газе́ты ка́ждый день.

1. You paid very dearly for it. 2. I am sorry for him. 3. He looks very depressed (sad). 4. It is easy to talk, but difficult to do. 5. Do they live far from here? 6. No, very near; five minutes on-foot. 7. We are sending (to-) you the goods to-day. 8. We will send (to-) you the newspapers every day.

125. The Comparative of Attributive Adjectives is formed by placing бо́лее (more) before the Adjective. (For explanation of Attribute and Predicate, see par. 56)

    a quicker train   бо́лее ско́рый по́езд
    a more difficult problem бо́лее тру́дная зада́ча

126. The Comparative of Predicate Adjectives is formed by changing the ending ый, etc., into ее.

This Comparative Form never changes in the Feminine, Neuter or Plural.

    1. бѣлый;   2. удобный;   3. прия́тный.

this paper is whiter   э́та бума́га бѣлѣе[1]
our flat is more convenient на́ша кварти́ра удо́бнѣе[2]

Instead of ее, ей may be added, but ее is the more usual.

    this is more pleasant э́то прия́тнѣе[3] or прия́тнѣй

127. The above is also the Comparative of Adverbs.

    quickly, ско́ро   more quickly, скорѣ́е
    slowly, ме́дленно   more slowly, ме́дленнѣй

The stress in the Comparative is always on ее (or ей) in words of two syllables; otherwise the stress remains as before.

128. THAN after the Comparative is rendered by putting the following word into the Genitive.

    she is more clever than она́ умнѣ́е сестры́
      her sister
    he is poorer than you   он беднѣ́е вас

129. After the Comparative Attributive, however, THAN must be translated by чѣм or не́жели.

(Sometimes these words are used instead of the Genitive in rule 128).

Either word can be used, but the first occurs more frequently. The word following чѣм or не́жели does not change.

    this is a quieter house э́то бо́лее споко́йный
    than yours   дом чѣм ваш

92. Translate into English.
(For Adjectives, see Vocabularies, pages 76, 83, and 90).

1. бо́лее лёгкий уро́к, бо́лее тяжёлый чемода́н; 2. с бо́лее стро́гим учи́телем, о бо́лее ва́жном де́ле; 3. по бо́лее краси́вым у́лицам, э́ти черни́ла черне́е; 4. ва́ша кни́га интере́снее, мой нож остре́й; 5. он хо́дит ме́дленнее, говори́те скоре́й; 6. он сильне́е своего́ бра́та, э́та карти́на краси́вее той; 7. ру́сский язы́к трудне́е англи́йского; 8. бо́лее бога́тый господи́н, чем тот; бо́лее чи́стая ко́мната, не́жели на́ша.

1. an easier lesson, the heavier bag; 2. with a stricter teacher, about more important business; 3. through (along) nicer streets, this ink[85] is blacker; 4. your book is more interesting, my knife is sharper; 5. he walks more slowly, speak more quickly; 6. he is stronger than his brother, this picture is nicer than that; 7. the Russian language is more difficult than the English; 8. a richer (gentle)man than that one; a cleaner room than ours.

93. Translate into English.

1. Почему́ вы ему́ не даёте бо́лее тру́дной рабо́ты? 2. Укажи́те* мне, пожа́луйста, бо́лее бли́зкую доро́гу. 3. Э́то трудне́е, чем вы ду́маете. 4. Он пришёл поздне́й,† чем вчера́. 5. В э́том рестора́не веселе́е,[271] чем в друго́м. 6. Его́ кварти́ра удо́бнее на́шей. † or по́зже.

1. Why do you not give (to-) him more difficult work? 2. Show (to-) me, please, the nearer way. 3. This is more difficult than you think. 4. He came later than yesterday. 5. In this restaurant it is more cheerful (jolly) than in the other-one. 6. His flat is more comfortable than ours. * literally: point out.

VOCABULARY TO PAGES 132-141.

Adjectives not on this page will be found in Vocabularies 76, 83, **90**.

444. accurate аккура́тный
ăh-koo-raht-nE͡e
445. child ребёнок
see rule 86   r,ĕh-b,aw-nok
446. Christmas Рождество́
răhj-d,ĕh-stfaw
447. cloth сукно́
sook-naw
448. clean чи́стый
tche-stE͡e
449. dinner обе́д
ăh-b,ed
450. drawer я́щик
box · yah-shtcheek
451. from here отсю́да
ăht-s,oo-dăh
452. goods това́р
merchandise   tăh-varr
453. heavy тяжёлый
t,ăh-jaw-wE͡e
454. hot горя́чий
not referring to weather
găh-r,ah-tche͡e
455. important ва́жный
vahj-nE͡e
456. interesting интере́сный
in-t,ĕh-r,ess-nE͡e
457. language язы́к
tongue   yăh-zEEk
458. near бли́зкий
ble-ske͡e

459. picture карти́на
karr-te-năh
459a. office конто́ра
kăhn-taw-răh
459b. to pain боле́ть
ache   băh-l,et,
460. people наро́д
năh-rod
461. pocket карма́н
karr-mahn
462. to put, stand
see rule 121
463. ,, lay
see rule 119
464. Russia Росси́я
răh-ce-yăh
465. to send
see rule 124
466. sharp о́стрый
aw-strE͡e
467. strong си́льный
ceel-nE͡e
468. shelf по́лка
poL-kăh
469. tailor портно́й
declined like an Adjective
parrt-noy
470. violin скри́пка
skreep-kăh
471. work рабо́та
răh-baw-tăh
472. what for ? заче́м ?
zăh-tch,em ?
473. yard арши́н
Russian yard, rule 82   arr-**sheen**

474. to try стара́ться постара́ться
endeavour   stăh-raht,-s,ăh   păh-stăh-raht,-s,ăh

CONVERSATIONAL PRACTICE.

(Numbers to Russian refer to the Vocabulary, and to English to the rules).

1. Приходи́те (or Приди́те) к нам сего́дня ве́чером.—Бу́дет о́чень ве́село.[271] 2. Хорошо́, постара́юсь прийти́. 3. Мы наде́емся,[215] что вы принесёте с собо́й скри́пку. 4. Мы все так лю́бим вас слу́шать! 5. К сожале́нию,* я не смогу́ игра́ть сего́дня.—Почему́? *p. 111, sent. 4.

1. Come to us this evening.—It will be very jolly. 2. All right, I shall try to come. 3. We hope that you will bring[107] your-violin with you.[116] 4. We all so like to listen (to) you! 5. To my-regret, I shall not be able to play to-day.—Why?

6. У меня́ боли́т пра́вая[29] рука́.[155]—Вы должны́ идти́ к до́ктору. 7. Я был у до́ктора — он сказа́л, что я не до́лжен игра́ть всю неде́лю.[333]— Э́то жа́лко[273]! 8. Вы придёте одни́?—Я ду́маю.

6. My-right hand pains me.—You must go to the doctor. 7. I was at the doctor's — he said that I must not play the whole week.†— That is a pity! 8. Will you come alone?— I think (so). † time in the Accusative.

9. Не могли́ бы вы привести́ ва́шего бра́та? 10. Нам всем бы́ло бы о́чень прия́тно. 11. Хорошо́, я постара́юсь. — Пожа́луйста. 12. В кото́ром часу́ вы бу́дете у нас?—В во́семь и́ли в де́вять. 13. Почему́ так по́здно? 14. Мой брат за́нят до семи́ в конто́ре.

9. Could you not bring[115] your brother? 10. To-us all —We all should be very pleased. 11. Very well, I shall-try. —Do (please). 12. At what time (which hour) will you be at our place? — At eight or at nine. 13. Why so late? 14. My brother is busy till seven (Genitive) in the office.

TWENTIETH LESSON.

130.   TO TAKE   брать, взять.
                    braht,   vz‚aht‚

PRESENT: I take, etc., я беру́, берёт, беру́т.
                            b‚ĕh-roo b‚ĕh-r‚ot b‚ĕh-root
FUTURE: I shall take, возьму́, возьмёт, возьму́т.
                      văhz‚-moo văhz‚-m‚ot văhz‚-moot
PAST: I took = I was taking, etc., я брал, etc.
   The forms not given are quite regular.   brahL

Perf.: I took, I have taken, взял, взяла́, взя́ли.
                             vz‚ăhL vz‚ăh-wah vz‚ah-le
IMPERATIVE: бери́те!   Perfective: возьми́те!
            b‚ĕh-re-t‚ĕh!   văhz‚-me-t‚ĕh!
   The SECOND PERSON of the IMPERATIVE was explained in par. 30.

131. The THIRD PERSON of the IMPERATIVE is formed by пусть followed by the Third Person.

   let him work   пусть рабо́тает
   let them read   пусть чита́ют

The terminations are always the same (page 48); but they are called Present endings in the Imperfective form, and Future endings in the Perfective form.

   let her think (it) over   пусть поду́мает

132. The FIRST PERSON PLURAL of the IMPERATIVE is simply the same Person of the PRESENT, without the Pronoun мы. (or of the Future—in Perfective Verbs).

   let us buy! ку́пим! ку́пим-те! *or* ку́пимте!
   те is often added; the form with the hyphen is now obsolete.

133. The numbers from FIVE to TWENTY (see par. 44) are declined exactly like Feminine Nouns in ь.

   six, шесть { Gen., Dat., Prep., шести́.
               { Instr., шестью́.

94. Translate into English.

1. мы берём, она́ возьмёт, он не брал: 2. берёте ли вы? возьму́т ли они́? не взяла́ ли она́? 3. возьми́те, не бери́те, я беру́; 4. пусть возьмёт, пусть берёт; 5. идём-те† *or* пойдём-те†; 6. пусть напи́шет, пусть пи́шет; 7. пусть возьму́т, пусть беру́т.

1. we take, she will take, he was not taking; 2. do you take? will they take? has she not taken? 3. take, do not take, I am taking; 4. let him take (once), let him take (frequently); 5. let us go (Imperfective or Perfective); 6. let him write (Perfective), let him write (Imperfective); 7. let them take (once), let them take (repeatedly).

95. Translate into English.

1. Он взял мой зо́нтик. 2. Не взя́ли ли вы его́ перча́ток[386]? 3. Мы берём ру́сские уро́ки. 4. Не бери́те э́той газе́ты. 5. Могу́ ли я взять э́тот каранда́ш?—Пожа́луйста. 6. Возьми́те э́то с собо́й. 7. Я не возьму́ ме́ньше[415] десяти́ фу́нтов. 8. Пусть вам ска́жет, что он хо́чет. 9. Пусть принесу́т э́то сюда́.[387] 10. Пое́демте во Фра́нцию. 11. Господа́, пойдёмте в теа́тр. 12. Я не взял часо́в с собо́й.

1. He took my umbrella. 2. Did you not take his gloves? 3. We are taking Russian lessons. 4. Don't take this newspaper. 5. May I take this pencil?—Please. 6. Take this with you.[116] 7. I shall not take less than ten pounds. 8. Let him tell (to-) you what he wants. 9. Let them bring it here=hither. 10. Let us go to France. 11. Gentlemen,[79] let us go to the theatre. 12. I did not take a watch with me.[116]

† see remark to par. 132.

LIST OF THE
MOST IMPORTANT IRREGULAR COMPARATIVES.

1. The ADVERBS of all the following Adjectives are formed regularly (rule 122). 2. The — shows that the COMPARATIVE is formed regularly (rule 125). 3. The form in the third column is that of the COMPARATIVE of ADVERBS (rule 127), as well as that of the PREDICATE.

	ORDINARY FORM of the Adjective.	ATTRIBUTIVE FORM (coming before Noun)	PREDICATIVE FORM (after Subject)
475.	bad, плохо́й pwäh-hoy	worse, ху́дший hood-she͡e	ху́же hoo-jĕh
476.	big, большо́й* large bǎhl,-shoy	bigger, бо́льший larger bol,-she͡e	бо́льше bol,-shĕh
477.	broad, широ́кий wide she-raw-ke͡e	broader, — wider	ши́ре she-r͵ĕh
478.	cheap, дешёвый d͵ĕh-shaw-vE͡e	cheaper, —	деше́вле d͵ĕh-shev-l͵ĕh
479.	clean, чи́стый tche-stE͡e	cleaner, —	чи́ще tche-shtchĕh
480.	dear, дорого́й expensive däh-räh-goy	dearer, — more expensive	доро́же däh-raw-jĕh
481.	distant, далёкий far däh-l͵aw-ke͡e	further, — more distant	да́льше dal,-shĕh
482.	easy, лёгкий l͵okh-ke͡e	easier, —	ле́гче l͵ekh-tchĕh
483.	good, хоро́ший häh-raw-she͡e	better, лу́чший wootch-she͡e	лу́чше wootch-shĕh
484.	hot, жа́ркий jarr-ke͡e	hotter, — (referring to weather only)	жа́рче jarr-tchĕh
485.	high, высо́кий tall vE-saw-ke͡e	higher, вы́сший taller vEEs-she͡e	вы́ше vE-shĕh
486.	little, ма́ленький small mah-l͵en͵-ke͡e	smaller, ме́ньший m͵en͵-she͡e	ме́ньше m͵en͵-shĕh
487.	low, ни́зкий nees-ke͡e	lower, ни́зший nees-she͡e	ни́же ne-jĕh
488.	near, бли́зкий blees-ke͡e	nearer, —	бли́же ble-jĕh

* The Adverb is бо́льше same as the Comparative.

Ordinary Form of the Adjective.	Attributive Form (coming before Noun)	Predicative Form (after Subject)
489. old, ста́рый stăh-rĕ͡e	older, ста́рший[1] senior starr-shĕ͡e	ста́рше starr-shĕh
490. rich, бога́тый băh-gah-tɛ͡e	richer, —	бога́че băh-gah-tchĕh
491. short, коро́ткий kăh-rot-ke͡e	shorter, —	коро́че kăh-raw-tchĕh
492. simple, просто́й prăh-stoy	simpler, —	про́ще praw-shtchĕh
493. thick, то́лстый stout toL-stɛ͡e	thicker, — stouter	то́лще toL-shtchĕh
494. young, молодо́й măh-wăh-doy	younger, мла́дший[1] мо́ложе junior mwahd-shĕ͡e măh-waw-jĕh	

1. the regular form only refers to AGE.

134. MUCH, before the COMPARATIVE, is rendered by гора́здо găh-rahz-daw. (see examples 6 and 7).

96. Translate into English.

1. э́то деше́вле, он моло́же; 2. кто из них вы́ше? э́та бума́га то́лще; 3. мой ста́рший брат, в лу́чшей гости́нице; 4. на́ша у́лица коро́че, но ши́ре ва́шей; 5. в э́той ко́мнате жа́рче, чем на у́лице; 6. ва́ша конто́ра гора́здо бо́льше мое́й; 7. в э́том до́ме чи́ще, не́жели в друго́м; да, но здесь гора́здо доро́же; 8. э́то ме́ньше и ху́же.

1. this is cheaper, he is younger; 2. who of them is taller? this paper is thicker; 3. my elder brother, in a better hotel; 4. our street is shorter, but broader than-yours; 5. in this room it is hotter than in the street; 6. your office is much bigger than-mine; 7. in this house it is cleaner than in the other-one; yes, but it is much more-expensive here; 8. this is smaller and worse.

135. TO SIT DOWN садѝться, сесть.
sǎh-deet,-s,ǎh   c,est,
Notice that the IMPERFECTIVE is reflective, but not the PERFECTIVE Form.

PRESENT : I sit down, etc., я сажу́сь, он сади́тся ;
мы сади́мся, вы сади́тесь, они́ садя́тся.
sǎh-jooss,, sǎh-deet-s,ǎh ; sǎh-deem-s,ǎh, sǎh-de-t,es,, sǎh-d,aht-s,ǎh

FUTURE : I shall sit down, ся́ду, ся́дет, ся́дут.
s,ah-doo   s,ah-d,et   s,ah-doot

PAST : I was sitting „ сади́лся, сади́лась, сади́лись.
sǎh-deeL-s,ǎh   sǎh-de-wahs,   sǎh-de-lees,

Perfective : I sat down, I have sat down, сел, etc.
c,eL

IMPERATIVE : сади́тесь !   Perfective : ся́дьте !
sǎh-de-t,es, !   s,ahd,-t,ěh !

The Imperfective is mostly used in this Verb.

---

136. The SUPERLATIVE of ADJECTIVES, when used as PREDICATE, is formed by adding всех (of all) to the COMPARATIVE.

    he is the tallest   он вы́ше всех
    this pen is the best э́то перо́ лу́чше всех

When OF ALL means OF EVERYTHING not referring to anything definite, it is rendered by всего́. PRON.: fc,ekh, fc,ěh-vaw
    this is the simplest э́то про́ще всего́

137. The SUPERLATIVE of ATTRIBUTIVE ADJECTIVES is formed by putting са́мый (r. 108) before it.
    the cleverest boy   са́мый у́мный ма́льчик
    the cleverest ladies   са́мые у́мные да́мы

When the ATTRIBUTE ADJECTIVE has a special form (see list 144), са́мый is put before the latter.
    the youngest daughter са́мая мла́дшая дочь

There is also a SUPERLATIVE ATTRIBUTE in ейший (or айший after a hisser). There are many irregularities ; but this form is little used.
    the cleverest one са́мый у́мный *or* умне́йший

97. Translate into English.
(For words, see pages 144 and 145, and Vocabulary 158).

1. я сажу́сь, садя́тся ли они́? не сади́тесь ли вы? 2. они́ се́ли, сел ли он? сади́тесь! *or* ся́дьте! 3. мы ся́дем, не ся́дут ли они́? не сади́тесь здесь; 4. когда́ вы сади́лись, я бы се́ла; 5. э́то лу́чше всего́, она́ красиве́е[272] всех; 6. э́тот уро́к трудне́е всех, э́та доро́га бли́же всех; 7. э́то са́мая бли́зкая доро́га, са́мый лу́чший сорт; 8. са́мый мла́дший офице́р в полку́.

1. I sit down, do they sit down? are you not sitting down? 2. they sat down, did he sit down? sit down! 3. we shall sit down, will they not sit down? do not sit down here; 4. as (when) you were sitting down, I (f.) should sit down; 5. this is the best *or* the best of all, she is the nicest *or* the prettiest; 6. this lesson is the most difficult, this way is the nearest; 7. this is the nearest way, the best quality; 8. the youngest officer in the regiment.

98. Translate into English.

1. Сади́тесь, пожа́луйста. 2. Кто́-то сел на моё ме́сто. 3. Я сейча́с ся́ду. 4. Не сади́тесь на э́тот стул. 5. Могу́ ли я сесть о́коло вас? 6. Он пришёл, когда́ мы сади́лись за стол. 7. Вчера́ был са́мый жа́ркий день в э́том году́. 8. Э́тот ма́льчик ни́же[487] всех.

1. Take a seat *or* sit down, please. 2. Somebody has sat down (seated himself) on my place. 3. I am going to sit down = I shall sit down presently. 4. Don't sit (down) on this chair. 5. May I sit down by (= near) you? 6. He came as we were sitting down at the table. 7. Yesterday was the hottest day in this year. 8. This boy is the shortest.

138. TO CALL, CALL TO   звать, позва́ть.
   not 'call on' or 'to wake'   zvăht,   păh-zvaht,

PRESENT : I call, etc., зову́, зовёт, зову́т.
   ză̆h-voo   ză̆h-v‚ot   ză̆h-voot

FUTURE : позову́, etc.   Conjugated like the Present.

PAST : звал, etc.   Perfective : позва́л.
   Quite regular.

IMPERATIVE : зови́те !   Perfective : позови́те !
   ză̆h-ve-t‚ĕh !   păh-ză̆h-ve-t‚ĕh !

---

139. TO WAIT, TO WAIT FOR   ждать, подожда́ть.
   TO EXPECT   jdăht,   păh-dă̆h-jdaht,

PRESENT : I wait-for, etc., жду, ждёт, ждут.
   jdoo   jd‚ot   jdoot

FUTURE : подожду́, etc.   PAST : quite regular.
   păh-dă̆h-jdoo   Future like Present.

IMPERATIVE : жди́те !   Perfective : подожди́те !
   jde-t‚ĕh !   păh-dă̆h-jde-t‚ĕh !

---

140. IN ORDER TO is rendered in Russian by что́бы or чтоб followed by the INFINITIVE.   tchtaw-be

I came (in order) to tell (to-) you   я пришёл что́бы вам сказа́ть

(in order) to kill time   что́бы уби́ть вре́мя

141. IN ORDER TO must be changed into IN ORDER THAT, after a REQUEST, ORDER, etc., and is rendered in Russian by the same что́бы, but followed by the PAST TENSE.

he asked (me) that I should go away   он проси́л что́бы я ушёл

SHORT, referring to a person, is translated by LOW (Vocabulary 487) in Russian.

99. Translate into English.

1. позовите его, не зовите их; 2. я позову такси[517a], он позвал городового; 3. как это называется? как его звали? 4. я подожду здесь, подождёте ли вы меня? 5. подождите минуту, не ждите больше; 6. мы ждали вас, они ждут писем*; 7. чтобы вам сделать удовольствие[396], чтобы не ждать так долго[339]; 8. чтобы я пришёл, чтобы он подождал.

1. call him, don't call them; 2. I shall call a taxicab, he called a policeman; 3. how is this called=how they call it? how was he called = how they called him? 4. I shall wait here, will you wait-for me? 5. wait a minute, don't wait (any) more; 6. we were waiting-for you, they are waiting-for their-letters; 7. in order to give (make) (to-) you pleasure, in order not to wait so long; 8. in order that I should come, in order that he should wait.

100. Translate into English.

1. Позовите их сюда.[387] 2. Кого вы зовёте? 3. Как вас зовут? 4. Он просил меня, чтобы я позвал вас. 5. Кого вы ждёте? — Никого. 6. Ждёте ли вы поезда? 7. Мы их ждали вчера весь день. 8. Он пришёл, чтобы поблагодарить вас.

1. Call them (to come here) hither. 2. Whom are you calling? 3. What is your name=how do they call you? 4. He requested me to call you=he asked me in order that I should call you. 5. Whom are you waiting-for? — Nobody. 6. Are you waiting-for the train? 7. We were waiting-for them the whole day yesterday. 8. He came (in order) to thank you.

* soft sign is changed into e.

TWENTY-FIRST LESSON.

142. TO WASH   МЫТЬ, ПОМЫ́ТЬ.
mɛɛt, păh-mɛɛt, (ɛ or ɛɛ like ɪ in pɪᴛ)

PRESENT : I wash, etc., мо́ю, мо́ет, мо́ют.
maw-yoo   maw-yet   maw-yoot

FUTURE : I shall wash, etc., помо́ю, etc.
Conjugated exactly like the Present.

PAST : both forms are quite regular.

IMPERATIVE : мо́йте !   Perfective : помо́йте !
moy-t‚ĕh !   păh-moy-t‚ĕh !

---

143.   TO SHAVE   брить, побри́ть.
breet‚   păh-breet‚

PRESENT : I shave, etc., бре́ю, бре́ет, бре́ют.
br‚eh-yoo   br‚eh-yet   br‚eh-yoot

FUTURE (exactly like the Present) : я побре́ю.

PAST : quite regular.

IMPERATIVE : бре́йте !   Perfective : побре́йте !
br‚eh^e-t‚ĕh !   păh-br‚eh^e-t‚ĕh !

The above Verbs are very much used REFLEXIVELY, (see pars. 49, 51), for : to get shaved, have a shave.

I wash myself	я мо́юсь
will you wash yourself ?	помо́етесь ли вы ?
yăh maw-yoos‚	păh-maw-yĕh-t‚es, le vɛ ?
he was washing himself	он мы́лся
wash yourselves !	помо́йтесь !
on mɛɛl-s‚ăh	păh-moy-t‚es‚ !
he is shaving himself	он бре́ется
we shall not shave ourselves	мы не побре́емся
on br‚eh-yet-s‚ăh	mɛ n‚ĕh păh-br‚eh-yem-s‚ăh
they have shaved themselves	они́ побри́лись
ăh-ne păh-bre-lees‚	

101. Translate into English.

1. я мо́ю, я мо́юсь; 2. кто мыл э́то? кто мы́лся здесь? 3. помо́ют ли они́ ру́ки? они́ помо́ются; 4. помо́йте э́то, пожа́луйста, не мо́йте э́того; 5. помо́йтесь, могу́ ли я помы́ться здесь? 6. он бре́ется, почему́ вы не бре́етесь? 7. бре́етесь ли вы са́ми*? нет, я не уме́ю бри́ться; 8. он бри́лся, побре́йтесь; 9. побре́йте меня́, я вас побре́ю о́чень ско́ро.

1. I am washing, I am washing myself; 2. who was washing this? who was washing himself here? 3. will they wash their-hands? they will wash themselves; 4. wash this, please, don't wash that; 5. wash yourself, can I wash myself here? 6. he is shaving himself, why don't you shave yourself? 7. do you shave yourself? No, I can't shave myself; 8. he was shaving himself, shave yourself; 9. shave me, I shall shave you very quickly.   * see page 115, par. 3.

102. Translate into English.

(For the various ways to render TO GO, see rules 68, 69, 90, 94).

1. Я иду́ домо́й. 2. Он е́дет за́втра во Фра́нцию. 3. Пойдёте ли вы с на́ми в музе́й? 4. Хо́дите ли вы ча́сто[303] в теа́тр? 5. Мы ско́ро пойдём. 6. Дождь шёл, дождь идёт, дождь пойдёт. 7. Шёл ли снег вчера́? 8. Куда́ они́ пошли́? 9. Не ходи́те с ни́ми!

1. I am going home. 2. He is going to France to-morrow. 3. Will you go with us to the museum? 4. Do you go often to the theatre? 5. We shall go soon. 6. It rained, it is raining, it will rain.* 7. Was it snowing* yesterday? 8. Where did they go to? 9. Don't go with them!

* Russians say: the rain goes, went, will go (same for snow and hail).

144. TO TRANSPORT, CONVEY везти́, повезти́.
to take or carry persons or things in a vehicle. v‚ĕh-ste păh-v‚ĕh-ste

PRESENT : I convey, etc., везу́, везёт, везу́т.
  v‚ĕh-zoo v‚ĕh-z‚ot v‚ĕh-zoot

FUTURE : I shall convey, etc., повезу́, etc.
  păh-v‚ĕh-zoo Conjugated like the Present.

PAST : I was conveying, etc., вёз, везла́, везли́.
  v‚oz v‚ez-wah v‚ez-le

Perfective : повёз, повезла́, повезли́.

IMPERATIVE : вези́те!   Perfective : повези́те!
  v‚ĕh-ze-t‚ĕh!   păh-v‚ĕh-ze-t‚ĕh!

145. The above Verb is generally used when a definite single action is referred to ; but when repetition or frequency is expressed вози́ть must be used.

Conjugated regularly, according to Rule 41 (з═ж in the 1st Person). For similar cases, see Rules 69, 93, and 114.

146. TO BRING привози́ть, привезти́.
things or persons in a vehicle. pre-văh-zeet‚ pre-v‚ez-te

The Imperfective Form is conjugated regularly, according to Rule 41 ; the Perfective is conjugated exactly like Verb in Rule 144.

PRESENT : привожу́, etc.   FUTURE : привезу́, etc.
  pre-văh-joo   pre-v‚ĕh-zoo

PAST : привози́л.   Perfective : привёз.
  pre-văh-zeeL   pre-v‚oz

IMPERATIVE : привози́те!   Perfective : привези́те!
  pre-văh-ze-t‚ĕh!   pre-v‚ĕh-ze-t‚ĕh!

Notice the important expressions :

they were sitting at the table (REST) } они́ сиде́ли за столо́м

they were sitting down at the table (MOVEMENT) } они́ сади́лись за стол

103. Translate into English.

1. мы везём, везёте ли вы? он не вёз; 2. повезут ли они? она повезла, повезите! 3. я всегда вожу, они возили, будете ли вы возить каждый день? 4. они привόзят, он привёз, привезёте ли вы? 5. привезите, не привозите, они привозили; 6. они везут товар⁴⁵²; 7. он возил солдат; 8. что вы мне привезли из Франции? 9. я вам привезу самовар из Р—.

1. Rule 144: we transport, do you convey? he did not transport; 2. will they convey? she has transported, transport (it)! 3. Rule 145: I always convey, they used to transport, will you transport every day? 4. Rule 146: they are bringing, he has brought, will you bring? 5. bring, do not bring, they were bringing; 6. they are carrying the goods; 7. he used to transport soldiers[82]; 8. what have you brought (to-) me from France? 9. I shall bring (to-) you a tea-urn from R—.

104. Translate into English.
(For translation of TO BRING, see Rules 107, 115, 146).

1. Принесите мне стакан воды. 2. Почему вы не привели вашего сына? 3. Я вам привёз гостей из деревни. 4. Мы вам принесём деньги завтра. 5. Он приводит каждый день кого нибудь к обеду. 6. Не привозите мне ничего из города.

1. Bring (to-) me a glass of water. 2. Why did you not bring your son? 3. I brought (to-) you some-visitors from the country. 4. We shall bring (to-) you the money[85] to-morrow. 5. He brings every day someone for (to) dinner. 6. Don't bring (to-) me anything from town.

147. TO SING петь, спеть.
   p‚et‚   sp‚et‚

PRESENT : I sing, etc., пою́, поёт ; пою́т.
   păh-yoo păh-yot păh-yoot

FUTURE : I shall sing, etc., спою́, etc.
   Exactly like the Present.

PAST : conjugated quite regularly.

IMPERATIVE : sing ! по́йте !   Perfective : спо́йте !
   poy-t‚ĕh !   spoy-t‚ĕh !

---

148. TO RUN бежа́ть, побежа́ть.
   b‚ĕh-jaht‚   păh-b‚ĕh-jaht‚

PRESENT : I run, etc., бегу́, бежи́т ; бегу́т.
   b‚ĕh-goo b‚ĕh-jeet b‚ĕh-goot

FUTURE : I shall run, etc., побегу́, etc.
   Exactly like the Present.

PAST : conjugated quite regularly.

IMPERATIVE : беги́те !   Perfective : побеги́те !
   b‚ĕh-ge-t‚ĕh !   păh-b‚ĕh-ge-t‚ĕh !

---

149. Important Impersonal Expressions (r. 64) are :

it is allowed   мо́жно | it is not allowed нельзя́
   one may   moj-naw   one may not   n‚el-z‚ah

"немо́жно" cannot be used instead.

it is necessary to   на́до *or* ну́жно { Either of these two
   one must, one has to nah-daw nooj-naw   words can be used.

it is necessary to go away   на́до уйти́
it is not allowed to enter   нельзя́ войти́

The PRESENT TENSE of TO BE (am, is, are) is not translated in Russian ; the PAST is rendered by the Neuter бы́ло, and the FUTURE by бу́дет. These Verbs come after the Adverbs.

have you not to *or* must you not ?   не на́до ли вам ?
=is it not necessary to you?   *or* не ну́жно ли вам ?

I was not allowed to   мне нельзя́ бы́ло
   =it was not allowed to me

will they be allowed to ?   мо́жно ли им бу́дет ?

105. Translate into English.

1. мы поём, поёте ли вы? она́ пе́ла; 2. я спою́, они́ спе́ли, не по́йте здесь; 3. он бежи́т, почему́ вы бежи́те? я не бежа́л; 4. побегу́т ли они́? не беги́те так ско́ро, беги́те скоре́е; 5. мне на́до *or* ну́жно, ему́ ну́жно бы́ло; 6. нам на́до бу́дет, не ну́жно ли им бу́дет? 7. ему́ нельзя́ бу́дет, мо́жно ли ей бы́ло? 8. мо́жно ли? нельзя́ ли?

1. we are singing, can—do you sing? she was singing; 2. I shall sing, they have sung, don't sing here; 3. he is running, why are you running? I was not running; 4. will they run? don't run (Imperf.) so quickly, run more quickly[127]; 5. I have to = I need,[149] he had to; 6. we shall want to, will they not have to? 7. he will not be allowed to, was she allowed to? 8. may one? may one not?

106. Translate into English.

1. Здесь нельзя́ кури́ть. 2. Мо́жно ли ходи́ть по траве́? 3. Нам на́до идти́ домо́й. 4. Ну́жно ли вам написа́ть что́-нибудь? 5. Ему́ нельзя́ бу́дет сто́лько[410] бежа́ть. 6. Ей на́до бы́ло петь ка́ждый день. 7. Мо́жно ли подожда́ть в э́той ко́мнате? 8. Куда́ они́ побежа́ли? 9. Поёте ли вы по-ру́сски, и́ли по-англи́йски?

1. It is not allowed to smoke here. 2. Is it allowed to walk on the grass? 3. We have to go home. 4. Have you to write anything? 5. He will not be allowed to run so-much. 6. She had to sing every day. 7. Is it allowed to wait in this room? 8. Where have they run to? 9. Do you sing in-Russian, or in-English?

150. Examples of the PRESENT GERUND:

ви́дя э́то	on seeing that
чита́я газе́ту	while reading the paper
встреча́я дру́га	on meeting a friend
е́здя по го́роду	whilst driving through town
выбира́я э́то	in choosing this

The PRESENT GERUND can only be formed from IMPERFECTIVE Verbs; it is obtained by changing the ending of the PRESENT* into я.

(after a hisser and in a few other cases а is put instead of я).
* of any Person except the 1st Singular.

151. Examples of the PAST GERUND:

уви́дев вас	having seen you
прочита́в кни́гу	„ read-through the book
встре́тив их	having met them
пое́хав домо́й	having gone home
написа́в *or* написа́вши э́то	having written that

The PAST GERUND can only be formed from PERFECTIVE Verbs; it is obtained by changing the ть of the INFINITIVE into в. (sometimes вши is put instead of в)

152. The PREPOSITIONS used in English with the GERUND are not translated in Russian (see par. 150).

The Preposition WITHOUT is rendered by не (not).

    without saying anything   не говоря́ ничего́

The GERUND can only be used in Russian when referring to the Subject of the Principal Sentence, as:

HAVING FINISHED work, he went home.
In the above sentence the subject HE is clearly understood.

The work HAVING BEEN FINISHED, he went home.
This must be translated 'when the work was finished, he went home,' because the Subject in the Principal Sentence is not HE but WORK.

The Gerund is mostly used in writing; in ordinary conversation it is generally rendered thus:

when he saw that **instead of** seeing that
когда́ он э́то уви́дел

when we had finished (reading through) the book
instead of having finished the book
когда́ мы прочита́ли кни́гу

107. Translate into English.

1. пока́зывая им кварти́ру; 2. ища́ вас; 3. ре́жа[164] хлеб; 4. не спра́шивая никого́; 5. заплати́в[175] счёт; 6. пригласи́в[173] госте́й; 7. позва́в соба́ку; 8. дав ему́ два рубля́; 9. взя́вши кни́гу со стола́; 10. смотря́ на меня́; 11. не зна́я ни о чём; 12. не прода́в ничего́.

1. in showing (to-) them the flat; 2. while looking for you; 3. in cutting[18] the bread; 4. without asking anybody; 5. having paid the bill; 6. having invited guests; 7. having called his dog; 8. having given (to-) him two roubles; 9. having taken the book from the table; 10. on looking at me; 11. without knowing anything[111]; 12. without having sold anything.

108. Translate into English.

1. Он шёл к нам, гро́мко смея́сь. 2. Она́ говори́ла со мной, чита́я письмо́. 3. Уви́дев своего́ дру́га, они́ пошли́ домо́й. 4. Игра́я на роя́ле, я услы́шал[196] шум. 5. Сказа́в э́то, он ушёл.* 6. Он смея́лся, смотря́ на нас.

1. He was walking towards us, laughing aloud. 2. She was speaking to me, while reading a letter. 3. Having seen their friend, they went home. 4. While playing the piano, I heard[48] a noise. 5. Having said this, he went away. 6. He was laughing, while looking at us. *see Rule 68: y=away.

VOCABULARY TO PAGES 143-159.

495. (it is) allowed мо́жно
  rule 149   moj-naw
496. not allowed нельзя́
  rule 149   n‚el‚-z‚ah
497. card   ка́рточка
  (diminutive) karr-totch-käh
498. drawing-room*
       гости́ная
       gäh-ste-näh-yäh
499. grass   трава́
       träh-vah
500. hurriedly спе́шно
       sp‚esh-naw
501. immediately = not
  slowly неме́дленно
       n‚ĕh-m‚ed-l‚en-naw
502. lesson   уро́к
       oo-rok
503. life ,   жизнь (f.)
       jeezn‚
504. luck   сча́стье
  happiness   shtchah-st-yĕh
505. manager*
       управля́ющий
       oo-präh-vl‚ah-yoo-shtche͡e
506. nephew племя́нник
       pl‚ĕh-m‚ahn-neek
507. policeman*
       городово́й
       gäh-räh-däh-voy
508. province
       прови́нция
       präh-veen-tse͡yäh
*declined like an Adjective.

509. quality   сорт
       sorrt
510. quite соверше́нно
  entirely   säh-v‚er-shen-naw
511. rain   дождь (m.)
       dojd‚
512. regiment полк
       poLk
513. snow   снег
       sn‚eg
514. son   сынъ
  see rule 79   seen
515. soon   ско́ро
       skaw-raw
516. situation
       до́лжность (f.)
  in a business   doL-jnost‚
517. sugar refinery
       са́харный заво́д
       sah-harr-nе͡e zäh-vod
517a. taxicab такси́
       täh-ksee
518. tea-urn самова́р
       säh-mäh-varr
519. thankful
       благода́рен
       bwäh-gäh-dah-r‚en
520. thence   отту́да
  from there   äht-too-däh
521. thither   туда́
  to there   too-dah
522. unexpectedly
       неожи́данно
       n‚ĕh-äh-je-dähn-naw

To Rule 139.—TO WAIT requires the OBJECT WAITED FOR in the GENITIVE.

		IMPERFECTIVE.	PERFECTIVE.
523.	to bid farewell	прощáться	простúться
		präh-sh-chaht,-s,äh	präh-steet,-s,äh

The Perfective conjugated according to Rule 41.

524.	to go away (not on foot)	уезжáть oo-yez-jaht,	уéхать oo-yeh-häht,

Conjugated exactly like Verb 95.

525.	to open	открывáть ăht-krĕ-vaht,	откры́ть ăht-krĕĕt,

The Perfective conjugates exactly like Verb 142.

526.	to ring	звонúть zväh-neet,	позвонúть päh-zväh-neet,
527.	to wire	телеграфúровать t,ĕh-l,ĕh-gräh-fe-raw-väht,	протелеграфúровать präh-t,ĕh-l,ĕh-gräh-fe-raw-väht,

CONVERSATIONAL PRACTICE.

1. Там звоня́т; откро́йте дверь, пожа́луйста. 2. Пришёл ли кто нибудь ко мне? 3. Да, како́й то господи́н вас спра́шивает; вот его́ ка́рточка. 4. Э́то мой племя́нник; попроси́те его́ в гости́ную; я сейча́с приду́ туда́. 5. Он проси́л сказа́ть вам, что он до́лго ждать не мо́жет. — Хорошо́. 6. Здра́вствуйте, дя́дя! — Здра́вствуй! Почему́ так спе́шно? 7. Я уезжа́ю че́рез два часа́.

1. Somebody is ringing (=there they-ring); open the door, please. 2. Has anyone come to me? 3. Yes, a certain gentleman is-asking-for you; here is his card. 4. This is my nephew; ask him to the drawing-room; I shall presently come there (thither). 5. He asked to tell (to-) you that he cannot wait long.—All right. 6. How-do-you-do, uncle?— How-do-you-do? Why are you in such a hurry (=why so hurriedly)? 7. I am going away in two hours.

TWENTY-SECOND LESSON.

153. TO LIE DOWN ложи́ться, лечь.
(movement) meaning also 'going to bed' wăh-jeet̸-s̸ăh l̸etch
to lie, to be in a recumbent position, is rendered by Verb 198, in Vocab.

PRESENT: I lie down, ложу́сь, ложи́тся; ложа́тся.
                       wăh-joos, wăh-jeet-s̸ăh wăh-jaht-s̸ăh

FUTURE: I shall lie down, ля́гу, ля́жет; ля́гут.
                             l̸ah-goo   l̸ah-jet   l̸ah-goot

PAST: ложи́лся. Perfective: лёг, легла́, легли́.
   wăh-jeeL-s̸ăh   l̸okh   l̸eg-wah   l̸eg-le

IMPERATIVE: ложи́тесь! Perfective: ля́гте!
   wăh-je-t̸es̸!   l̸akh-t̸ĕh!

154. TO EAT есть, с'есть.*
                     yest, s'yest

PRESENT: ем, ешь, ест; еди́м, еди́те, едя́т.
I am eating yem yesh yest yĕh-deem yĕh-de-t̸ĕh yĕh-d̸aht

FUTURE: I shall eat, etc., с'ем, etc.
Conjugated exactly like the Present. s'yem

PAST: I was eating, ел, etc. Perfective: с'ел.
                  yeL   s'yeL

IMPERATIVE: е́шьте! Perfective: с'е́шьте!
          yesh-t̸ĕh!   s'yesh-t̸ĕh!

There is also another Verb for TO EAT, ку́шать and поку́шать, which is quite regular. This Verb is not so much used as есть, except in the Imperative.

      eat!   ку́шайте! поку́шайте!

155. на́до and ну́жно (explained in par. 149) are only used when followed by a Verb.

   I want to write   мне на́до *or* ну́жно писа́ть

But when a Noun follows, ну́жен must be used.
        This word is an Adjective in the Short Form.

Fem. нужна́, Neut. ну́жно, Plur. нужны́.
we want a room   нам нужна́ ко́мната
he wanted money   ему́ нужны́ де́ньги

        * For use of apostrophe, see page 8.

109. Translate into English.

1. он не ложи́тся, ложи́тесь ли вы? они́ не ложа́тся; 2. мы ля́жем, не ля́жете ли вы? я ложи́лась; 3. они́ легли́, ложи́тесь *or* ля́гте, не ложи́тесь; 4. я не ем, еди́те ли вы? они́ не едя́т; 5. мы с'еди́м, он не с'ест, я е́ла; 6. мы не с'е́ли, ку́шайте, не ку́шайте; 7. мне ну́жен слова́рь, им нужны́ перча́тки[386]; 8. нужна́ ли вам кварти́ра? нам ну́жен был учи́тель; 9. ей ну́жен бу́дет зо́нтик.

1. he does not lie down, are you lying down? they are not lying down; 2. we shall lie down, will you not lie down? I (f.) was lying down; 3. they have lain down, lie down, don't lie down; 4. I am not eating, are you eating? they are not eating; 5. we shall eat, he will not eat, I (f.) was eating; 6. we have not eaten, eat, don't eat; 7. I want a dictionary, they want gloves; 8. do you want rooms (=flat)? we wanted a teacher; 9. she will want a parasol (=umbrella).

110. Translate into English.

1. Не ложи́тесь* так ра́но. 2. Почему́ вы легли́ вчера́ так по́здно? 3. Скажи́те ва́шей соба́ке, что́бы она́ легла́.—Ложи́сь! 4. Я бы хоте́л с'есть что нибу́дь. 5. Он с'ел всё, что бы́ло. 6. Не ну́жно ли вам э́то перо́?

1. Don't lie down so early. 2. Why did you lie down so late yesterday? 3. Tell (to-) your dog to lie down—in-order-that she (should) lie down.—Lie down! 4. I should like (want) to eat something (anything). 5. He has eaten everything (=all that was). 6. Don't you want this pen?

* спать often added.

156. TO BURN (something) жечь, сжечь.
(j like s in 'measure') jetch, sjetch,

PRESENT: I burn, etc., жгу, жжёт ; жгут.
j'goo j'jot j'goot

FUTURE: I shall burn, сожгу́, сожжёт ; сожгу́т.
săh-jgoo săh-j'jot săh-jgoot

PAST: I was burning, etc., жёг, жгла, жгли.
jog jgwăh jgle

Perfective: I burnt, сжёг, сожгла́, сожгли́.
sjog săh-jgwah săh-jgle

IMPERATIVE: жги́те ! Perfective: сожги́те !
jghe-t,ĕh ! săh-jghe-t,ĕh !

TO LIGHT, зажечь (P.) is conjugated exactly like сжечь.
The Imperfective зажига́ть is quite regular.

TO BE ALIGHT, TO BE BURNING, TO BE ON FIRE, are translated горе́ть, сгоре́ть. găh-r,et, sgăh-r,et,
The Perfective means TO BE BURNT DOWN. This Verb is quite regular.

157. TO DRINK пить, вы́пить.
peet, VE-peet,

PRESENT: I drink, etc., пью, пьёт ; пьют.
p'yoo p'yot p'yoot

FUTURE: I shall drink, вы́пью, вы́пьет ; вы́пьют.
VE-p'yoo VE-p'yet VE-p'yoot

PAST: conjugated quite regularly.

IMPERATIVE: пе́йте ! Perfective: вы́пейте !
p,eh^e-t,ĕh ! VE-p,eh^e-t,ĕh !

158. IMPERSONAL VERBS are often formed in Russian from the REFLECTIVE VERBS.
They are then in the 3rd Person Singular; the English Subject is in the Dative as usual.

хоте́ться, захоте́ться (see par. 60).

I want to drink мне хо́чется пить
(I have a desire to drink) mn,ĕh haw-tchet-s,ăh peet,

will he not want to eat ? не захо́чется ли ему́ есть ?

we did not want to go нам не хоте́лось итти́
(we had no inclination to go) năhm n,ĕh hăh-t,eh-wos, eet-te

111. Translate into English.

1. он жжёт, жжёте ли вы? они не жгут; 2. я не сожгу, сожгли ли они? не жгите; 3. дом горит, бумаги горели; 4. зажгите лампу, не зажигайте огня; 5. свеча горит, зажгите спичку; 6. мы не пьём, выпьете ли вы? он пил; 7. выпейте, не пейте; 8. я никогда не пью коньяк, мы всегда пьём чай.

1. Rule 156: he is burning, do you burn? they do not burn; 2. I shall not burn, did they burn? do not burn; 3. the house is on fire, the papers were burning; 4. light the lamp, don't light the fire⁷²; 5. the candle is burning, light (or strike) a match; 6. we do not drink, will you drink? he was drinking; 7. drink, do not drink; 8. I never drink brandy, we always drink tea.

112. Translate into English.

1. Почему вы не зажгли лампы? 2. Он сжёг ваши письма. 3. Все дома на этой улице сгорели. 4. Что вы пили? 5. Я ничего не буду пить. 6. Выпейте ещё один стакан. 7. Ему нельзя так много пить. 8. Мне хочется пойти на концерт. 9. Хотелось ли вам спать? 10. Им не захочется это сделать.

1. Why did you not light the lamp? 2. He has burnt your letters. 3. All the houses in this street have been burnt-down. 4. What did you drink? 5. I shall not drink* anything. 6. Drink one glass more (=yet). 7. He must not (is not allowed to) drink so much. 8. I want to go to (on) the concert. 9. Did you want to sleep? 10. They will not want to do it.

* Imperfective Future preferable. Perfective means: finish drinking.

159. TO SEEM казáться, показáться.
kăh-zaht,-s,ăh păh-kăh-zaht,-s,ăh

This is another important impersonal Verb, similar to the one in rule 158.

it seems to me мне кáжется
  mn,ĕh kah-jet-s,ăh

did it seem to you ? казáлось ли вам ?
  kăh-zah-wos, le văhm ?

will it not seem to him ? не покáжется ли емý ?
  n,ĕh păh-kah-jet-s,ăh le yĕh-moo ?

---

160. TO BELIEVE, THINK, SUPPOSE, are also rendered by the above Impersonal Verbs, when the same meaning could be expressed by IT SEEMS, etc.

I believe, that he is at мне кáжется, что он
home дóма

he thought, that you емý казáлось, что вы
were in the country в деревне
  (WERE = ARE, and is therefore not translated).

they will think, that we им покáжется, что мы
were dissatisfied недовóльны

These Verbs may also be translated literally in this meaning by дý́мать (vocabulary 147) and полагáть, to suppose.

I think *or* suppose, that я дý́маю *or* полагáю,
he will come что он прийдёт
  yăh doo-măh-yoo *or* păh-wăh-gah-yoo shtaw on pre-d,ot

---

161. TO BELIEVE (voc. 133) can only be translated literally when meaning : to believe in someone or thing.
(This Verb is followed by the Dative).

I believe, that they are мне кáжется, что онú
here здесь
  mn,ĕh kah-jet-s,ăh shtaw ăh-ne zd,es,

I do not believe (to-) him я емý не вéрю
  yăh yĕh-moo n,ĕh v,eh-r,yoo

113. Translate into English.

1. ей кажется, показалось ли им? 2. нам будет казаться, ему может показаться; 3. думаете ли вы? *or* кажется ли вам? 4. не полагали ли они? *or* не казалось ли им? 5. мне кажется, мы им не верим; 6. кажется, я думаю.

1. it seems to her, did it seem to them? 2. it will (Imperf.) seem to us, it may seem (Perf.) to him; 3. do you think *or* does it seem to you? 4. did they not suppose *or* did it not seem (so) to them? 5. I believe *or* it seems to me, we do not believe (to-) them; 6. it seems (so), I think (so).

114. Translate into English.

1. Мне кажется, что это неправда. 2. Ему показалось, что русский язык очень труден. 3. Я полагаю *or* мне кажется, что это так. 4. Они думали *or* им казалось, что мы больше не придём. 5. Нам казалось, что вы заграницей. 6. Поверили ли вы всему, что он сказал? 7. Нам кажется, что им не хочется идти. 8. Не хотелось ли ему пить? 9. Что вы ели сегодня к завтраку?—Холодное мясо и салат. 10. Пили ли вы что нибудь?

1. It seems to me, that this is not true. 2. It seemed to him, that the Russian language was very difficult. 3. I suppose, that this is so. 4. They thought, we should not come any more. 5. We believed, that you were abroad. 6. Did you believe (to-) all (that) he said? 7. It seems to us, that they do not want to go. 8. Did he not want to drink? 9. What did you have for (=eat to) lunch to-day?— Cold meat and salad. 10. Did you drink anything?

162. TO PLEASE   нра́виться, понра́виться.
     TO LIKE   nrah-veet,-s,ăh păh-nrah-veet,-s,ăh
         Conjugated regularly according to rule 47.

he pleases me   он мне́ нра́вится
=I like him   on mn,ĕh nrah-veet-s,ăh
I do not please him   я ему́ не нра́влюсь
=he does not like me   yăh yĕh-moo n,ĕh nrah-vl,oos,
did that please him?   понра́вилось ли э́то ему́?
=did he like that?   păh-nrah-ve-wos, le a-to yĕh-moo?
he likes this book   э́та кни́га ему́ нра́вится
=this book pleases him   a-tăh k-ne-găh yĕh-moo nrah-veet-s,ăh

   This Verb is very much used for TO LIKE and TO BE FOND OF (not in the meaning of 'to be in love') when the English Object is a Noun or Pronoun. The English Object then becomes the Subject in Russian.

---

163. But when TO LIKE is followed by a VERB, it must be translated literally in Russian by люби́ть.
    he likes to smoke   он лю́бит кури́ть
    I do not like to write   я не люблю́ писа́ть

164. When the Object is something to eat or to drink, TO LIKE must also be translated by люби́ть.
    do you like chocolate? лю́бите ли вы шокола́д?

---

165. TO UNDERSTAND понима́ть, поня́ть.
                                  păh-ne-maht, păh-n,aht,
       The Imperfective Form is quite regular.

PRESENT: I understand, etc., я понима́ю, etc.
                                            păh-ne-mah-yoo
FUTURE: я пойму́, поймёт; пойму́т.
I shall understand   păh^e-moo păh^e-m,ot păh^e-moot
PAST: я понима́л, etc.   Perfective: по́нял.
I understood păh-ne-mahl   I have understood paw-n,ăhl
IMPERATIVE: понима́йте! Perfective: пойми́те!
        păh-ne-mah^e-t,ĕh!   păh^e-me-t,ĕh!

115. Translate into English.

1. я ему́ нра́влюсь, они́ нам нра́вятся, мы им не нра́вимся; 2. понра́вилось ли ей э́то? э́то вам не понра́вится; 3. э́то мне не нра́вилось; 4. они́ ему́ не понра́вятся; 5. я люблю́ е́здить, мне не нра́вится э́тот рома́н; 6. лю́бите ли вы ходи́ть пешко́м? нам не нра́вится э́та ко́мната; 7. вы их не поймёте, по́нял ли он вас? пойми́те!

1. I please (to-) him, they please (to-) us, we do not please (to-) them; 2. did it please (to-) her? this will not please (to-) you; 3. this did not please (to-) me *or* I did not like it; 4. he will not like them *or* they will not please (to-) him; 5. I like to travel, I do not like this novel; 6. do you like walking (go on foot)? we don't like this room; 7. you will not understand them, did he understand you? understand!

116. Translate into English.

1. Как вам понра́вился мой друг? 2. Ей не понра́вится э́та гости́ница. 3. Лю́бите ли вы игра́ть на роя́ле? 4. Понра́вился ли им конце́рт? 5. Мне не нра́вится Ло́ндон, сказа́л ли́чный секрета́рь. 6. Лю́бите ли вы ко́фе? 7. Нет, я всегда́ пью чай и́ли шокола́д. 8. Понра́вилась ли вам пье́са?—О́чень. 9. Я не могу́ поня́ть, почему́ вам э́то не нра́вится.

1. How did you like my friend? 2. She will not like this hotel. 3. Do you like to play (on) the piano? 4. Did they like the concert? 5. I don't like London, said the Private (=personal) Secretary. 6. Do you like coffee? 7. No, I always drink tea or chocolate. 8. Did the play please (to-) you? — Very much. 9. I cannot understand why this does not please (to-) you.

166. The Verb приходи́ть, прийти́ (rule 71), forms the example for the whole group of similar Verbs. The most important are :

528. go in, come in	входи́ть	войти́
529. go out, come out	выходи́ть	вы́йти
530. find, recover	находи́ть	найти́
531. go away	уходи́ть	уйти́

(continued in par. 169).

IMITATED PRONUNCIATION.—528. f'hăh-deet, văh^e-te; 529. vɛ-hăh-deet, vɛ^e-te; 530. năh-hăh-deet, năh^e-te; 531. oo-hăh-deet, oo^e-te.

They are all conjugated exactly like the Verb in rule 71, and can also only be used when the meaning is : to go ON FOOT.

167. Although these Verbs begin with a PREPOSITION, the NOUN that follows must be preceded by another Preposition.

I went-in into the room	я вошёл в ко́мнату
they are coming-out out-of the shop	они́ выхо́дят из магази́на
go-away from here !	уйди́те отсю́да !
go out out-of the room !	вы́йдите из ко́мнаты !

168. INDIRECT QUESTIONS are translated in Russian exactly as if they were DIRECT QUESTIONS.

DIRECT QUESTION.

will you be at home ?   бу́дете ли вы до́ма ?

INDIRECT QUESTIONS.

he asks, whether you would be at home ?	он спра́шивает, бу́дете ли вы до́ма ?
they were asking, if you had sold the books ?	они́ спра́шивали, про́дали ли вы кни́ги ?

=did you sell or have you sold the books ?

CONJUNCTIONS are of course not translated in such cases.

117. Translate into English.

1. войди́те, не входи́те, они́ вошли́; 2. мы не войдём, входи́те ли вы? не входи́ли ли они́? 3. я ухожу́, не уходи́те ли вы? он уйдёт; 4. уйди́те, не уходи́те, она́ ушла́; 5. я нахожу́, не нахо́дите ли вы? мы найдём; 6. она́ нашла́, найди́те! они́ находи́ли; 7. я выхожу́, он вы́шел, вы́йдете ли вы? 8. вы́йдите, не выходи́те.

1. come *or* go in, don't come *or* go in, they came in; 2. we shall not go in, are you coming in? were they not coming in? 3. I am going away, are you not going away? he will go away; 4. go away, don't go away, she went away; 5. I find, do you not find? we shall find; 6. she found, find! they were finding; 7. I am going out, he went out, will you go out? 8. go out, don't go out.

118. Translate into English.

1. Выхо́дите ли вы сего́дня из до́му*? 2. Нашли́ ли вы доро́гу? 3. Не уходи́те так ра́но. 4. Мы вошли́ в дом. 5. Я войду́ в э́тот рестора́н. 6. Вы э́того нигде́ не найдёте. 7. Я вы́шел на у́лицу. 8. Они́ вошли́, когда́ мы выходи́ли. 9. Я до́лжен сейча́с уйти́. 10. Когда́ вы придёте?

* pronounced: eez-daw-moo.

1. Are you going out (of-the-house) to-day? 2. Did you find the way? 3. Don't go away so early. 4. We came into the house. 5. I shall go in this restaurant. 6. You will not find it anywhere. 7. I went out into (on) the street. 8. They came in, as (when) we were going out. 9. I must go away presently. 10. When will you come?

CONVERSATIONAL PRACTICE.
(Continued from page 159 ; see Vocabulary 158, 159).

1. Я пришёл проститься с вами. 2. Куда ты едешь? Мне никто об этом ничего не говорил. 3. Я получил²⁸⁸ совершенно неожиданно должность управляющего сахарным заводом в провинции. 4. Сегодня мне телеграфировали оттуда, чтобы приехать немедленно. 5. Ну, желаю тебе счастливого пути и много счастья на новой дороге жизни. — Спасибо! Я вам очень благодарен.

1. I came to bid-farewell to (=with) you. 2. Where art thou going to ? Nobody told me anything about it. 3. I received quite unexpectedly a situation of a manager in-a-sugar refinery in the province(s). 4. To-day they-wired (to-) me from-there to come immediately. 5. Well, I wish (to-) thee a happy journey* and much luck in your-new way of life.—Thanks ! I am to you very thankful.

* Genitive after ' wish '.

1. Можно ли попросить¹⁹³ вас на минуту?— Пожалуйста. 2. Мне хочется погулять немножко; открыт ли парк теперь? 3. Мне кажется, что открыт, но я не уверен. 4. Хотите пойти посмотреть? — С большим удовольствием. 5. Как вам нравится этот парк? 6. Не очень. Здесь слишком мало деревьев. 7. Это правда, но зато сколько цветов.

1. May I speak¹ to you¹ for² a minute ? — Certainly. 2. I should like³ to walk a little ; is the park open now⁴ ? 3. I⁵ believe⁵ that it is open, but I am not sure. 4. Shall⁶ we go and see⁶?—With great pleasure. 5. How⁷ do you like⁷ this park ? 6. Not much. There⁸ are⁸ too few trees here.

VOCABULARY TO PAGES 160-171.

532. abroad заграни́цей
(state) zăh-grăh-ne-tséh͡e
see page 180
533. bill счёт
account sh-chot
534. brandy конья́к
kăhn,-yahk
535. candle свеча́
sf,ĕh-tchah
536. chocolate шокола́д
shăh-kăh-wahd
537. concert конце́рт
kăhn-ts,errt
538. fire ого́нь
rule 72 ăh-gon,
539. flower цвето́к
tsf,ĕh-tok
540. fresh све́жий
sf,eh-je͡e
541. lamp ла́мпа
wahm-păh
542. match спи́чка
speetch-kăh
543. music му́зыка
moo-zE-kăh
544. nowhere нигде́
not anywhere ne-gd,eh
545. open откры́тый
ăht-kre-tE͡e
546. private ча́стный
tchah-stnE͡e

546a. personal ли́чный
leech-nE͡e
547. salad сала́т
săh-waht
548. secretary секрета́рь
c,ĕh-kr,ĕh-tarr,
549. sure уве́рен
assured oo-v,eh-r,en
                      paragraph
550. to burn, light   156
to be alight
551. to be on fire   156
552. to bring   146
not on foot
553. to call   138
554. to drink   157
555. to eat   154
556. to lie down   153
557. to run   148
558. to shave   143
559. to sing   147
560. to sit down   135
561. to transport   144-145
convey
562. to wash   142
563. to wait   139
expect
564. to suppose полага́ть
no Perfective pă-wăh-gaht,

continued from opposite page.

7. This is true,[9] but[10] then look at the many flowers.[10]

    1 ask you; 2 on, time in the Accusative; 3 to-me it-wants-itself; 4 Adverbs when emphatic are put last; 5 to me it-seems; 6 do you want to-go to see? 7 how to-you pleases? 8 'there are' is as a rule not translated; 9 truth; 10 but for-that how-many flowers.

TWENTY-THIRD LESSON.

169. Other important Verbs belonging to the group in par. 166, expressing movement on foot, are:

565.	to call on	заходи́ть	зайти́
		zăh-hăh-deet,	zăh^e-te
566.	to approach come near	подходи́ть	подойти́
		păhd-hăh-deet,	păh-dăh^e-te
567.	to pass	проходи́ть	пройти́
		prăh-hăh-deet,	prăh^e-te
568.	to cross, traverse go beyond	переходи́ть	перейти́
		p‚ĕh-r‚ĕh-hăh-deet,	p‚ĕh-r‚ĕh^e-te

170. In DEPENDENT SENTENCES after Verbs like: think, say, write, imagine, believe, etc., the Russian construction remains the same as in a Principal Sentence.

I thought, that you were playing (now)	я ду́мал, что вы игра́ете

<small>If not referring to the present moment, the Past is of course used.</small>

we believed, that you would not come	нам каза́лось, что вы не придёте
he supposed, that they were at home	он полага́л, что они́ до́ма

<small>WAS or WERE are not translated here, because they mean AM, IS or ARE in Russian.</small>

171. The THIRD PERSON PLURAL is often used in Russian to express the PASSIVE VOICE.

<small>(The Pronoun THEY must not be expressed).</small>

it is said = they say	говоря́т
it was supposed = they supposed	полага́ли
he is called = they call him	его́ зову́т
you will be requested = they will request you	вас попро́сят
Russian spoken here = they speak Russian here	здесь говоря́т по-ру́сски

119. Translate into English.

1. я захожу́, он зайдёт, мы зашли́; 2. подхо́дят ли они́? не подходи́те; 3. он прохо́дит, они́ не проходи́ли; 4. перейдём, вы перешли́; 5. он сказа́л, что прийдёт; мы ду́мали, что вы до́ма; 6. им каза́лось, что они́ пра́вы; 7. полага́ли ли вы, что он э́то сде́лает? 8. мы зайдём к вам; 9. они́ подошли́ к нам; 10. их не зна́ют здесь; 11. э́тот рома́н легко́ чита́ется.

1. I call on, he will call on, we called on; 2. are they coming near? don't come near; 3. he is passing, they did not pass (Imperf.); 4. let us cross, you crossed *or* you went beyond; 5. he said he would come; we thought you were at home; 6. they believed that they were right; 7. did you suppose that he would do it? 8. we shall call on you (to you); 9. they approached us (to us); 10. they are not known here; 11. this novel is very readable (=easily read).

120. Translate into English.

1. Так не говоря́т. 2. Сказа́ли раз навсегда́. 3. Э́того не де́лают. 4. Вре́мя прохо́дит о́чень ско́ро. 5. Зайди́те к нам сего́дня ве́чером. 6. Уви́дев меня́, он перешёл на другу́ю сто́рону у́лицы. 7. Не подходи́те так бли́зко к маши́не.

1. One should* not say so. 2. It was said once for always. 3. One should* not do this. 4. The time passes very quickly. 5. Call on us this evening. 6. Having seen me he crossed-over on the other side of the street. 7. Don't approach so close (near) to the machine.

* this is not said *or* done.

172. The Verb приезжа́ть, прие́хать (rule 95) forms the example for the whole group of similar Verbs. The most important are:

569.	to go away drive away, leave	уезжа́ть oo-yez-jaht,	уе́хать oo-yeh-hăht,
570.	to drive in ride in, enter	в'езжа́ть v'yez-jaht,	в'е́хать v'yeh-hăht,
571.	to cross, traverse run (someone) over	переезжа́ть p,ĕh-r,ĕh-yez-jaht,	перее́хать p,ĕh-r,ĕh-yeh-hăht,
572.	to drive up	под'езжа́ть păhd'-yez-jaht,	под'е́хать păhd'-yeh-hăht,
573.	to call in, visit (when driving past)	заезжа́ть zăh-yez-jaht,	зае́хать zăh-yeh-hăht,
574.	to pass through (not on foot)	проезжа́ть prăh-yez-jaht,	прое́хать prăh-yeh-hăht,
575.	to drive out of a place	выезжа́ть vɛ-yez-jaht,	вы́ехать vɛ-yĕh-hăht,

173. Russian VERBS with REFLEXIVE FORMS are very much used in sentences like the following:

stamps sold here =stamps sell themselves here	ма́рки продаю́тся здесь
prospectus sent gratis =prospectus sends itself gratis	проспе́кт высыла́ется беспла́тно
this material wears well =this stuff well wears itself	э́то сукно́ хорошо́ но́сится
this will finish badly =this badly will finish itself	э́то пло́хо ко́нчится
it happens, it happened	случа́ется, случи́лось
the concert begins at 7 o'clock sharp=straight	конце́рт начина́ется ро́вно в семь часо́в
that is easily explained	э́то легко́ об'ясня́ется

121. Translate into English.

1. я уезжа́ю, он уе́хал; 2. мы в'е́дем, не в'езжа́йте; 3. переезжа́ете ли вы? вы перее́дете кого́ нибу́дь; 4. они́ не под'е́хали, кто под'езжа́л? 5. мы зае́дем к вам, зае́хала ли она́ к ней? 6. он прое́хал весь го́род; 7. я прое́ду всю Англию; 8. выезжа́ете ли вы? мы вы́ехали из Москвы́.

1. I am leaving, he went away; 2. we shall drive in, don't drive in; 3. are you crossing? you will run-over somebody (=anybody); 4. they did not drive up, who was driving up? 5. we shall call on you, did she call on her? 6. he passed-through the whole town; 7. I shall pass-through the whole of England; 8. do you drive out? we left (went out of) Moscow.

122. Translate into English.

1. Когда́ вы уезжа́ете? 2. Когда́ вы бу́дете проезжа́ть наш магази́н, заходи́те к нам. 3. Таки́е лю́ди не о́чень ча́сто встреча́ются. 4. Этот това́р о́чень хорошо́ продаётся. 5. Это случа́ется со мной пе́рвый раз. 6. Тре́буется ру́сский учи́тель. 7. Францу́зская гуверна́нтка тре́буется сейча́с. 8. Он написа́л из Пари́жа, что прие́дет за́втра.

1. When are you going away? 2. Call on us when you drive-past (Future Imperfect) our shop. 3. One does not meet such people very often. 4. These goods sell very well. 5. It happened (=it happens) to me for the first time. 6. A Russian teacher wanted. 7. A French governess wanted at once. 8. He wrote from Paris that he would come to-morrow.

The Participles in Russian are practically Adjectives formed from Verbs, and are treated as such.

174. The Past Participle is generally formed by changing the ть of the Perfective Form into нный.

Infinitive of Perfective Form.	Past Participle. Long Form.	Short Form.
make, сде́лать	made, сде́ланный	сде́лан
sell, прода́ть	sold, про́данный	про́дан
send, посла́ть	sent, по́сланный	по́слан
write, написа́ть	written, напи́санный	напи́сан

Imitated Pronunciation: sd‚eh-wăhn-nĕ͡e; praw-dăhn-nĕ͡e; paw-swăhn-nĕ͡e; năh-pe-săhn-nĕ͡e

This is called in Russian the Past Participle Passive.

175. There are some Verbs that change the ть into тый instead of into нный.

open, откры́ть	opened, откры́тый	откры́т
break, разби́ть	broken, разби́тый	разби́т
shave, побри́ть	shaven, побри́тый	побри́т

ăht-krɛ-tɛ͡e; răhz-be-tɛ͡e; păh-bre-tɛ͡e

176. The Present Participle is generally formed from the Third Person Plural of the Present Tense by changing the т into щий.

This is called the Present Participle Active, and has no Short Form.

they speak, говоря́т	speaking, говоря́щий
they write, пи́шут	writing, пи́шущий
they go, иду́т	going, иду́щий

găh-văh-r‚ah-sh-che͡e; pe-shoo-sh-che͡e; e-doo-sh-che͡e

They are declined like ordinary Adjectives,—see rules 53-57, and table p. 88.

| the books are sold | кни́ги про́даны |
| a writing machine | пи́шущая маши́на |

123. Translate into English.

1. написанное письмо́, напеча́танная статья́; 2. сва́ренные я́йца, спя́щий ребёнок; 3. лю́бящая мать, пи́шущие маши́ны; 4. ку́пленный това́р,⁴⁵² жда́нные го́сти; 5. все, е́дущие заграни́цу; игра́ющие де́ти; 6. уча́щиеся, разби́тое стекло́; 7. откры́тое окно́, уби́тые и ра́неные; 8. окно́ помы́то, дверь была́ откры́та; 9. э́ти часы́ про́даны, моё письмо́ ото́слано.

1. a written letter, a published article; 2. boiled eggs, a sleeping child; 3. a loving mother, typewriters=writing machines; 4. bought goods (Sing.), expected guests; 5. all (those) going abroad; playing children; 6. students=learning ones, the broken glass; 7. an open window, killed and wounded; 8. the window is cleaned (washed), the door was open(ed); 9. this clock is sold, my letter has been sent off.

124. Translate into English.

1. Бы́ли ли ва́ши часы́ на́йдены? 2. Э́тот това́р был ку́плен на́ми в Пари́же. 3. Был ли э́тот счёт заплачен? 4. Где был потерян кошелёк? 5. Я не куря́щий. 6. Ра́неных всегда́ бо́льше, чем уби́тых. 7. Где ваго́н для некуря́щих? 8. Това́р про́данный на́ми.

1. Has your watch been found? 2. These goods* were bought by us in Paris. 3. Has this bill been paid? 4. Where was the purse lost? 5. I am not a smoker=a smoking-one. 6. There are always more wounded than killed. 7. Where is the carriage for non-smokers? 8. The goods* that have been sold by us.

* 'goods' generally in Singular.

The two PARTICIPLES on page 176 are the only ones which students need use, but the following forms are often met with in the written language.

177. The PAST PARTICIPLE ACTIVE is generally formed by changing the Infinitive ending ть into вший.

кури́вший	koo-reef-she͡e	one who smoked
ви́девший	ve-d͡ef-she͡e	one who saw
е́хавший	yeh-hähf-she͡e	one who was travelling

я ви́дел да́му, сиде́вшую* на сту́ле — I saw the lady, who-was-sitting on the chair

мы стоя́ли у горе́вшего села́ — we were standing near the village, that-was-burning

она́ встре́тила учи́теля учи́вшего* меня́ по-ру́сски — she met the teacher, who-was-teaching me Russian

* Accusative.

178. The PRESENT PARTICIPLE PASSIVE is formed from the FIRST PERSON PLURAL of the PRESENT TENSE by adding ый.

люби́мый	loo-be-mе͡e	that is being loved
чита́емый	che-tah-yĕh-mе͡e	that is being read
кури́мый	koo-re-mе͡e	that is being smoked

Formed from 1st Person Plural: лю́бим, чита́ем, ку́рим.

The PARTICIPLES in pars. 177-178 can be translated in English only by relative sentences.

чита́емая на́ми кни́га о́чень интере́сна — the book being-read by us is very interesting

собира́емые ва́ми цветы́ хорошо́ па́хнут — the flowers being-gathered by you smell nice

това́р производи́мый у них — the goods being-produced at their place

Examples of Present Participle Passive Predicate.

э́та да́ма все́ми уважа́ема	this lady (is) by everybody being respected
он и́ми не люби́м	he (is) by them not being liked
они́ охраня́емы солда́тами	they (are) being guarded by soldiers

125. Translate into English.

1. Англича́нин, стоя́вший во главе́ э́той фи́рмы. 2. Вояжёр фи́рмы, торгу́ющей вино́м. 3. Компа́ния, получи́вшая э́то письмо́. 4. Финанси́ст, собира́вший свои́х акционе́ров. 5. Собира́емые и́ми де́ньги иду́т в по́льзу бе́дных. 6. Чита́емая мно́ю кни́га о́чень интере́сна.

1. The Englishman who was (standing) at the head of this firm. 2. A traveller of a firm trading in wine. 3. The company that received this letter. 4. A financier who-was-gathering (meeting) his shareholders. 5. The money collected by-them is for the poor (goes to the-benefit of-the-poor). 6. The book which is being read by-me is very interesting.

126. Translate into English.

1. Прика́зчик, люби́вший пошути́ть, отве́тил... 2. Уважа́емый господи́н Петро́в! 3. Шля́па, вися́щая на стене́, моя́. 4. Напи́санная ва́ми статья́ не годи́тся. 5. Вы не бы́ли приглашены́. 6. Его́ друг был уби́т на войне́.

1. The clerk, who-liked to-joke, answered... 2. Respected Mr. Petroff! 3. The hat, hanging on the wall, is mine. 4. The article, written by you, is not suitable. 5. You were not invited. 6. His friend was killed in the war.

179. The PARTICIPLES are sometimes used as NOUNS.

a scientist, savant   учёный (Past Passive)
=one, that was taught   oo-tchaw-nĕ͡e

an acquaintance   знакómый (Present Passive)
=one that is being known   znäh-kaw-mĕ͡e

[знакóмить, познакóмить = to acquaint]

manager   управляющий (Pres. Active)
=one that manages

---

180. ABROAD, is rendered by : beyond the frontier.

he went abroad (Accusative: where to?)   он поéхал заграницу

they were abroad (Instrumental: where?)   они́ бы́ли заграни́цей

we came from abroad   мы приéхали из заграни́цы
(Genitive : where from ?)

---

181. THESE and THOSE ARE are rendered in Russian exactly like THIS IS; THESE WERE by THIS WERE.

these are his friends   э́то егó друзья́

those are not good gloves   э́то не хорóшие перчáтки

these were your mistakes   э́то бы́ли вáши оши́бки

those are not her handkerchiefs   э́то не её платки́

they (these) were my nephews   э́то бы́ли мои́ племя́нники

---

182. In QUESTIONS, and especially in NEGATIVE QUESTIONS, ли is seldom used after э́то. The Question is mostly rendered by simply raising the voice at the end of the sentence.

is that all ?   э́то всё ?

is this your paper ?   э́то вáша газéта ?

is that not her purse ?   э́то не её портмонé ?

are those not your scissors ?   э́то не вáши нóжницы ?

127. Translate into English.

1. это кто? *or* кто это? это не они; 2. это чьё? это не вы? *or* не вы ли это? 3. это не её почерк, это ваши картины? 4. это не их фабрика? 5. это были мои компаньоны, это будут его наследники? 6. не были ли это ваши сыновья? *or* это не были ваши сыновья? 7. это будет в порядке? не было ли это глупо? 8. поедете ли вы заграницу? 9. они заграницей; 10. управляющий приехал из заграницы.

1. who is that? these are not they; 2. whose is this? is that not you? 3. this is not her handwriting, are those your pictures? 4. is that not their factory? 5. they were my partners, will they be his heirs? 6. were those not your sons? 7. will this be in order? was that not stupid? 8. will you go abroad? 9. they are abroad; 10. the manager came from abroad.

128. Translate into English.

1. Это не их вина. 2. Это ещё не готово. 3. Это были не они. 4. Это были его гости? 5. Это будет слишком дорого? 6. Эта дама ваша знакомая? 7. Все служащие в нашем банке пошли на войну. 8. Мы не знали что делать с полученным товаром.

1. This is not their fault. 2. It is not yet ready. 3. It was not they. 4. Were those his guests (*or* visitors)? 5. Will that be too expensive? 6. Is this lady an acquaintance of yours = this lady your acquaintance? 7. All the employés in our bank went to the war. 8. We did not know what to do with the goods received = received goods.

TWENTY-FOURTH LESSON.

183. The INSTRUMENTAL must be used after the Verbs: to be, to appoint, to find, to become, to call, to make, to consider, etc.

he was a soldier	он был солда́том
will he be a doctor?	бу́дет ли он до́ктором?
I am called Peter	меня́ зову́т Петро́м
they consider him an idiot	его́ счита́ют идио́том

As the Present Tense of TO BE (am, is, are) is not expressed in Russian, the following Noun MUST BE IN THE NOMINATIVE.

he is a manufacturer   он фабрика́нт

184. TO APPOINT назнача́ть, назна́чить.

năh-znăh-tchăht, năh-znah-tcheet,

he was appointed a director	его́ назна́чили дире́ктором *or*: он был назна́чен дире́ктором
I shall be made an officer	меня́ сде́лают офице́ром

TO BECOME is generally rendered in Russian by TO BE, or by the Reflective of TO MAKE (сде́латься).

he will become a member of the Stock Exchange	он бу́дет чле́ном Би́ржи
she became a great artist	она́ сде́лалась вели́кой арти́сткой

185. ADJECTIVES also take the INSTRUMENTAL, following the same rule.

do you find it difficult? { нахо́дите ли вы э́то тру́дным?

186. The above rule applies also to the PRONOUNS.

what (= who) would you like to become?   кем вы бы хоте́ли быть?

129. Translate into English.

1. я никогда́ не́ был его́ дру́гом; 2. он купе́ц; 3. не назна́чат ли вас управля́ющим? 4. сде́лали ли её нача́льницей? 5. она́ счита́ет себя́ прекра́сной; 6. он не счита́ется (*or* его́ не счита́ют) о́чень бога́тым; 7. его́ зову́т (*or* называ́ют) мини́стром; 8. не называ́ли (*or* не́ зва́ли) ли вас гра́фом? 9. он э́то найдёт стра́нным; 10. мы его́ нашли́ больны́м; 11. э́то ли бы́ли его́ го́сти?

1. I have never been his friend; 2. he is a merchant; 3. won't you be appointed manager? 4. did they make her headmistress (*or* matron)? 5. she considers herself beautiful; 6. he is not considered very rich; 7. they call him minister; 8. didn't they call you count? 9. he will find it strange; 10. we found him ill; 11. were those his guests (*or* visitors)?

130. Translate into English.

1. Его́ сде́лали учи́телем. 2. Почему́ вас все называ́ют профе́ссором? 3. Она́ счита́ется о́чень симпати́чной. 4. Он сам счита́ет себя́ у́мным, но други́е его́ счита́ют идио́том. 5. Как они́ вас зва́ли? 6. Я не ваш друг. 7. Бу́дете ли вы его́ насле́дником? 8. Он был всем: купцо́м, учи́телем, солда́том.

1. He was made a teacher. 2. Why does everybody call you a professor? 3. She is considered very sympathetic. 4. He (himself) considers himself very clever, but others consider him an idiot. 5. How (= what) did they call you? 6. I am not your friend. 7. Will you become his heir? 8. He was everything: a merchant, a teacher, a soldier.

187. There is and there are are not translated.

there is somebody waiting-for you   кто-то вас ждёт

Expressions of PLACE and TIME begin the sentence.

    there are ten pupils in this class   в э́том кла́ссе де́сять ученико́в

    there was a fire here (on) last week   на про́шлой неде́ле здесь был пожа́р

Questions and Negations are rendered as in pars. 15 and 33.

188. There is not and there are not are rendered by нет, followed by the Genitive.

    there is no telephone here   здесь нет телефо́на

    are there no papers?   нет ли газе́т?

189. Is there? are there? must be rendered by есть ли?

    Is there a lift in this hotel?—There is.   Есть ли лифт в э́той гости́нице?—Есть.

    Are there any trams in this town?—There are.   Есть ли трамва́и в э́том го́роде?—Есть.

These examples show that есть is also used in emphatic answers.

    Isn't there anything to eat?—There is not.   Нет ли чего́ нибу́дь пое́сть?—Нет.

190. There is not translated in the Past and Future, but the Verb must be expressed.

    there was not any money   не́ было де́нег

    was there no noise?   не́ было ли шу́ма?

    there will be no room   не бу́дет ме́ста

    will there be many people?   бу́дет мно́го наро́ду?

131. Translate into English.

1. нет горчи́цы; 2. есть ли здесь кто нибудь? —есть; 3. на э́той у́лице краси́вые магази́ны; 4. нет ли ме́ста для вас?—нет; 5. за́втра бу́дет конце́рт, сего́дня никого́ не́ было; 6. бу́дут ли я́йца к за́втраку? 7. у меня́ в ко́мнате, у нас в Росси́и; 8. у него́ на лице́, у них на фа́брике; 9. не́ было бы удово́льствия; 10. бы́ли ли на столе́ ножи́ и ви́лки? 11. в э́том году́ не́ было сне́га.

1. there is not any mustard; 2. is there anybody here?—there is; 3. there are nice shops in this street; 4. is there no room for you?—there is not; 5. there will be a concert to-morrow, there has not been anybody to-day; 6. will there be eggs for (=to) breakfast? 7. in my room, by us in Russia; 8. on his face, in their factory; 9. there would not be any pleasure; 10. were there any knives and forks on the table? 11. there was not any snow (in) this year.

132. Translate into English.

1. У неё в ко́мнате нет карти́н. 2. Есть ли ещё биле́ты?— Есть, но то́лько о́чень дороги́е. 3. Нет ли пи́сем для меня́?— Есть три. 4. В ка́ссе нет де́нег. Что мне де́лать? 5. Бу́дет ли ме́сто у них* в ба́нке? 6. Не бу́дет, но у нас в конто́ре есть ме́сто.   * see Rule 193.

1. There are not any pictures in her room. 2. Are there any tickets left (=yet)?—There are, but only very expensive ones. 3. Are there no letters for me?—There are three. 4. There is no money in the cashbox. What shall I do (=to-me to-do)? 5. Will there be a situation in their bank? 6. There will not be, but in our office there is a situation.

The Neuter of the Past Tense can generally be formed from the Masculine by adding o.
<small>The stress is generally the same as in the Masculine.</small>

191. The Neuter is used if the Subject is Neuter.

the letter was lying on the table ; it was sent by-my aunt	письмо́ лежа́ло на столе́ ; оно́ бы́ло по́слано мое́й тётей

The Neuter must even be used after Pronouns, Adverbs, etc.

all was burnt	всё сгоре́ло
what has happened ?	что случи́лось ?
have many guests come ?	мно́го ли госте́й пришло́ ?

192. Impersonal Expressions are in the Neuter.

it was lucky for him	ему́ повезло́

<small>literally : it has conveyed to him (see par. 144).</small>

it finished badly	пло́хо ко́нчилось
it could happen*	могло́ случи́ться
everything would be well	всё бы́ло бы хорошо́

*The meaning is Conditional, but the Past only is used as in English.

The Neuter is always used unless the Russian Subject is Masculine, Feminine or in the Plural.

how much did it cost ?	ско́лько э́то сто́ило ?
where was it ?	где э́то бы́ло ?
it resulted in nothing =it led up to nothing	э́то ни к чему́ не привело́

193. This idiomatic form is very usual :

1. in our school	у нас в шко́ле
2. at their house	у них до́ма
3. in my pocket	у меня́ в карма́не

1. =by us in school. 2. =by them at home. 3. =by me in pocket.

133. Translate into English.

1. пальто́ висе́ло, со́лнце свети́ло; 2. на́ше село́ лежа́ло..., моё перо́ упа́ло; 3. хорошо́ ли сиде́ло моё пла́тье? 4. мне не повезло́, повезло́ ли вам? 5. где, когда́ э́то бы́ло? что случи́лось? 6. мно́го наро́ду стоя́ло там, сто́лько люде́й жда́ло! 7. э́то наде́лало мно́го шу́ма, э́то не дава́ло мне поко́я; 8. мно́го госте́й ушло́, но ещё бо́льше пришло́; 9. могло́ быть пло́хо.

1. the overcoat was hanging, the sun was shining; 2. our village was situated (=lying)..., I dropped my pen=my pen has fallen; 3. did my dress fit (sit) well? 4. I had no luck, had you any luck? 5. where, when was it? what has happened? 6. many people were standing there, so many people were waiting! 7. it has made* much noise, it did not give me (any) rest; 8. many guests went away, but still more arrived; 9. it could end (=be) badly.

134. Translate into English.

1. Я купи́л плоху́ю бума́гу и не могу́ на ней писа́ть. 2. Нра́вятся ли вам мои́ часы́?—О́чень. 3. Хоте́ли бы вы их купи́ть?—Нет, спаси́бо. 4. Мы бы про́дали наш дом, е́сли бы кто нибудь хоте́л его́ купи́ть. 5. Э́то о́чень удо́бный чемода́н; я его́ всегда́ беру́ с собо́й. 6. Где его́ дом?—Вы стои́те пе́ред ним.

1. I bought bad paper and cannot write on it. 2. Do you like my watch?—Very much. 3. Would you like to buy it (them)?—No, thanks. 4. We would sell our house, if anybody should want to buy it. 5. This is a very convenient bag; I always take it with me. 6. Where is his house?—You are standing in front of it.   *=caused, наде́лало.

194. IT, when referring to a NOUN, must take the same Gender as the Noun.

Nouns can be Masculine or Feminine in Russian, even when referring to a thing or a name; others are Neuter.

IT, as SUBJECT or NOMINATIVE of the sentence is:

MASC. он (he).   FEM. она́ (she).   NEUT. оно́ (it).

IT is on the table   он на столе́
(referring to a MASCULINE)

IT is on the table   она́ на столе́
(referring to a FEMININE)

195. The OBJECT is put in the GENITIVE after ждать (to wait for).

I am waiting for the train   я жду по́езда
whom are you waiting for?   кого́ вы ждёте?

576. TO AVOID   избега́ть   избежа́ть.
followed by Genitive   eez-b,ĕh-gaht,   eez-b,ĕh-jaht,
Imperfective regular; Perfective conjugated like 'to run,' par. 163.

PRESENT: I avoid, избега́ю, избега́ет, избега́ют.
FUTURE: I shall avoid, избегу́, избежи́т, избегу́т.
PAST: избега́л.   Perfective: избежа́л.
IMPERATIVE: избега́йте!   Perfective: not usual.

577. TO BEGIN   начина́ть   нача́ть.
    năh-che-naht,   năh-chaht,
Imperfective regular; Perfective inserts an н before the regular е endings; е becomes ё when the stress is on it.

PRESENT: начина́ю, начина́ет, начина́ют.
FUTURE: I shall begin, начну́, начнёт, начну́т.
PAST: начина́л, etc.   Perfective: на́чал, etc.
IMPERATIVE: начина́йте!   Perfective: начни́те!

THIS AFTERNOON is translated like: to-day after dinner (mid-day meal), сего́дня по́сле обе́да.

135. Translate into English.

1. он избегáет, избегáете ли вы? мы избежи́м; 2. не избежи́те ли вы? онá избегáла, мы избежáли; 3. избегáйте э́того, не избегáйте его́, я бу́ду избегáть; 4. он начинáет, когдá вы начнёте? мы нáчали; 5. начни́те сейчáс, не начинáйте тепéрь, я начинáл нéсколько раз; 6. где вáше перó? вот онó; 7. зáнят ли э́тот стул? нет, он не зáнят; 8. скóлько стóит э́та бумáга? не знáю, онá óчень дорогá.

1. he avoids, do you avoid? we shall avoid; 2. will you not avoid? she was avoiding, we have avoided; 3. avoid this, don't avoid him, I shall avoid (Imperfective); 4. he begins, when will you begin? we have begun; 5. begin at once, don't begin now, I was beginning several times; 6. where is your pen? here it is; 7. is this chair engaged? no, it is not engaged; 8. how much does this paper cost? I don't know, it is very dear.

136. Translate into English.

1. Почему́ он меня́ избегáет? 2. Вы ошибáетесь, он вас не избегáет. 3. Мне казáлось, что вы нас избегáли. 4. Почему́ вы не начинáете? 5. Чегó вы ждёте? 6. Они́ начну́т сегóдня пóсле обéда. 7. Это неизбéжно. 8. Кни́га у вас? Нет, онá у негó.

1. Why does he avoid me? 2. You are mistaken, he does not avoid you. 3. It seemed to me that you were avoiding us. 4. Why don't you begin? 5. What are you waiting for? 6. They will begin this afternoon. 7. This is unavoidable. 8. Have you got the book? No, he has got it.

196. IT, if not Subject of the sentence, is translated like HIM when referring to MASCULINES.

(see List of Personal Pronouns,—page 112).

this is a good table	э́то хоро́ший стол
yes, IT is good (Subject)	да, он хоро́ш
where did you buy IT?	где вы его́ купи́ли?
what will you do with IT?	что вы с ним сде́лаете?

578. TO CHOOSE   выбира́ть   вы́брать.
                       VE-be-raht,   VE-bräht,

Imperfective regular; Perfective conjugated like 'to take,' par. 130.

PRESENT: выбира́ю, выбира́ет, выбира́ют.
FUTURE: вы́беру, вы́берет, вы́берут.
PAST: выбира́л, etc.   Perfective: вы́брал.
IMPERATIVE: выбира́йте!   Perfective: вы́берите!

579. TO FORGET   забыва́ть   забы́ть.
                       zăh-be-vaht,   zăh-beet,

Imperfective regular; Perfective conjugated like 'to be,' par. 22.

PRESENT: забыва́ю, забыва́ет, забыва́ют.
FUTURE: I shall forget, забу́ду, забу́дет, забу́дут.
PAST: забыва́л, etc.   Perfective: забы́л, etc.
IMPERATIVE: забыва́йте!   Perfective: забу́дьте!

580. TO DIE   умира́ть   умере́ть.
               oo-me-raht,   oo-m,ĕh-r,et,

Imperfective regular; Perfective slightly irregular.

PRESENT: умира́ю, умира́ет, умира́ют.
FUTURE: I shall die, умру́, умрёт, умру́т.
PAST: умира́л.   Perf. у́мер, умерла́, умерли́.
IMPERATIVE: умира́йте!   Perfective: умри́те!

ЛИ in the CONDITIONAL is mostly omitted, especially with ВЫ.

137. Translate into English.

1. он выбира́ет, не выбира́ете ли вы? она́ выбира́ла; 2. вы́берут ли они́? мы не вы́берем, выбира́ли бы вы*? 3. они́ бы не вы́брали, вы́берите что́ нибудь, не выбира́йте так до́лго; 4. она́ забыва́ет, мы не забыва́ем, они́ забы́ли; 5. вы всегда́ забыва́ете, они́ э́то забу́дут, не забыва́йте э́того; 6. его́, ему́, им; 7. за ним, о нём, к нему́; 8. на нём, над ним, под ним, в нём; 9. он у́мер, умерла́ ли она́? они́ не у́мерли.   * see footnote, page 190.

1. he chooses, do you not choose? she was choosing; 2. will they choose? we shall not choose, would you choose? 3. they would not have chosen, choose something, don't choose so long; 4. she forgets, we do not forget, they have forgotten; 5. you always forget, they will forget it, don't forget it. IT in the following phrases refers to a Masculine (see Rule 196): 6. of-it, to-it, with-it; 7. behind it, about it, towards it; 8. on it, above it, under it, in it; 9. he died, has she died? they did not die.

138. Translate into English.

1. Что вы вы́брали? 2. Она́ вы́брала краси́вую шля́пу. 3. Ско́лько она́ за неё заплати́ла? 4. Он всегда́ забыва́ет, что говори́т. 5. Не забу́дьте придти́* за́втра. 6. Я э́того не забу́ду. 7. Он у́мер на про́шлой неде́ле. 8. Он умрёт бе́дным челове́ком.   * or прийти.

1. What did you choose? 2. She has chosen a nice hat. 3. How much has she paid for it (her)? 4. He always forgets, what (he) says. 5. Don't forget to come to-morrow. 6. I shall not forget it. 7. He died (on) last week. 8. He will die a poor man (Instr.).

VOCABULARY TO PAGES 172-191.

581. acquaintance
declined like an Adj. ЗНАКОМЫЙ
znăh-kaw-mᴇ͡e

582. article   статья́
(in a paper) stäht,-yah

583. for always навсегда́
năh-fc,eg-dah

584. breakfast за́втрак
or lunch zahf-trăhk

585. bank банк
băhnk

586. cashbox ка́сса
or booking-office kah-ssăh

587. clerk слу́жащий
=serving-one swoo-jăh-shche͡e

588. clock часы́
or watch (rule 85) chăh-cᴇ

589. cleaned помы́тый
=washed păh-mᴇ-tᴇ͡e

590. concert конце́рт
kăhn-ts,errt

591. convenient удо́бный
oo-dob-nᴇ͡e

592. to cost сто́ить
=to be worth staw-eet,

593. Count граф
(title) grăhf

594. employé (see 'clerk')

595. engaged за́нят
=busy zah-n,ăht

596. expensive дорого́й
=dear dăh-răh-goy

597. England А́нглия
ahn-gle͡yăh

598. financier финанси́ст
fe-năhn-cist

599. face лицо́
le-tsaw

600. glass стекло́
(material) st,ek-waw

601. goods това́р
=merchandise tăh-varr

602. governess
гуверна́нтка
goo-v,err-nahnt-kăh

603. headmistress,
principal нача́льница
năh-chahl,-ne-tsăh

604. ill больно́й
see rule 73 băhl,-noy

605. to joke шути́ть
shoo-teet,

606. killed уби́тый
oo-be-tᴇ͡e

607. luck сча́стье
=happiness sh-chah-st-yŏh

608. manager
управля́ющий
oo-präh-vl,ah,yoo-ah-che͡e

609. merchant купе́ц
see rule 72 koo-pets

610. minister мини́стр
me-neestrr

611. to be mistaken,
make a mistake
ошиба́ться
Perf. ошиби́ться
ăh-she-baht,-s,ăh ăh-she-beet,-s,ăh

612. nice краси́вый
krăh-ce-vᴇ͡e

613. noise шум
shoom
614. once раз
răhz
615. overcoat пальто́
(undeclinable) păhl,-taw
616. people наро́д
=nation năh-rod
617. partner компаньо́н
kom-păh-neˆyon
618. purse кошелёк
see rule 72   kăh-shĕh-l,ok
619. purse портмоне́
(undeclinable) porrt-maw-neh
620. receive получа́ть
получи́ть
păh-woo-chaht, păh-woo-cheet,
621. respected
уважа́емый
oo-văh-jah-yĕh-mᴇˆe
622. rest поко́й
păh-koy
623. Russia Росси́я
răh-ce-yăh
624. situation до́лжность
dolj-nost,
625. ,, ме́сто
=place   m,eh-staw
626. suitable
подходя́щий
păhd-hăh-d,ah-sh-cheˆe
627. stand стоя́ть
постоя́ть
stăh-yaht, păh-stăh-yaht,
628. sun со́лнце
soʟn-tsĕh
629. servant слуга́
Masc. or Fem.   swoo-gah

630. smoker куря́щий
koo-r,ah-shcheˆe
631. several не́сколько
n,eh-skol-kaw
632. stupid глу́пый
gwoo-pᴇˆe
633. strange стра́нный
strahn-nᴇˆe
634. sympathetic
симпати́чный
ceem-păh-teech-nᴇˆe
635. shop
магази́н or ла́вка
măh-găh-zeen   wahf-kăh
636. side сторона́
stăh-răh-nah
637. snow снег
sn,eg
638. shareholder
акционе́р
ăhk-tseˆyaw-n,err
638a. Stock Exchange
би́ржа beer-jăh
639. trading торгу́ющий
tarr-goo-yoo-shcheˆe
640. unavoidable
неизбе́жный
n,ĕh-eez-b,ej-nᴇˆe
641. war война́
văhˆe-nah
642. wanted тре́буется
tr,eh-boo-yet-s,ăh
643. the whole of весь
=whole v,es,
644. wounded ра́неный
rah-n,ĕh-nᴇˆe
645. year год
see rule 96   god

TWENTY-FIFTH LESSON.

197. IT, if not the Subject of the sentence, is translated like HER when referring to FEMININES.

where is my book?	где моя книга?
I don't know where IT is	я не знаю, где она
what have you done with IT?—I haven't seen IT.	что вы с ней сделали? —я её не видел.

---

646. TO GET UP   вставать   встать.
                                fstäh-vaht,   fstäht,
Imperfective conjugated like 'to give,' par. 87; Perfective slightly irregular.

PRESENT: I am getting up, встаю, встаёт, встают.
FUTURE: I shall get up, встану, встанет, встанут.
PAST: вставал.   Perfective: встал.
IMPERATIVE: вставайте!   Perfective: встаньте!

---

647. TO HELP   помогать   помочь.
                      päh-mäh-gaht,   päh-motch
Imperfective regular; Perfective conjugated like 'to be able,' par. 59.

PRESENT: I help, помогаю, помогает, помогают.
FUTURE: I shall help, помогу, поможет, помогут.
PAST: помогал.   P. помог, помогла, помогли.
IMPERATIVE: помогайте!   Perfective: помогите!

---

648. TO SELL   продавать   продать.
                     präh-däh-vaht,   präh-daht,
Conjugated exactly like 'to give,' par. 87.

PRESENT: I sell, продаю, продаёт, продают.
FUTURE: я продам, продашь, он продаст;
           продадим, продадите, продадут.
PAST: продавал.   Perf. продал *or* продал.
IMPERATIVE: продавайте!   Perfective: продайте!

139. TRANSLATE INTO ENGLISH.

1. мы встаём, встаньте; 2. не встанут ли они? когда она вставала ..., не вставайте; 3. поможете ли вы? они не помогли, он помогает; 4. помогите нам, не помогайте ему; 5. он не продаст, продадите ли вы? не продавайте этого; 6. мы не продаём, продайте это; 7. у меня была фабрика, но я её продал; 8. где ваша комната? вот она; вы в ней давно живёте?

1. we get up, get up; 2. will they not get up? when she was getting up..., don't get up; 3. will you help? they did not help, he is helping; 4. help (to-) us, don't help (to-) him; 5. he will not sell, will you sell? don't sell it; 6. we are not selling, sell this; 7. I had a factory, but I sold it; 8. where is your room? here it is; have you lived (=do you live) long in it?

140. TRANSLATE INTO ENGLISH.

1. Мы встаём всегда очень рано. 2. Когда вы встанете завтра? 3. Он пришёл, когда я вставал. 4. Не вставайте, если вы плохо себя чувствуете. 5. Чем (я) могу вам помочь? 6. Они никогда никому не помогают. 7. Я бы не продавал так дёшево. 8. Продаст ли он вам весь товар? 9. Я ищу свою палку.

1. We always get up very early. 2. When will you get up to-morrow? 3. He came when I was getting up. 4. Do not get up, if you feel (yourself) not well (=badly). 5. How (=with-what) can I help (to-) you? 6. They never help (to-) anybody. 7. I should not sell so cheaply. 8. Will he sell all the goods to you? 9. I am looking for my stick.

198. IT, if not Subject of the sentence, is translated like HIM when referring to NEUTERS.

> here is his letter — вот его письмо
> where is IT? — где оно (Subject)?
> when did you receive IT? — когда вы его получили?
> did you believe (to-) IT? — поверили ли вы ему?

649. TO KILL убивать убить.
     oo-be-vaht, oo-beet,

Imperfective regular; Perfective conjugated like 'to drink,' par. 157.

PRESENT: I kill, etc., убиваю, убивает, убивают.
FUTURE: I shall kill, etc., убью, убьёт, убьют.
PAST: убивал.   Perfective: убил, —а, —и.
IMPERATIVE: убивайте! Perfective: убейте!

650. TO FALL падать упасть (for пасть).
     pah-däht, oo-pahst, (the real Perfective)

The Imperfective Form is quite regular; the Perfective is conjugated like 'to put,' par. 119.

PRESENT: I fall, etc., падаю, падаёт, падают.
FUTURE: I shall fall, etc., упаду, упадет, упадут.
PAST: падал, etc. Perfective: упал, —а, —и.
IMPERATIVE: падайте! Perfective: упадите!

651. TO GROW расти вырости.
 to grow up räh-ste ve-räh-ste

PRESENT: I grow, etc., расту, растет, растут.
FUTURE: выросту, выростёт, выростут.

Conjugated exactly like the Present, except that the stress is on the first syllable.

PAST: рос, росла, росли. P. вырос, выросла, etc.
IMPERATIVE: растите! Perfective: выростите!

The Imperfective Imperative is mostly used.

141. Translate into English.

1. мы не убьём, не убивайте; 2. вы упадёте, не падайте, упали ли они? 3. мы не упадём, что упало? не падают ли они? 4. как он вырос! оно не растёт, когда мы выростём …; 5. ваше пальто висело здесь, но оно упало; 6. я знал это слово, но я его забыл; 7. вы писали моим пером, что вы с ним сделали? 8. его, ему, им; 9. за ним, о нём, к нему; 10. на нём, над ним, под ним.

1. we shall not kill, do not kill; 2. you will fall, don't fall, did they fall? 3. we shall not fall, what fell? are they not falling? 4. how he has grown-up! it is not growing, when we shall grow up …; 5. your overcoat was hanging here, but it fell; 6. I knew this word, but I forgot it; 7. you were writing with my pen, what have you done with it? It, referring to Neuters: 8. of-it, to-it, with-it; 9. behind it, about it, towards it; 10. on it, above it, under it.

142. Translate into English.

1. Нашего знакомого убили на войне. 2. На бирже все бумаги падают. 3. Чем ты будешь, когда выростёшь? 4. Моё кольцо упало, но я его нашёл. 5. В его саду растут красные и белые розы. 6. Это ваше место?—Да, но вы можете сидеть на нём.

1. An[1] acquaintance of ours was killed[1] in the war. 2. On the Stock Exchange all stocks[2] are falling. 3. What will[3] you be[3] when you[4] grow up[4]? 4. I[5] dropped my ring,[5] but I[6] picked it up again.[6] 5. There are red and white roses growing in his garden. 6. Is this your seat?—Yes, but you may sit on it.

1 =they killed our acquaintance; 2 =papers; 3 =wilt thou be; 4 =thou wilt grow-up; 5 =my ring fell; 6 =I found it.

199. Verbs in ять add the e endings in the usual way by cutting off the ть of the INFINITIVE (rule 13).

652. TO ALLOW	позволять păh-zvăh-l‚aht,	позво́лить păh-zvaw-leet,
653. TO ADVERTISE announce (Rule 47)	объявля́ть ăhb-yăhv-l‚aht,	объяви́ть ăhb-yăh-veet,
654. TO CHANGE	меня́ть m‚ĕh-n‚aht,	поменя́ть păh-m‚ĕh-n‚aht,
655. TO LEAVE (something) abandon (Rule 47)	оставля́ть ăh-stăhv-l‚aht,	оста́вить ăh-stah-veet,
656. TO LOSE	теря́ть t‚ĕh-r‚aht,	потеря́ть păh-t‚ĕh-r‚aht,
657. TO REPEAT	повторя́ть păh-ftăh-r‚aht,	повтори́ть păh-ftăh-reet,

200. If the ending ять is preceded by a Vowel, the e endings are added, after cutting off ять.

658. TO MELT, та́ять tah-yăht,	it melts, та́ет tah-yet
659. TO LAUGH, смея́ться sm‚ĕh-yaht‚-s‚ăh	I laugh, я смею́сь (yăh) sm‚ĕh-yoos,

When ять is preceded by о, the Verb takes и ending:

660. TO STAND	стоя́ть stăh-yaht,	постоя́ть păh-stăh-yaht,
661. TO FEAR to be afraid of (requires the Genitive)	боя́ться băh-yaht‚-s‚ăh	побоя́ться păh-băh-yaht‚-s‚ăh

he stands, он стои́т on stăh-eet	we are afraid, мы бои́мся mE băh-eem-s‚ăh

201. CHRISTIAN NAMES in Russian are declined like ordinary Nouns.

with Peter and Vera   с Петро́м и Ве́рой
for Olga and Nicholas   для Ольги и Никола́я
s'p‚et-rom e v‚eh-roy   dl‚ăh ol‚-ghe e ne-kăh-wah-yăh

Nominatives: Пётр, Ве́ра, Никола́й, Ольга.

143. Translate into English.

1. он потерял, мы не теряем, не теряйте; 2. я не позволяю, позволите ли вы? позвольте; 3. они повторяют, она не повторила, повторите ещё раз; 4. оставляете ли вы? я не оставлю, оставьте, пожалуйста! 5. они стоят, почему вы стоите? постойте! 6. чего вы боитесь? я его не боюсь, не бойтесь; 7. почему они смеются? не смейтесь, я не смеялся; 8. от Николая для Веры.

1. he lost, we do not lose, don't lose; 2. I do not allow, will you allow? allow (me); 3. they are repeating, she did not repeat, repeat-it once more; 4. do you leave-it? I shall not leave-it, leave off, please! 5. they are standing, why do you stand? wait! (=stand!) 6. what are you afraid of? I am not afraid of him, don't fear; 7. why do they laugh? don't laugh, I did not laugh; 8. from Nicholas for Vera.

144. Translate into English.

1. Он ищет то, чего не потерял. 2. Не позволяйте вашим детям так громко смеяться. 3. Садитесь, пожалуйста! — (Нет,) спасибо, я постою. 4. Мне говорили, что вы меняете квартиру. 5. Они никого не боятся. 6. Сегодня теплее, чем вчера; снег тает на улице. 7. Человек сеет, а ветер веет.*

1. He is looking for something (=for that what) he did not lose. 2. Don't allow your children to laugh so loud. 3. Sit down, please!—No, thanks, I can (=shall) stand. 4. I was told (=to-me they told) that you were moving (=are changing the flat). 5. They are not afraid of anybody. 6. To-day is warmer than yesterday; the snow melts in the street. 7. The man sows, and the wind blows.*   *proverb.

There is a small number of Russian Verbs ending in the INFINITIVE in ти or чь, instead of in ть.

202. Most Verbs in ти really end in сти.
(Notable exceptions are the compounds with идти′)
to carry, нести   to grow, расти
to shake, tremble, трясти to sweep, мести
IMITATED PRONUNCIATION.—n‚ĕh-stee, răh-stee, tr‚ăh-stee, m‚ĕh-stee.

They all take ё endings; in the First Person Singular and the Third Person Plural they take ту or су.

I carry, я несу does he grow? растёт ли он?
 do they sweep? метут ли они?
 we don't shake мы не трясём

The л in the Past Tense Masculine is mostly omitted after г, к, з, and с (also after б and р).

662. TO DUST мести or подметать подмести.
 TO SWEEP m‚ĕh-ste (regular) păhd-m‚ĕh-ste
PRESENT: I dust, etc., мету, метёт, метут.
FUTURE: I shall dust, etc., подмету, etc.
PAST: I dusted, etc., подметал, etc.
  Perfective: подмёл, подмела, подмели.
In the Imperfective the Past of подметать is mostly used.
IMPERATIVE: метите! Perfective: подметите!

663. TO PRESERVE, TAKE CARE OF беречь сберечь.
SAVE (money), TO WATCH (in Imperf. only) b‚ĕh-r‚ech sb‚ĕh-r‚ech
PRESENT: берегу, бережёт, берегут.
FUTURE: сберегу, etc. Conjugated exactly like the Present.
PAST: берёг, берегла, берегли. Р. сберёг.
IMPERATIVE: берегите! Perfective: сберегите!
  The REFLECTIVE IMPERATIVE is much used:
берегитесь! beware! take care!
берегись! look out! (colloquial form is generally used)

145. Translate into English.

1. мы метём, подметут ли они? почему вы не метёте? 2. он подметал, подмела ли она? не метите; 3. бережёте ли вы? мы сбережём, она не сберегла; 4. берегли ли они? сберегите! берегитесь! 5. кто это трясёт? не трясите, я не тряс; 6. берегитесь воров! 7. эти улицы метутся два раза в день; 8. почему вы трясётесь? они тряслись; 9. они несут, они несутся; 10. он нёс, он нёсся.

1. we sweep, will they dust? why are you not dusting? 2. he was dusting, did she sweep? don't dust; 3. do you preserve? we shall save, she did not save; 4. were they taking care? save! beware! 5. who shakes this? don't shake (it), I did not shake (it); 6. beware of pickpockets (=thieves)! 7. these streets are swept twice a day; 8. why do you tremble? they trembled; 9. they carry, they are running; 10. he carried, he was running.

146. Translate into English.

1. Подметите мою комнату. 2. Он сберёг очень много денег. 3. Потрясите это дерево. 4. Этот пол, мне кажется, никогда не подметался. 5. Я берегусь его, как огня. 6. Она тряслась от страха. 7. Подмели ли вы уже весь зал? 8. Берегитесь, а Бог вас сбережёт.

1. Dust my room. 2. He saved a[1] lot of[1] money. 3. Shake this tree. 4. This floor, it seems to me, has never been swept. 5. I beware of him, like of the fire. 6. She trembled from fear. 7. Have you already dusted the whole hall? 8. Take care of yourself, and God will take care of you.

1. very much.

203. Most Verbs in чь really end in ечь.
   (principal exception : мочь, to be able)
   to flow, течь   to drag, draw, влечь
   to burn, жечь   to preserve, беречь
   IMITATED PRONUNCIATION : t‚ech, vl‚ech, jech, b‚ĕh-r‚ech,

All these Verbs take the ё endings ; in the First Person Singular and Third Person Plural they take y and ут.

The y endings are preceded by a guttural г or к ; the other endings by a hisser ж or ч.

   I drag, я влеку   they preserve, они берегут
   do you bake ?   печёте ли вы ?
   we don't burn   мы не жжём

664. TO FLOW, LEAK   течь   потечь.
                              t‚ech‚   păh-t‚ech‚

PRESENT : теку, течёт, текут.
FUTURE : потеку, etc. Conjugated exactly like the Present.
PAST : тёк, текла, текли. Perfective : потёк.
IMPERATIVE : теките ! потеките !
(used only in poetical speech)

665. TO BAKE   печь   спечь.
   (not meat)   p‚etch‚   sp‚etch‚

PRESENT : I bake, etc., пеку, печёт, пекут.
FUTURE : спеку, etc. Conjugated exactly like the Present.
PAST : пёк, пекла, пекли. Perfective: спёк.
IMPERATIVE : пеките ! спеките !

666. TO CUT HAIR   стричь   постричь.
                         streetch‚   păh-streetch‚

PRESENT : стригу, стрижёт, стригут.
FUTURE : I shall cut hair, etc., постригу, etc.
Conjugated exactly like the Present.
PAST : стриг, стригла, стригли. P. постриг.
IMPERATIVE : стригите ! Perfective : постригите !

147. Translate into English.

1. течёт, текло́, потечёт; 2. не течёт ли? не текло́, не потечёт ли? 3. я пеку́, не печёт ли она́? мы пекли́; 4. что вы спекли́? я спеку́, он не спечёт; 5. она́ стрижёт ему́ во́лосы, постри́г ли он вам во́лосы? 6. я не бу́ду стричь их, постриж́ёте ли вы его́ за́втра? 7. я берегу́, он не бережёт, она́ сберегла́; 8. я берёг, мы не берегли́, береги́те его́, береги́тесь! 9. влеку́т ли они́? он повлёк.

    1. it flows *or* it leaks, it flowed, it will flow; 2. does it not leak? it was not flowing, will it not flow? 3. I bake, does she not bake? we were baking; 4. what have you baked? I shall bake, he will not bake; 5. she cuts his hair, did he cut your hair? 6. I shall not cut (their hair) (Imperf.), will you cut (his hair=him) to-morrow? 7. I watch, he does not watch, she saved; 8. I took care of, we did not take care of, take care of him, look out!=be careful! 9. do they drag? he dragged.

148. Translate into English.

1. Парикма́хер спра́шивает: постри́чь и́ли побри́ть? 2. Клие́нт отвеча́ет: постри́чь! побри́ть! 3. Постриги́те мне во́лосы,* побре́йте мне бо́роду. 4. Эта река́ течёт о́чень бы́стро. 5. Спеки́те мне пиро́жное. 6. Сожги́те э́ти бума́ги сейча́с-же. 7. Сбереги́те де́ньги.

    1. The hairdresser asks: haircut or shave? 2. The customer replies: cut my hair=to cut hair! shaving=to shave! 3. Cut my hair, shave my beard. 4. This river flows very swiftly. 5. Bake me a cake. 6. Burn these papers at once. 7. Save (your) money.

* literally: cut to-me the-hairs.

TWENTY-SIXTH LESSON.

204. Verbs ending in нуть are conjugated by taking off уть, and adding the **e** endings: **y** and **ут** used for ю and ют. (when stressed, e becomes ё)

667. TO PULL, DRAW	тянуть t‚äh-noot,	потянуть päh-t‚äh-noot,
668. TO RETURN *something*	возвращать vähz-vrähsh-tchaht,	вернуть v‚err-noot,
669. TO MOVE *put into motion*	двигать dve-gäht,	двинуть dve-noot,
670. TO SHOUT, CALL (Rule 43)	кричать kre-chaht,	крикнуть kreek-noot,
671. TO TOUCH, STIR *move*	трогать traw-gäht,	тронуть traw-noot,
672. TO BE DROWNING	тонуть täh-noot,	утонуть oo-täh-noot,

205. Family names with endings of ordinary Adjectives are declined like such.

граф Толстой   Достоевский
grähf tähl-stoy   däh-stäh-yef-ske͡e
at Count Tolstoy's   у графа Толстого
Mrs. Kurskaya   госпожа Курская
to Dostoyefsky   Достоевскому

206. Family names in **в** or **н** have a special declension. They form Fem. in **a**, and Plural in **ы**.

(Mr.) Petroff, Петров   (Mrs.) Petroff, Петрова
(Mr. and Mrs.) Petroff, Петровы

They are declined like NOUNS in the Sing. Masc. (except Instr. ым), and like ADJECTIVES in the Plural and Fem. Sing. (except Fem. Accus. which ends in **y**, and Nom. Plur. in **ы**).

about Mr. & Mrs. Tchekhoff   о Чехове и Чеховой
with Pushkin   с Пушкиным

149. Translate into English.

1. не тяни́те, не та́нете ли вы? он потяну́л; 2. верну́ли ли они́? она́ верну́лась; 3. не кричи́те, когда́ он кри́кнет; 4. я не дви́ну, дви́ньте э́то, не дви́гайтесь; 5. мы уто́нем, тону́л ли он? 6. о Че́хове и Достое́вском; 7. Пу́шкина и Чайко́вского; 8. пе́ред Турге́невым, к Степа́новым; 9. когда́ вы вернётесь? 10. он не дви́нулся с ме́ста.

1. don't pull, do you not pull? he pulled; 2. did they return (it)? she came back (=returned herself); 3. don't shout, when he will call (=shout); 4. I shall not move (it), move this, don't move (yourself); 5. we shall get drowned, was he drowning? 6. about Tchekhoff[1] and Dostoyefsky[1]; 7. by=of-Pushkin[2] and Tchaikowsky[3]; 8. before Turgeneff, to Stepanoffs (Plur.); 9. when will you come back? 10. he did not move (himself) from the place.

1 famous Russian writers; 2 famous Russian poet; 3 Russian composer.

150. Translate into English.

1. Почему́ вы всегда́ кричи́те на него́? 2. Говоря́т, что два и́ли три корабля́ утону́ли.* 3. Про́сят не тро́гать карти́н. 4. Я вчера́ верну́лся из Фра́нции. 5. Кем напи́сана о́пера „Пи́ковая да́ма"? 6. Сюже́т—Пу́шкиным, а му́зыка—Чайко́вским.

* better: went to the bottom, пошли́ ко дну.

1. Why do you always shout at (=on) him? 2. They say that two or three ships were sunk (=drowned). 3. You are requested (=they beg) not to touch the pictures. 4. I returned yesterday from France. 5. By whom is written the opera "Queen of Spades"? 6. The plot by Pushkin and music by Tchaikowsky.

207. Verbs in еть generally take и endings; a certain group, however, take е endings added after е.

673. TO BE ILL to suffer from (with)	болѣть băh-l‚et‚	заболѣть păh-băh-l‚et‚
674. TO REGRET, pity be sorry for	жалѣть jăh-l‚et‚	пожалѣть păh-jăh-l‚et‚

he is ill   онъ болѣетъ   I regret   я жалѣю
                băh-l‚eh-yet   jăh-l‚eh-yoo

The majority of these Verbs denote a GROWING action, and are derived from Adjectives.

675. TO GROW DARK	темнѣть t‚ĕm-n‚et‚	потемнѣть păh-t‚ĕm-n‚et‚
676. TO GROW RED to blush	краснѣть krăh-sn‚et‚	покраснѣть păh-krăh-sn‚et‚
677. TO GROW PALE	блѣднѣть bl‚ĕd-n‚et‚	поблѣднѣть păh-bl‚ĕd-n‚et‚
678. TO GROW THIN	худѣть hoo-d‚et‚	похудѣть păh-hoo-d‚et‚
679. TO GROW THICK GET STOUT	толстѣть tăhL-st‚et‚	потолстѣть păh-tăhL-st‚et‚
680. TO GROW OLD	старѣть stăh-r‚et‚	постарѣть păh-stăh-r‚et‚

208. TO HAVE, имѣть (no Perfective), belongs to the same group.

This Verb is mostly used with abstract Nouns, like:
we had the PLEASURE   мы имѣли удовольствіе
I have the HONOUR   честь имѣю

When TO HAVE means 'possession of a thing,' the idiomatic construction in par. 15 should be used.

Sentences like: я имѣю книгу, имѣете ли вы карандашъ? are not correct, although occasionally used (not in Central Russia).

209. болѣть with ordinary и endings means: to pain, ache, ail.   голова болитъ   the head aches
                зубы болятъ   the teeth ache

151. Translate into English.

1. мы болеем, не болели ли вы? 2. мы жалеем, не жалел ли он? 3. темнеет, потемнело; 4. почему вы краснеете? не краснейте; 5. как вы побледнели! не побледнела ли она? 6. он всё толстеет, не потолстели ли они? 7. я худею с каждым днём, вы не похудели; 8. как он постарел! не стареет ли она? 9. вы имели счастье! 10. они болеют, у них болят зубы.

1. we are ill, were you not ill? 2. we regret, was he not sorry for ...? 3. it grows dark, it has grown dark; 4. why do you blush? don't blush; 5. how pale you grew! did she not grow pale? 6. he is still getting stout, did they not get stout? 7. I grow thin (with) every day, you did not grow thin; 8. how he grew old! does she not grow old? 9. you had luck! 10. they are ill, they have the toothache (=by them teeth ache).

152. Translate into English.

1. Они всегда болеют; то[1] у них зубы болят, то[1] голова болит, то[1] горло. 2. Я имел желание пойти в театр, но у меня не было денег. 3. Почему вы так побледнели? Болит ли у вас что-нибудь? 4. Он всегда жалеет бедных, но не даёт им ни гроша.

[1] =now ..., then ..., then ....

1. They are always ill; now they have the toothache, then headache, then a sore throat. 2. I wanted to=I had a desire to go to the theatre, but I had no money. 3. Why have you grown so pale? Does anything hurt you? 4. He always pities the poor, but does not give (to-) them even a farthing.

210. The NUMERALS from 11 to 20 are formed by adding надцать (used for на десять, 'on ten') to the units (ь and е, final letter of the first word is dropped).
(For numbers 1 to 10, see pars. 11 and 44, also page 218).

    11 одиннадцать   ăh-deen-năht-tsăht,
    12 двенадцать   14 четырнадцать
      dv‚ĕh-naht-tsăht,   chĕh-tɛrr-năht-tsăht,

The stress is always on на except in 11 and 14. Those numerals are declined like Feminine Nouns in ь (see par. 133).

211. Russian Nouns are often used in the so-called DIMINUTIVE Form to render the English LITTLE, or to express affection, politeness, etc.

    This DIMINUTIVE is mostly formed by inserting к (or к preceded by е, и, о) before or to the ending of the Noun:
    little hat, шляпка   little table, столик

The preceding consonant often changes into a hissing sound:
    книга becomes книжка   лицо becomes личико

Similarly, a Noun may be changed to express SPITE, DEPRECATION by inserting ишк, онк, etc.; LARGENESS of the thing ищ, etc., or simply when the speaker is in a good mood and wants to show it, ушк, еньк, etc.
    little town, городок   dirty town, городишка
    big   „   городище   nice little „ городушка

All these are niceties which students need not use, but which they may come across sometimes in reading.

---

681. TO PROMISE   обещать   пообещать
    sometimes used reflectively ăh-b‚ĕh-shohaht, păh-ăh-b‚ĕh-shohaht,

682. TO HANG   вешать   повесить
    (Rule 41)   v‚eh-shăht,   păh-v‚eh-ceet

    Imperative Perfect: повесьте păh-v‚es‚-t‚ĕh

683. TO REMEMBER   помнить   вспомнить
    TO RECOLLECT   pom-neet,   fspom-neet,
    The Perfective used only in the meaning of: remember again.

153. TRANSLATE INTO ENGLISH.

1. пообещáйте мне, обещáют ли они́ вам? мы им не обещáли; 2. мы вéшаем, не вéшайте э́того, повéсьте э́то; 3. я не повéшу, повéсят ли они́? не повéсили ли вы? 4. пóмните ли вы? мы бýдем пóмнить, пóмните! 5. я вспóмнил, когдá онá вспóмнит; 6. пятнáдцать, восемнáдцать, девятнáдцать; 7. с шестнáдцатью солдáтами, в двенáдцати частя́х; 8. кусóчек, билéтик, бутылочка, рýчка, окóшко; кáрточки.

1. promise me, do they promise you? we did not promise them; 2. we are hanging, do not hang this, hang it; 3. I shall not hang it, will they hang it? did you not hang it? 4. do you remember? we shall remember, remember! 5. I recollected, when she will recollect; 6. fifteen, eighteen, nineteen; 7. with sixteen soldiers, in twelve parts; 8. Diminutive of: a piece, a ticket, a bottle, hand, window; visiting-cards.

154. TRANSLATE INTO ENGLISH.

1. Я вам обещáю, что я бýду пóмнить об э́том. 2. Повéсьте, пожáлуйста, моё пальтó. 3. Они́ нам обещáлись э́то устрóить. 4. Вчерá нóчью ктó то повéсился в пáрке. 5. Не мóжете ли вы вспóмнить, что он вам сказáл? 6. Он мне дóлжен шестнáдцать фýнтов.

1. I promise (to-) you that I shall remember (about) it. 2. Hang up my overcoat, please. 3. They promised (to-) us to arrange this. 4. Last (yesterday) night someone hanged himself in the park. 5. Can you not remember what he told (to-) you? 6. He **owes** (to-) me sixteen pounds.

212. TWO, THREE, FOUR, given in par. 18, are declined as follows:

	two двух	three трёх	four четырёх
G. P.	двух	трёх	четырёх
D.	двум	трём	четырём
I.	двумя́	тремя́	четырьмя́

G. P. dvookh tr͵okh chĕh-tɛ-r͵okh. D. dvoom tr͵om chĕh-tɛ-r͵om.
I. dvoo-m͵ah tr͵ĕh-m͵ah chĕh-tɛr-m͵ah.

In all cases, except in the NOMINATIVE or ACCUSATIVE, they agree with the Noun. (In the Nominative they require Genitive Sing.—see par. 11).

213. The usual way of address in Russian (except to strangers) is that by Christian name and father's name (о́тчество ot-tchĕh-stfaw, from оте́ц, father).

This is generally obtained by adding ович or евич (or simply ыч) to the father's name.

Ivan Ivan's-son Ива́н Ива́нович or Ива́ныч.
      e-vahn e-vah-naw-veech *or* e-vah-nɛch

Алекса́ндр Серге́евич or Серге́ич.
(This was Pushkin's Christian name and father's name).

Father's name for Feminine is овна or евна.

О́льга Никола́евна Olga Nicholas'-daughter.

214. All NEUTER NOUNS ending in ко, and a few others, form the NOMINATIVE PLURAL irregularly in и.

apple, я́блоко, я́блоки knee, коле́но, коле́ни
shoulder, плечо́, пле́чи ear, у́хо, у́ши
  exception: о́блако cloud; облака́ clouds.
1. yahb-waw-kaw yahb-waw-ke. 2. pl͵ĕh-chaw pl͵eh-che.
3. kăh-l͵eh-naw kăh-l͵eh-ne. 4. oo-haw oo-she.

684.	TO ACCOMPANY	провожа́ть	проводи́ть
	Rule 41	prăh-văh-jaht,	prăh-văh-deet,
685.	TO ACCEPT	принима́ть	приня́ть.
	RECEIVE, TAKE	pre-ne-maht,	pre-n͵aht,

Future: приму́, при́мет, при́мут
    pre-moo pree-met pree-moot
Imperative Perfective: прими́те!
      pre-me-t͵ĕh! (otherwise regular)

155. Translate into English.

1. проводи́те меня́, не провожа́йте их; 2. я провожу́ вас, не провожа́ете ли вы нас? 3. при́мете ли вы? я не приня́л бы, не принима́йте; 4. мы принима́ем госте́й, принима́ют ли они́ лека́рство? 5. он при́мет во внима́ние, при́няли ли вы ме́ры? 6. с двумя́ господа́ми, о трёх сёстрах; 7. для четырёх солда́т, двум да́мам; 8. с Ива́ном Петро́вичем, для Ве́ры Ива́новны; 9. я́блоки, я́блок, у́ши, уше́й.

1. accompany me, don't accompany them; 2. I shall accompany you, don't you accompany us? 3. will you accept? I should not accept, don't accept; 4. we receive visitors, do they take medicine? 5. he will take into consideration (=attention), did you take measures? 6. with two gentlemen, about three sisters; 7. for four soldiers, to two ladies; 8. with Ivan Peter's son, for Vera Ivan's daughter; 9. apples, of apples, ears, of ears.

156. Translate into English.

1. Я вас провожу́ домо́й, О́льга Ива́новна. 2. Мы при́няли трёх но́вых слу́жащих в на́шу конто́ру. 3. Кто провожа́ет Мари́ю Петро́вну? —Никола́й Серге́ич. 4. Мы провожа́ли двух знако́мых, кото́рые е́хали заграни́цу. 5. Вы лю́бите я́блоки? 6. У меня́ у́ши боля́т.

1. I shall accompany you home, Olga Ivan's-daughter. 2. We took three new clerks into our office. 3. Who accompanies Mary Peter's-daughter? —Nicolas Sergius'-son. 4. We accompanied two friends (=acquaintances) that were going abroad. 5. Do you like apples? 6. I have the earache.

215. Numerals from 20 to 40 are :

 20 двáдцать 30 трúдцать 40 сóрок
  dvaht-tsäht,   treet-tsäht,   saw-rok

From 50 to 80 they are formed by adding десят (tens) after ordinary numerals :

 50 пятьдесят 80 вóсемьдесят
 90 девянóсто 100 сто (staw)

50. p‚äht-d‚ĕh-s‚aht ; 80. vaw-c‚em-d‚ĕh-s‚äht ; 90. d‚ĕh-v‚äh-naw-staw.

These Numerals are declined like Feminine Nouns in soft sign ь (from 50 to 80 both parts are declined).

 with 60 pounds шестьюдесятью фýнтами
        shest‚-yoo-d‚ĕh-s‚äht‚-yoo foon-täh-me
 on 70 pages на семúдесяти странúцах
      näh c‚ĕh-me-d‚ĕh-s‚ĕh-te sträh-ne-tsähkh

40, 90, and 100, form an exception : they end in **а** in all cases (Accusative like Nominative).

 to 100 soldiers ста солдáтам
 for 40 roubles за сóрок рублéй
  stäh sähL-dah-tähm zäh-saw-rock roob-l‚eh^e

216. to read (Voc. 143) has also an abbreviate Perfective form very much used :

  to read through прочéсть präh-chest,

Future : прочтý, прочтёт, прочтýт.
    präh-chtoo präh-cht‚ot präh-chtoot

Past (Perfective) : прочёл, прочлá, прочлú.
     präh-chol präh-chwah präh-chle

Imperative (Perfective) : прочтúте ! präh-cht‚ee-t‚ĕh!

217. to hear (par. 43) has also another form much used, but only in the Past.

  слыхáть swE-haht, услыхáть oo-swE-haht,

686. to clean Rule 41	чúстить che-steet,	почúстить päh-che-steet,
687. to spoil Rule 41	пóртить porr-teet,	испóртить iss-porr-teet,

157. Translate into English.

1. я не прочту, не прочтёте ли вы? прочтите; 2. мы прочли, прочёл ли он? 3. она услыхала, слыхали ли вы? 4. я почищу, чистят ли они? она не чистила; 5. я не порчу, не испортите ли вы? они испортили; 6. шестьдесят фунтов, семьдесят рублей; 7. перед тридцатью солдатами, в восьмидесяти домах; 8. для девяноста учеников, без сорока копеек.

1. I shall not read through, will you not read through? read it through; 2. we have read through, did he read through? 3. she heard, did you hear? 4. I shall clean, do they clean? she did not clean; 5. I don't spoil, will you not spoil-it? they have spoiled; 6. sixty pounds, seventy roubles; 7. before thirty soldiers, in eighty houses; 8. for ninety pupils, less (=without) forty copecks.

158. Translate into English.

1. Можете ли вы дать мне прочесть вашу газету? 2. Я её ещё сам не прочёл. 3. Мы услыхали такой шум, что все подумали: не аэроплан ли это? 4. Слыхали ли вы, что с нами вчера случилось? 5. Он портит всё, что берёт в руки. 6. Почистите мне, пожалуйста, платье и ботинки. 7. У меня не было ста рублей, я обещал дать остальные сорок сегодня.

1. Can you give me your newspaper to read? 2. I have not read it yet myself. 3. We heard such a noise, that everybody thought: not an aeroplane this? 4. Have you heard what happened to (=with) us yesterday? 5. He spoils everything that he takes in hand(s). 6. Clean my suit and boots, please. 7. I did not have hundred roubles, (so) I promised to pay (=give) the remaining forty to-day.

218. The IMPERATIVE can be formed from the Second Person Plural of the Present.

Perfective Verbs, having no Present, form the Imperative from the FUTURE.

(*a*) In Verbs having и endings the Imperative and the Second Person Plural are alike, except that the stress always rests on the и in ите in the IMPERATIVE.

    you speak говори́те   you smoke ку́рите
    speak ! говори́те !   smoke ! кури́те !

(*b*) In Verbs having е endings, the ете is changed in the Imperative into ите. ите becomes йте after a vowel. (The stress is generally on the same vowel as in the Infinitive).

    you wash мо́ете   wash ! мо́йте !
    you write пи́шете   write ! пиши́те !
    you live живёте   live ! живи́те !

(*c*) There is a small number of Verbs where the stress is not on the termination; they therefore take ьте in the IMPERATIVE. If the termination follows a vowel йте is used.

    to cut ре́зать   cut ! ре́жьте !
    to answer отве́тить   answer ! отве́тьте !
    to get up встать   get up ! вста́ньте !
    to be быть   be ! бу́дьте !

ANOTHER WAY OF FORMING THE IMPERATIVE.

The IMPERATIVE can also be formed from the THIRD PERSON PLURAL of the PRESENT.

    1. they work, рабо́тают   work ! рабо́тайте !
    2. „ speak, говоря́т   speak ! говори́те !
    3. „ believe, ве́рят   believe ! ве́рьте !
    4. „ clean, чи́стят   clean ! чи́стите !

The above examples show that the Terminations of the Present are taken off, and those of the Imperative added, thus :

    1. After a Vowel й or йте. 2. After a Consonant и' or и'те. 3. After a Consonant where Infin. Term. is NOT accented ь or ьте. 4. After two Consonants, however, и or ите (и unstressed).

It depends on the last letter that remains of the word, after the termination is cut off, what ending the Imperative takes.

159. Translate into English.

1. пошлите, не посылайте; 2. возьмите, не берите; 3. попробуйте, не пробуйте; 4. принесите, привезите, приведите; 5. не приносите, не привозите, не приводите; 6. спрячьте, не прячьте; 7. ответьте, не отвечайте; 8. повесьте, не вешайте; 9. не плачьте, не режьте этого; 10. садитесь *or* сядьте; 11. ложитесь *or* лягте; 12. помойтесь, не купайтесь в море; 13. спрячьтесь, не жалуйтесь; 14. пойдёмте, поедемте, выпьем; 15. пусть (он) принесёт сюда, пусть (они) напишут вам.

1. send, do not send; 2. take, do not take; 3. try, do not try; 4. bring, bring (a person *or* thing not on foot), bring (a person on foot); 5. do not bring, do not bring, do not bring; 6. hide, do not hide; 7. answer, do not answer; 8. hang it, don't hang it; 9. don't cry, do not cut this; 10. sit down; 11. lie down; 12. wash yourself, don't bathe in the sea; 13. hide yourselves, don't complain; 14. let us go (on foot), let us go (not on foot), let us drink; 15. let him *or* her bring it hither, let them write to you.

160. Translate into English.

1. Спойте нам что-нибудь, София Андреевна. 2. Подождите секунду, они сейчас придут. 3. Не брейтесь этой бритвой. 4. Заходите к нам, Борис Андреевич; мы всегда по вечерам дома. 5. Подвиньте ваши стулья.

1. Sing (to-) us something, Sophie Andrew's-daughter. 2. Wait a second, they will come presently. 3. Do not shave with that razor. 4. Call on us, Boris Andrew's-son; we are always at home in the evenings. 5. Move your chairs.

VOCABULARY TO PAGES 194-217.

688. apple я́блоко
 yahb-waw-kaw
689. arrange устра́ивать
 устро́ить
 oo-strah-e-väht, oo-straw-eet,
690. beard борода́
 băh-räh-dah
691. to blow ве́ять
 v,eh-yäht,
692. cake пиро́жное
 pe-roj-naw-yĕh
693. to take care бере́чь
 сбере́чь
 b,ĕh-r,ech, sb,ĕh-r,ech,
694. consideration
 attention внима́ние
 vne-mah-ne-yĕh
695. copeck копе́йка
 käh-p,eh^e-käh
696. customer клие́нт
 kle-yent
697. cut hair стричь
 постри́чь
 streech, päh-streech,
698. ear у́хо
 oo-haw
699. farthing грош
 grosh
700. fear страх
 (Noun) sträkh
701. God Бог
 bokh
702. hair во́лос
 vaw-wos

703. hairdresser
 парикма́хер
 päh-reek-mah-herr
704. hall зал
 zähL
705. handle ру́чка
 rooch-käh
706. measure ме́ра
 m,eh-räh
707. medicine лека́рство
 drug l,ĕh-karr-stfaw
708. music му́зыка
 moo-zE-käh
709. opera о́пера
 aw-p,ĕh-räh
710. once more ещё раз
 yĕh-shchaw rähz
711. part часть (f.)
 chähst,
712. pickpocket вор
 thief vorr
713. plot сюже́т
 subject s,oo-jet
714. queen (in cards) да́ма
 =lady dah-mäh
715. razor бри́тва
 breet-fäh
716. to reply
 see 'to answer,' No. 171
717. river река́
 r,ĕh-kah
718. rose ро́за
 raw-zäh
719. remaining
 остально́й
 äh-stähl,-noy

720. seat, place ме́сто
  m,eh-staw
721. second секу́нда
  (Noun) c,ĕh-koon-dăh
722. sink тону́ть
  be drowned утону́ть
  tăh-noot, oo-tăh-noot,
723. snow снег
  sn,eg
724. stick па́лка
  pahL-kăh
725. Stock Exchange
  би́ржа
  beer-jăh
726. spade пи́ковый
  in cards (Adj.) pe-kaw-vɛ͡e
727. student студе́нт
  stoo-d,ent

728. swift бы́стрый
  bɛ-strɛ͡e
729. to take брать
  взять
  brăht, vz,ăht,
730. tooth зуб
  zoob
731. twice два ра́за *or*
  два́жды
  dvăh rah-zăh *or* dvahj-dɛ
732. visiting card
  (визи́тная) ка́рточка
  ve-zeet-năh-yăh karr-toch-kăh
733. Vera Ве́ра
  v,eh-răh
734. warm тёплый
  t,op-wɛ͡e

January янва́рь yăhn-vahr,	Sunday воскресе́нье văhss-kr,ĕh-c,en,-yĕh
February февра́ль fĕhv-rahl,	Monday понеде́льник păh-n,ĕh-d,el,-nik
March март măhrt	Tuesday вто́рник ft-orr-nik
April апре́ль ăh-pr,ehl,	Wednesday среда́ sr,ĕh-dah
May май my *or* măh͡e	Thursday четве́рг chĕt-f,erg
June ию́нь yoon,	Friday пя́тница p,aht-ne-tsăh
July ию́ль yool,	Saturday суббо́та soob-baw-tăh
August а́вгуст ahv-goost	
September сентя́брь c,en-t,ahbr,	November ноя́брь năh-yahbr,
October октя́брь ăhk-t,ahbr,	December дека́брь d,ĕh-kahbr,

THE NUMBERS (CARDINAL AND ORDINAL).

1 оди́н	10 де́сять	19 девятна́дцать
2 два*	11 оди́ннадцать	20 два́дцать
3 три	12 двена́дцать	30 три́дцать
4 четы́ре	13 трина́дцать	40 со́рок
5 пя́ть	14 четы́рнадцать	50 пятьдеся́т
6 шесть	15 пятна́дцать	60 шестьдеся́т
7 семь	16 шестна́дцать	70 се́мьдесят
8 во́семь	17 семна́дцать	80 во́семьдесят
9 де́вять	18 восемна́дцать	90 девяно́сто

* две is the Feminine for 'two', and is used in 12, 200, 2,000. Zero or nought (0) is нуль.

For explanation to the above, see rules 210, 212, 215.

100 сто	400 четы́реста	700 семьсо́т
200 две́сти	500 пятьсо́т	800 восемьсо́т
300 три́ста	600 шестьсо́т	900 девятьсо́т

See rules 219 and 220.

1,000 ты́сяча	10,000 де́сять ты́сяч
2,000 две ты́сячи	100,000 сто ты́сяч
3,000 три ты́сячи	1,000,000 миллио́н
4,000 четы́ре ,,	2,000,000 два миллио́на
5,000 пять ты́сяч	5,000,000 пять миллио́нов

1,000 is declined like a Feminine Noun.

1st пе́рвый	4th четвёртый	7th седьмо́й
2nd второ́й	5th пя́тый	8th восьмо́й
3rd тре́тий	6th шесто́й	9th девя́тый

11th оди́ннадцатый	40th сороково́й
12th двена́дцатый	50th пятидеся́тый
15th пятна́дцатый	100th со́тый
20th двадца́тый	1,000th ты́сячный

219. Declension of the Numerals (for 2, 3, 4, see rule 212).

	NOM., ACC.	GEN., DAT., PREP.	INSTR.
5	пять	пяти́	пятью́
8	во́семь	восьми́	восьмью́
40	со́рок	in all other cases : сорока́	
50	пятьдеся́т	пяти́десяти	пятью́десятью

The Dative of the numerals 40, 90, and 100 may take **у** instead of **а**, when coming after the Preposition **по**.

220. In the HUNDREDS both parts are declined. The DECLENSION of **сто, сти,** and **ста** is as follows :

Gen. сот   Dat. стам   Instr. ста́ми   Prep. ста

with two hundred   с двумяста́ми
about six hundred   о шестиста́х, etc.

221. The ORDINAL NUMBERS are irregular in the first four, but from the fifth upwards (7th and 8th excepted) they are formed regularly from the Cardinals, by changing the last letter into **ый**, or **о́й** if stressed ; 40th adds **ово́й**.

1st пе́рвый p‚err-vĕ˘e   2nd второ́й ftăh-roy
3rd тре́тий tr‚eh-tĕ˘e   4th четвёртый chet-f‚orr-tĕ˘e

The Ordinals have the same form for Masculine, Feminine, Neuter and Plural as Adjectives with full endings (page 72).
From 50, the first part of the Ordinal is put in the GENITIVE.

60th шестидеся́тый   80th восьмидеся́тый

Ordinal for 100th and compounds is **со́тый** ;
for 1000th, **ты́сячный**

400th четырёхсо́тый   2,000th двухты́сячный

222. Examples of COMPOUND NUMBERS in letters :
207 две́сти семь   1,001 ты́сяча оди́н
3,792 три ты́сячи семьсо́т девяно́сто два
21st двадцать пе́рвый   32nd тридцать второ́й
43rd со́рок тре́тий   54th пятьдеся́т четвёртый

223. a half (½) полови́на   one third (⅓) треть
one fourth (¼) че́тверть

The above are Feminine Nouns, declined as such. They can be expressed also by часть (part) added to corresponding Ordinals.

From 'one-fifth,' there are no special names for the Fractions, and they are all formed with часть, thus:

    one-seventh   седьма́я часть
    one-hundredth   со́тая часть

If the word часть is omitted, the Numeral одна́ (one, fem.) must be placed before the Ordinals, thus:

one-twentieth двадца́тая часть *or* одна́ двадца́тая

224. In Fractions like 'five-sevenths,' 'eight-ninths,' etc., the first part is expressed by Cardinals, and the second by Ordinals; the latter are put in the Genitive Plural.

    five-sevenths   пять седьмы́х
    two-thirds   две тре́тьих *or* две тре́ти

    Notice: two and a half   два с полови́ной

(полови́ной,—Instrumental of полови́на, after the Preposition с, with; the stress is always on ви).

    three and a half   три с полови́ной, etc.

BUT: one and a half полтора́ (полторы́ for Feminine)

225. Notice the following combinations with 'half.'

half a pound полфу́нта	half a hundred полсо́тни
half an hour получаса́	half a minute полмину́ты
half a bottle полбуты́лки	half a dozen полдю́жины

о is not pronounced 'ăh' here, as пол is a separate word.

The above compounds are formed from пол (a half—abbreviation of полови́на) and the Noun, which is put in the Genitive.

When declined, пол becomes полу in all cases except Nominative, the Noun taking the usual terminations.

226. simple *or* one fold   ординáрный
double *or* two fold   двойнóй
triple, treble, *or* three fold   тройнóй

227. The Accusative is much used in expressions of TIME :
on a hot day   в жáркий день
at the same time   в то же (сáмое) врéмя
for-another time   другóй раз

228. IN, referring to TIME, is rendered by **чéрез**.
in two years   чéрез два гóда
in six years   чéрез шесть лет
in an hour чéрез час   in a month чéрез мéсяц

229. FOR, when not required in English, is not translated :
we lived there (for) three years   мы жúли там три гóда
we shall be here (for) two days   мы бýдем здесь два дня

But FOR is rendered by **на** in sentences like :
he only came for a (*or* one) week   он приéхал тóлько на недéлю

230. The Prepositional is used with TIME when referring to weeks, months, years, and centuries.
in which year ?   в котóром годý ?
in September   в сентябрé
in the 20th century   в двадцáтом вéке
(in) this week   на э́той недéле

231. Notice the Russian translation :
on the next (=following) day   на слéдующий день
(in) the next (=future) week   на бýдущей недéле
(in the) last (=past) week   на прóшлой недéле

232. In DATES, the day of the month, the month and the year are put in the GENITIVE.

17th July, 1936   семна́дцатого ию́ля ты́сяча девятьсо́т три́дцать шесто́го го́да

When abbreviated: 17го ию́ля 1936г.

Notice that in the Compound Ordinals only the last number is Ordinal and declined.

30th May, 1564   тридца́того ма́я ты́сяча пятьсо́т
30го ма́я 1564г.   шестьдеся́т четвёртого го́да

233. ONCE раз is used instead of оди́н in counting 1, 2, 3.
    twice   два ра́за *or* два́жды
    three times   три ра́за ,, три́жды
    five times   пять раз (Gen. Plural)

234. To express an approximate number о́коло may be used.   about two hours   о́коло двух часо́в

This can also be done more idiomatically by simply putting the Noun before the Numeral.
    about twenty men   челове́к два́дцать
    between thirty and forty copecks   копе́ек три́дцать-со́рок
    for about two hours   часа́ два

235. Adjectives coming between the Nominative of 2, 3, 4, and a Noun are put in the GENITIVE or NOMINATIVE Plural.
    three red pencils   три кра́сных карандаша́
    two pretty ladies   две краси́вые да́мы
    This is the same in the ACCUSATIVE.

When the sentence is not in the Nominative or Accusative, the Adjective simply agrees with the other words.
    with four young soldiers   с четырьмя́ молоды́ми солда́тами

236. For Numbers 2 to 10, special Numerals, called COLLECTIVE, are sometimes used:

2 дво́е   3 тро́е   4 че́тверо
  dvaw-yĕh   traw-yĕh   chet-f͜ĕh-raw

The others from five upwards are formed by adding **еро** to the ordinary Numerals instead of the **ь** : 5 пять, пя́теро.

They are all declined like the PLURAL of ordinary Adjectives (except дво́е, тро́е, which take **и** instead of **ы**).

N. пя́теро   G. & P. пятеры́х   D. пятеры́м   I. пятеры́ми

These numerals are used with Nouns having no Singular, or living beings of the two genders (workpeople, children, animals, etc.). Their use is very idiomatic, and students need not employ them yet.

three children   тро́е дете́й

237. Notice the idiomatic use of **по** with the numerals 2, 3, 4. All other numerals must be in the Dative after **по**.

we have two books each   у нас по две кни́ги
they sell it at five roubles per yard   они́ продаю́т э́то по пяти́ рубле́й за арши́н
he gave a rouble to each   он дал ка́ждому по рублю́

238. EACH OTHER or ONE ANOTHER are rendered by друг дру́га (friend of friend).

they like each other   они́ лю́бят друг дру́га
do you understand one another?   понима́ете ли вы друг дру́га?

Only the second word of this phrase is declined.

they went with each other   они́ пошли́ друг с дру́гом
they never speak about one another   они́ никогда́ не говоря́т друг о дру́ге

239. The Particle **же** is very much used in Russian for emphasis. It can be put practically after every word, thus:

but I told (to-) him   я же ему́ говори́л
where then have you been?   где же вы бы́ли?
he will pay (to-) me even to-day   он мне заплатит сего́дня же

240. AND is rendered by **и** in Russian when used in a CONJUNCTIVE sense.

| he and I | он и я |
| we wrote and read | мы писа́ли и чита́ли |

241. When AND is DISJUNCTIVE it is rendered by **а** in Russian.

| he works, and you do nothing | он рабо́тает, а вы ничего́ не де́лаете |
| she is there, and he is here | она́ там, а он здесь |

242. и, when enumerating objects or actions, may be put either before the last word, or when emphatic, before each word.

meat, cheese, and fruit	мя́со, сыр и фру́кты
they have eaten (both) meat, cheese, and fruit	они́ скуша́ли и мя́со, и сыр, и фру́кты
he drank, ate, and read at one and the same time	он и пил, и ел, и чита́л в одно́ и то́-же вре́мя

The following are the principal Verbs that require the Object in a different Case than in English.

243. The GENITIVE must be used with:

to be afraid of, боя́ться	to hold one's self, держа́ться
to avoid, избега́ть	to await, ждать
to desire, жела́ть	to seek, иска́ть
to deprive, лиша́ть	to concern, каса́ться
used reflexively it means: to be deprived, to lose	to ask, проси́ть
they are afraid of air and water	они́ боя́тся во́здуха и воды́
he avoids all labour and difficulties	он избега́ет вся́кого труда́ и затрудне́ний
did they ask for money or for work?	проси́ли ли они́ де́нег и́ли рабо́ты?

I shall ask him the permission	я попрошу у него позволения

When there are two Objects **у** *is put before the Person.*

I wish (to-) you a happy journey, all best (= good), happiness	(я) желаю вам счастливого пути, всего хорошего, счастья
they deprived him of situation and lodgings	его лишили места и квартиры
I was nearly killed	я почти лишился жизни
concerning this business	что касается этого дела
do you expect any letters or wires from home?	ждёте ли вы писем, или телеграмм из дому?
I seek freedom and rest	я ищу свободы и покоя
BUT: I am waiting for my sister	я жду мою сестру (A.)

244. The DATIVE must be used after:

to believe, верить	to learn, учиться
to disturb, мешать	to complain, жаловаться
to threaten, грозить	*the matter (or Person complained about) is in the Accusative, preceded by* на.
to teach, учить	
(the Object after TO TEACH *is in the Accusative)*	to greet, кланяться =to bow
they believe nothing and nobody	они ничему и никому не верят
he disturbs everybody and everything	он всем и всему мешает
did they threaten your friends?	грозили ли они вашим друзьям?
we taught them the Russian language	мы их учили русскому языку
did you learn that?	учились ли вы этому?

I shall complain to the director about (on) you	я пожа́луюсь на вас дире́ктору
greet your friends!	кла́няйтесь ва́шим друзья́м!

245. The INSTRUMENTAL must be used after:

to breathe, дыша́ть	to profit, по́льзоваться *use, take advantage of*
to manage, управля́ть	to rule, владе́ть *be in possession of*
to be proud of, горди́ться (Rule 41)	to sacrifice, же́ртвовать
I should like to breathe fresh air	я бы хоте́л подыша́ть све́жим во́здухом

a common expression, meaning: to go to the country, for a walk, etc.

who manages your office?	кто управля́ет ва́шей конто́рой?
you may be proud of your sons	вы мо́жете горди́ться ва́шими сыновья́ми
what dictionary are they using?	каки́м словарём они́ по́льзуются?
they are sacrificing money and life	они́ же́ртвуют деньга́ми и жи́знью
he owns all the cinemas in this town	он владе́ет все́ми кинемато́графами в э́том го́роде

246. TO MARRY (a girl) =to wife one's self — жени́ться *Perfective unusual* jĕh-neet,-s,ăh

he married her	он жени́лся на ней
whom is he marrying?	на ком он же́нится?
a married man	жена́тый челове́к
is he married?	он жена́т?
he is single	он хо́лост
he is a bachelor	он холостя́к

247. TO MARRY (a man) } выходи́ть за́муж
　　=to go out for husband } вы́йти за́муж
　she married him　　　она́ вы́шла за него́ за́муж
　she gets married to-　она́ выхо́дит за́муж
　　morrow　　　　　　за́втра
　she is married　　　 она́ за́мужем
　a married woman　　 заму́жняя же́нщина
to give (a girl) in marriage } выдава́ть за́муж
　=to give out for husband　} вы́дать за́муж

248. WHAT O'CLOCK ?　кото́рый час ?
　one o'clock, час　　　 five o'clock, пять часо́в
　two, three, four o'clock　два, три, четы́ре часа́
　　quarter to eight　　　без че́тверти во́семь
　　　=without a quarter eight
　　twenty-five minutes to ten　без двадцати́ пяти́
　=without twenty-five (minutes) ten　　(мину́т) де́сять
　　half past six　　　　полови́на седьмо́го
　　　=half of the seventh
　　quarter past five　　 че́тверть шесто́го
　　　=quarter of the sixth
　　ten minutes past ten　де́сять мину́т
　　　=ten minutes of the eleventh　　оди́ннадцатого
　quarter of an hour, half an hour　че́тверть часа́, полчаса́
　eight o'clock sharp (exactly)　ро́вно во́семь
　before (earlier than) six　ра́ньше шести́
　after three　　　　　 по́сле трёх

249. TIME, referring to HOURS OF THE DAY or DAYS OF THE WEEK, is expressed by the Preposition в followed by the Accusative.
　　at half past one　　в полови́не второ́го
　　at quarter past three　в че́тверть четвёртого
　　on Monday, on Tuesday,　в понеде́льник, во
　　　on Saturday　　　　вто́рник, в суббо́ту

RUSSIAN HANDWRITING.

1. дом, комната, перо;
2. наш билет, наша газета, наше письмо; 3. ваш багаж, ваша гостиница, ваше дело; 4. улица, наш адрес, ваш стол; 5. наше дело, ваша телеграмма, наш ресторан.

The above is given in printed characters in Exercise 1, page 11.

1. Где гостиница? 2. Это ресторан. 3. Вот касса. 4. Ваш багаж там. 5. Это наш стол. 6. Где

RUSSIAN HANDWRITING (continued).

ваша комната? 7. Вот наша улица. 8. Ваше перо там. 9. Это наш дом. 10. Вот ваше письмо. 11. Где ваш билет? 12. Вот наш адрес.

These sentences are given in printed characters in Exercise 2, page 11.

1. его гостиница, её адрес, их дело; 2. ресторана, телеграммы, пера; 3. его письма, их улицы; 4. кассы, её багажа; 5. номер дома; 6. багаж дамы.

The above is given in printed characters in Exercise 3, page 13.

CONTENTS.

How to read the Imitated Pronunciation	page 3
Russian Alphabet	„ 4
„ Written Alphabet	„ 5
Rules on Pronunciation	„ 6-9
Specimen Handwriting	„ 228

ARTICLES:
& DISTINGUISHING ADJECTIVES
see Determinative Adjectives p. 231

NOUNS (Singular):

Nominative	page 10
How to tell the Gender	„ 10
Table of Terminations	„ 89
REMARKS ON DECLENSION	„ 26
SOFT DECLENSIONS	„ 32
ENGLISH OBJECT becomes Subject in Russian	rule 15
Genitive and Possessive	„ 2
GENITIVE after Negative	„ 9, 33
„ Sing. after 2, 3, 4	„ 11
„ after Prepositions	„ 14
„ after Measures	„ 118
„ „ Adverbs of Quantity	„ 117
DATIVE	„ 20
„ after Prepositions	„ 46
ACCUSATIVE	„ 8
„ living beings	„ 8A
„ of Feminines	„ 8B
„ with Negations	„ 9
INSTRUMENTAL	„ 23
with TO BE, etc.	page 183
PREPOSITIONAL	rule 29

PLURAL of NOUNS:

NOMINATIVE	rule 39
EXCEPTIONS	„ 78-81
GENITIVE 42, Exceptions	„ 82, 83
„ after numbers from 5	44
DATIVE	„ 45
Accusative	„ 39
Instrumental	„ 48
Prepositional	„ 48

IRREGULARITY IN NOUNS: Change of Endings after hissers and gutturals	rule 40
Genitive of Nouns in consonants preceded by hissing sound	„ 83
Instrumental of these Nouns	„ 84
Nouns only used in Plural	„ 85
„ dropping o or e	„ 72
„ inserting o or e	„ 72
NEUTERS in МЯ	„ 74
Genitive Sing. Masc. in у	„ 76
Prepositional „ „ in у	„ 77
Nominative Plural in а or я	„ 78
Nominative Plur. irregular	„ 79
Genitive „ „	„ 79
Nouns with Two Plurals	„ 81
Nouns alike in Genitive Plural and Nominative Singular	„ 82
Nouns of Persons ending in ИН	„ 80
Mother, daughter, child	„ 75, 86
Russian Diminutive	„ 211
Neuter Nouns in КО	„ 214
Declension of Family Names	205, 206

ADJECTIVES:

Table of Terminations	page 89
PREDICATE Endings	rule 6
Formation of PREDICATE	„ 57
ATTRIBUTIVE Endings	53 to 56
„ Soft Declensions rule	58, 67
GENITIVE Endings	„ 66
Change of Endings after hissers and gutturals	„ 40
Predicate formed by inserting or omitting o or e	„ 73
COMPARATIVE:	
Attributive	„ 125
Predicative	„ 126
Irregular	List page 144
SUPERLATIVE:	
Attributive	rule 137
Predicative	„ 136

HUGO'S RUSSIAN GRAMMAR SIMPLIFIED.

Determinative Adjectives and Pronouns:

How to render A, THE	page 11
Table of Terminations	pp. 88, 114
OUR, YOUR	page 10
HIS, HER, THEIR	rule 3, 12
THIS, THAT, MY	„ 16
Genitive, Dative, Accus.	16, 18, 21
Prepositional, Instr.	24, 42, 45, 48
THAT in opposition to THIS	rule 97
THIS IS or THAT IS	„ 32
THESE and THOSE rendered by THIS	„ 181
THE SAME	„ 108
MYSELF (not emphatic)	„ 116
ALL, WHOLE, EVERYTHING	page 115
SELF (emphatic)	„ 115
ALONE, ONE	„ 115

PRONOUNS:

PERSONAL „ Table	page 112
NOMINATIVE, Sing. & Plur.	rule 5
GENITIVE & ACCUSATIVE	„ 12
Dative or Indirect Object	„ 19
Instrumental 26 Prepositional	„ 31
Prefixing н after Preposition	„ 14
Position of Pronouns	91, 92
INTERROGATIVE „	88, 100 to 103
RELATIVE „	88, 100 „ 103
DEMONSTRATIVE „	32, 181
DISTRIBUTIVE „	98-99, 110-112
IT referring to a Noun	194, 198

Indefinite Adjectives or Pronouns ... pages 117, 118
Table of Declension ... page 114
List of Indefinite Pronouns „ 124
such as: NOBODY, NOTHING, SOMEBODY, SOMETHING, ANYBODY, ANYTHING, ALL, etc.

VERBS: Regular & Irregular
Perfective & Imperfective pp. 46-49

PRESENT TENSE	„ 46, 47
FUTURE	page 48
PAST	„ 49
IMPERATIVE	page 49
List of Regular Verbs	18, 47, 56, 64
INFINITIVE	rule 10
How to find STEM	„ 36
Negative Form	„ 9, 34
Interrogative Form	„ 8, 35
PRESENT of TO BE (am, is, are)	„ 5
PAST of TO BE (was, were)	„ 4
PAST TENSE, Formation of	„ 7, 10
English for the RUSSIAN PAST	„ 10
How to change the English for the auxiliaries, HAS, HAVE, DID	8, 17
How to render DO and DOES	13, 17
NEUTER of the PAST	191, 192
PRESENT of TO HAVE (=possess)	15
PAST, negative and interrogative	33
TO HAVE with Abstract Nouns	208
FUTURE of TO BE	„ 22
„ other Verbs	rule 25, page 48
CONDITIONAL „	rule 28
IMPERATIVE „	30, 131-132
PRESENT of ать, ять	13, 199, 200
„ ить, еть	17, 207
„ овать	„ 52
„ ать, preceded by a hisser	„ 43
CHANGES OF STEM	rule 36
„ in Verbs in ать	37, 43
Ditto in ить, еть	„ 40
Verbs in ить, еть taking л	„ 47
REFLEXIVE VERBS, i.e., Verbs with reflexive forms	„ 51
Present 49 Past & Future	„ 50
Verb list of Reflexives	page 70
Impersonal of Reflexives	rule 158
PASSIVE VOICE:	
by Third Person Plural	„ 171
by Reflexive Forms	„ 173
Auxiliaries:	
CAN, MAY, TO BE ABLE TO	„ 59
WANT TO, WISH TO	„ 60
CAN=to know how to	„ 61
MUST, TO BE OBLIGED TO	„ 62
TO HAVE, иметь	„ 208

GERUNDS:
Present rule 150 Past... rule 151
Use of Gerunds ... ... „ 152
How to render English Prepositions with Gerunds „ 152

PARTICIPLES:
Past rule 174, 175 Present „ 176
Russian Past Part. Active 176, 177
Present Participle Passive rule 178
Participles as Nouns ... „ 179

IRREGULAR VERBS: 52 to 217
see Vocabulary pages 233 to 238
(The number after the Verb indicates where the Conjugation is given)
Compounds of TO GO
  rule 166, 169, 172
in ЯТЬ ... ... rule 199, 200
in СТИ' ... ... rule 202
in ЧЬ ... ... „ 203
in НУТЬ ... ... „ 204
in ЕТЬ ... ... „ 207
How to render TO OWE ... „ 63
PUT rule 121   SEND ... „ 124
TO SIT AT table, SIT DOWN TO „ 146
TO READ rule 216 TO HEAR „ 217
TO HAVE „ 208 TO MARRY „ 246
TO PAIN ... ... „ 209
Verbs requiring GENITIVE „ 243
  „   „   DATIVE „ 244
  „   „   INSTRUMENTAL 245

ADVERBS:
of Negation ... ...rule 9, 34
of Quantity requiring Genit. „ 117
Formation of Adverbs ... „ 122
IRREGULAR „ pages 144-145
COMPARATIVE „ rule 125-129
POSITION „ ... rule 123
MUCH before Comparative „ 134
THERE IS, THERE ARE, etc. 187-190
ABROAD (how to render) rule 180
НАДО' and НУ'ЖНО ... 149, 155

PREPOSITIONS:
List of Prepositions ... page 132
Remarks on Prepositions rule 120
IN ORDER TO 140, 141
(see also Cases under Nouns)

CONJUNCTIONS:
IF in Conditional ... rule 28
AND 240, 241, 242

IDIOMATIC FORMS:
'at our school,' 'in your house' ... ... rule 193
THESE and THOSE ARE ... „ 181
INSTRUMENTAL after TO BE and some other Verbs 183, 185, 186
Colloquial Idioms page 85, 111
Idiomatic Answers „ 104
English Adjectives equal Russian Adverbs ... ... rule 64
English Subject (Nominative) becomes Dative ... „ 65
Indirect Phrases ... 168, 170
How to render YEAR ... rule 96
Usual Russian mode of Address 213
NEUTER FORM ... ... „ 192
SHORT, referring to a person „ 141
JUST AS, SIMILAR TO ... „ 109
THIS AFTERNOON ...page 188
Position of TO BE in IMPERSONAL EXPRESSIONS ... rule 149
Days and Months ...page 217
How to tell the Time ... „ 227
Interrogation by Intonation, rule 182

NUMBERS: page 218
one ... page 114 and rule 233
2, 3, 4 and Declensions rule 11, 212
5 upwards „ „ 44, 219
11-20 ... ... rule 210
20-40 and 50 to 100 ... „ 215
Declension of Hundreds „ 220
Cardinal & Ordinal Numbers „ 221
Compound Numbers ... „ 222
Fractions 223-225
once, twice, etc. ... ... rule 233
Collective Numbers ... „ 236

LIST OF WORDS,

with number referring to the Vocabulary in which the Russian is given with the Imitated Pronunciation.

(to) abandon, 655
(to be) able to, 284
about, 369, 418-19, 435
above, 420
abroad, 532
(to) accept, 685
„ accompany, 684
accurate, 444
acquaintance, 581
address, 1
(to) advertize, 653
„ advise, 205
aeroplane, 220
(to be) afraid of, 661
after, 375, 422
all, 355
(to) allow, 652
it is allowed, 495, 496
ally, 289
alone, 354
along, 421
already, 334
always, 75
(for) always, 583
among, 426
(to) announce, 653
„ answer, 76, 171
anybody, 376, 377
anyone, 377
anything, 378, 379
(not) anywhere, 544

(to) apologize, 208
apple, 688
(to) approach, 566
army, 123
(to) arrange, 689
„ arrive, 347, 348
article, 582
(to) ask, 45, 172
„ beg, 193
assured, 549
at, 24, 423, 433, 437
at last, 264
at once, 151, 178
attention, 694
author, 89
(to) avoid, 576

bad, 475
badly, 152
bag, 179
(to) bake, 665
bank, 585
(to) bath, 209
„ be on fire, 551
beard, 690
because, 230
beer, 231
before, 424
(to) beg, 193
„ begin, 577
behind, beyond, 425

(to) believe, 77, 133
beside(s), 427
between, 426
(to) bid farewell, 523
big, 476
bill, 533
(to) bind, 169
black, 232
(to) blow, 691
blue, 233
(to) boil, 134
book, 49
booking-office, 7, 586
bottle, 314
box, 181
boy, 180
brandy, 534
bread, 182
breakfast, 380, 584
(to) bring, 402, 552
broad, 299, 477
brother(s), 16, 315, 335
bullet, 183
burden, 381
(to) burn, 550
business, 13
busy, 26, 595
but, 90
butter, 382
(to) buy, 30, 194
by, 423

INDEX TO THE VOCABULARIES.

Nos.	page	Nos.	page	Nos.	page	Nos.	page
1-15	10	133-150	47	375-406	126	581-645	192
16-23	12	151-177	56	407-417	130	646-648	194
24-29	14	178-204	64	418-443	132	649-651	196
30-41	16	205-207	68	444-474	140	652-661	198
42-44	18	208-229	70	475-494	144	662-663	200
45-48	20	230-263	76	495-527	158	664-666	202
49-66	24	264-288	83	528-531	168	667-672	204
67-74	26	289-298	86	532-564	171	673-680	206
75-84	28	299-313	90	565-568	172	681-683	208
85-88	30	314-333	104	569-575	174	684-685	210
89-122	41	334-353	110	576-577	188	686-687	212
123-132	42	354-374	117	578-580	190	688-734	216

234 HUGO'S RUSSIAN GRAMMAR SIMPLIFIED.

cake, 692
(to) call, 553
  ,, call in, 573
  ,, call on, 565
  ,, call out, 670
can, 284 (Verb)
candle, 535
card, 497
(to take) care, 693
(to) carry, 177, 403
cash-box, 586
(a) certain, 356
chair, 91, 317
chairs, 317
(to) change, 654
cheap, 234, 478
child, 445
children, 318
chocolate, 536
(to) choose, 578
Christmas, 446
cigar, 38
cigarette, 184
clean, 448, 479
(to) clean, 686
cleaned=washed, 589
clerk, 587
clever, 235
clock, 332, 588
cloth, 447
club, 336
coffee, 383
cold, 265
(to) come (kindly), 404
  ,, come near, 566
company, 300
(to) complain, 210
concert, 537, 590
consideration, 694
convenient, 266, 591
(to) convey, 561
copeck, 695
(to) cost, 316, 592

Count, 593
(to) count, 135
country, 236
(to) cross, 568, 571
  ,, crush, 200
  ,, cry, 163
cup, 319
customer, 696
(to) cut, 164
  ,, cut hair, 666, 697

daughter, 320
day, 301
dear, 237, 480, 596
dentist, 302
dictionary, 124
(to) die, 580
difficult, 238
(to) dine, 92, 137
dining-room, 384
dinner, 449
distant, 481
(to) do, 31, 136
doctor, 17
dog, 50
door, 239
(to) draw, 667
drawer, 450
drawing-room, 498
(to) dress, 211
(the) dress, 240
(to) drink, 554
  ,, drive away, 569
  ,, drive in, 570
  ,, drive out, 575
  ,, drive up, 572
  ,, drown=be drowning, 672
dull, 267
(to) dust, 662

each, 362

ear, 698
early, 153, 241
earth, 96
easy, 242, 482
(to) eat, 405
  ,, eat, 555
egg, 385
employé, 594
(to) endeavour, 474
engaged, 595
England, 597
(in) English, 51
English, 243
Englishman, 321
enough, 244, 416
(to) enter, 570
entirely, 510
envelope, 52
evening, 93
(in the) evening, 67
every, 363
every day, 221
except, 427
(to) expect, 563
expensive, 237, 480, 596
face, 599
factory, 125
(to) fall, 650
far, 481
(to) bid farewell, 523
farthing, 268, 699
father, 322
fault, 94
fear (Noun), 700
(to) fear, 661
  ,, feel, 206
a few, 412
few, 413
fewer, 415
field, 222
financier, 598
(to) find, 530

INDEX TO THE VOCABULARIES.

Nos.	page	Nos.	page	Nos.	page	Nos.	page
1-15	10	49-66	24	133-150	47	264-288	83
16-23	12	67-74	26	151-177	56	289-298	86
24-29	14	75-84	28	178-204	64	299-313	90
30-41	16	85-88	30	205-207	68	314-333	104
42-44	18	89-122	41	208-229	70	334-353	110
45-48	20	123-132	42	230-263	76	354-374	117

fire, 538
flat, 18
floor, 323
(to) flow, 664
flower, 539
(to) fly, 195
for, 428, 429
(to) forget, 579
fork, 95
four, 44
French, 245
(in) French, 223
frequent, 303
fresh, 540
friend, 19
from, 432
  ,, here, 451
from, off, 431
from, out of, 430
front(al), 246
(in) front of, 424

gentleman, 53
gentlemen, 324
(to) get up, 646
  ,, give, 78
glad, 27
glass, 20
  ,, (material), 600
glove, 386
(to) go=drive away, 569
  ,, ,, away, 524, 531,
  ,, ,, beyond, 568 [569
  ,, ,, in, 528
  ,, ,, often, 350, 352
  ,, ,, out, 529
  ,, ,, past, 567
  ,, go, travel, 351
  ,, go, walk, 349
God, 701
good, 247, 483
good-looking, 272

goods, 452, 601
governess, 602
grass, 499
ground, 96
(to) grow, grow up, 651
  ,, grow dark, 675
  ,, ,, old, 680
  ,, ,, pale, 677
  ,, ,, red, 676
  ,, ,, stout, 679
  ,, ,, thin, 678
(to) guarantee, 212

hair, 702
hairdresser, 703
hall, 704
hand, 155
(to) hand, 406
handle, 705
(to) hang, 682
happiness, 504, 607
happy, 337
hat, 54
(to) have to, 285
headmistress, 603
(to) hear, 196
heavy, 453
(to) help, 647
here, 28
(to) hide, 165, 213
high, 248, 485
hither, 387
(to) hold, 197, 214
(at) home, 25
home(wards), 304
(to) hope, 215
horse, 126
hot, 269, 454, 484
hotel, 8
hour, 42
house, 2
how, 154

how many? } 86, 411
how much? }
hungry, 388
hurriedly, 500

idiot, 370
if, 97
ill, 270, 604
(to be) ill, 673
immediately, 501
important, 455
in, 433
ink, 325
interesting, 456
into, to, 434
(to) invite, 46, 173

(to) joke, 326, 605
jolly, 271
journey, 338

(to) keep, 197
key, 156
(to) kill, 649
killed, 606
knife, 98
(to) know, 32, 138

lady, 21
lamp, 541
landlord, 99
language, 457
large, 299, 476
late, 249
(to) laugh, 216, 659
  ,, lay, 463
  ,, leak, 664
  ,, learn, 217
  ,, leave, 569
  ,, ,, something, 655
lemon, 100
Leningrad, 344
less, 415
lesson, 502

INDEX TO THE VOCABULARIES (continued from opposite page).							
Nos.	page	Nos.	page	Nos.	page	Nos.	page
375-406	126	528-531	168	581-645	192	667-672	204
407-417	130	532-564	171	646-648	194	673-680	206
418-443	132	565-568	172	649-651	196	681-683	208
444-474	140	569-575	174	652-661	198	684-685	210
475-494	144	576-577	188	662-663	200	686-687	212
495-527	158	578-580	190	664-666	202	688-734	216

letter, 14
(to) lie, 198
  „ „ down, 556
life, 503
(to) light, 550
like, 154
(to) like, 199
little, 305, 389, 413, 486
(a) little, 55, 408, 409
long, 339, 340
(to) look, 139
  „ „ for, 166
  „ lose, 656
  „ love, 199
low, 487
luck, 504, 607
luggage, 3
lunch, 380, 584

machine, 224
(to) make, 31, 136
  „ make a mistake, be mistaken, 611
manager, 505, 608
many, 327, 407
match, 542
may, 284
means, 371
measure, 706
meat, 290
medicine, 707
(to) meet, 47, 174
  „ melt, 658
merchant, 609
merchandise, 452, 601
milk, 101
minister, 610
minute, 43
mistake, 225
more, 390, 414
morning, 103
(in the) morning, 68

motor car, 307
(to) move, put in motion, 669, 671
much, 157, 327, 407
much (diminutive), 409
museum, 102
music, 543, 708
must, 285
mustard, 391

name, 291, 328
nation, 616
near, 423, 435, 436, 458,
nephew, 506
never, 329
new, 292
newspaper, 9
nice, 272, 612
night, 104
no, 56
nobody, 392
noise, 185, 613
nothing, 353, 393
not many } 408, 409
  „ much }
novel, 186
now, 178
nowhere, 544
number, 22

(to be) obliged, 285
(to) occupy oneself, 218
of course, 105
office, 459A
officer, 39
often, 303, 341
old, 293, 489
on, 437, 438
on foot, 342
on the other side of, 425
on to, 438

once, 158, 614
once more, 710
one, 357
only, 69
open, 525, 545
opera, 709
opinion, 250
or, 106
order, 372
other, 364
overcoat, 615

page, 373
(to) pain, 459B
paper, 107
Paris, 343
park, 188
part, 711
partner, 617
(to) pass, 406, 567
  „ „ through, 574
  „ pay, 79, 175
pen, 15
pencil, 57
people, 460, 616
personal, 546A
Peter, 127
piano, 159
pickpocket, 712
picture, 459
piece, 394
(it is a) pity, 273
(to) pity, 674
place, 58, 625
(to) play, 140
pleasant, 274
please, 306
pleasure, 396
plot=subject, 713
pocket, 461
policeman, 507
poor, 308

[488

INDEX TO THE VOCABULARIES.

Nos.	page	Nos.	page	Nos.	page	Nos.	page
1-15	10	49-66	24	133-150	47	264-288	83
16-23	12	67-74	26	151-177	56	289-298	86
24-29	14	75-84	28	178-204	64	299-313	90
30-41	16	85-88	30	205-207	68	314-333	104
42-44	18	89-122	41	208-229	70	334-353	110
45-48	20	123-132	42	230-263	76	354-374	117

portion, 294
possible, 275, 395
post-office, 128
pound, 80
(to) praise, 63, 141
present, 81
(to) present, 287
presently, 108
(to) preserve, 663
„ press, 200
price, 295
(to) print, 142
private, 546
problem, 251
(to) promise, 681
province, 508
(to) publish, 142
„ pull, 667
pupil, 109
purse, 618, 619
(to) put, 462, 463

quality, 509
queen (in cards), 714
question, 189
quick, 309
quiet, 252
quite, 510

(to) rain, 511
razor, 715
(to) read, 33, 143
ready, 41
really, 110
(to) receive, 288, 620
„ recollect, 683
„ recover, 530
red, 253
regiment, 310, 512
(to) regret, 674
remaining, 719
(to) remember, 683
„ repeat, 657

(to) reply=answer, 171
„ request, 193
respected, 621
rest, 622
restaurant, 4
(to) return=give back, 668
rich, 254, 490
(to) ride in, 570
ridiculous, 276
right, 29
(to) ring, 526
river, 717
room, 10
rose, 718
rouble, 190
(to) run, 557
„ run over one, 571
Russia, 464, 623
Russian, 255
(in) Russian, 59

sad, 278
salad, 547
salt, 397
same, 365
(to) sample, 207
satisfied, 160
(to) save money, 663
„ say, 167
school, 129, 226
seat, place, 720
second (Noun), 721
secretary, 548
(to) see, 34, 176
(it) seems, 161
self, 358
(to) sell, 35, 648
„ send, 82, 465
servant, 629
several, 631
shareholder, 638
sharp, 466

(to) shave, 558
shelf, 468
ship, 296
shop, 191, 635
short, 491
(to) shout, 670
„ show, 168
sick, 270
side, 636
(to be) silent, 203
simple, 492
(to) sing, 559 [722
„ sink=be drowned,
sister, 40
(to) sit, 202
„ sit down, 560
situation, 516, 624, 625
(to) sleep, 201
slow, 311
slowly, 227
small, 486
(to) smoke, 36, 64, 144
smoker, 630
snow, 513, 637, 723
so, 111
so many, so much, 410
society, 300
soldier, 191A
some, 412
somebody, 398, 399
someone, 398, 399
something, 400, 401
son, 514
sons, 345
soon, 515
sorry, 330
spade (in cards), 726
(to) spoil, 687
spoon, 112
(postage) stamp, 312
(to) stand, 462, 627, 660
station, 130
stick, 724

INDEX TO THE VOCABULARIES (continued from opposite page).

Nos.	page	Nos.	page	Nos.	page	Nos.	page
375-406	126	528-531	168	581-645	192	667-672	204
407-417	130	532-564	171	646-648	194	673-680	206
418-443	132	565-568	172	649-651	196	681-683	208
444-474	140	569-575	174	652-661	198	684-685	210
475-494	144	576-577	188	662-663	200	686-687	212
495-527	158	578-580	190	664-666	202	688-734	216

(to) stir, 671
Stock Exchange, 638A,
story, 186   [725
strange, 277, 633
street, 11
(to) stretch, 406
strict, 256
strong, 467
student, 727
stupid, 257, 632
such, 366
(to) suffer, 204
sufficient, 417
sugar, 113
sugar refinery, 517
suitable, 626
summer, 258
sun, 628
(to) suppose, 564
sure, 549
(to) sweep, 662
swift, 728
sympathetic, 634

table, 5
tailor, 469
(to) take, 729
" take a walk, 149
" take care of, 663
tall, 248, 485
taxi driver, 85
taxicab, 517A
tea, 114, 331
tea-urn, 518
(to) teach, 145
teacher, 115
(to) tease, 65
telegram, 12
(to) tell, 167
(to) thank, 66, 146
thankful, 519
thanks, 70
that, 359
theatre, 117
thence, 520
(from) there, 520
(to) there, thither, 521
thick, stout, 493
thing, 131
(to) think, 147
three, 43

thus, 111
ticket, 6
tie, 297
(to) tie, 169
till, 441
to, into, 434, 439
to-day, 71
(to) tolerate, 204
to-morrow, 87
tongue, 457
too, 346
tooth, 730
(to) touch, 671
towards, 439
town, 259
trading, 639
train, 116
(to) transport, 561
" travel, 351, 352
" traverse, 568, 571
tree, 228
trip, 279
truth, 83
(to) try, 207, 474
Tsar, 132
twice, 731
two, 42

umbrella, 280
unavoidable, 640
uncle, 118
under, 440
(to) understand, 48
unexpectedly, 522
unpleasant, 281
up to, 441
upon, 437
useful, 282
useless, 283

very, 72
village, 236
violin, 470
(to) visit, 573
visiting card, 732
visitor, 260
voyage, 338

(to) wait, 563
" walk, 349
(take a) walk, 149

(to) want, 286
wanted, 642
war, 641
warm, 734
(to) warm oneself, 219
" wash, 562
watch, 332, 588
(to) watch, 663
water, 298
(to) wear, 177
week, 333
(to) weep, 163
well, 192
what ? 61, 367
what for, 472
when, 73
where to, 162
which ? 368
white, 261
who, 60
whole, 119
the whole, 360
(the) whole of, 643
whose, 361
why, 88
wide, 477
wife, 120
(to be) willing, 286
window, 262, 374
wine, 23
(to) wire, 527
" wish, 148
with, 442
with what ? 229
without, 443
woman, 313
wood, 228
word, 44
work, 471
(to) work, 121, 150
(to be) worth, 592
wounded, 644
(to) write, 37, 170
written, 122

yard, 473
year, 645
yes, 62
yesterday, 74
yet, 84
young, 263, 494